BATH
HISTORY

BATH
HISTORY

VOLUME X

edited by Brenda J. Buchanan

Millstream Books
2005

The Editor wishes to thank the expert readers who have helped so greatly in the preparation of this volume.

The Editor and authors are always pleased to receive comments and information from readers. In the first instance please contact the Editor through the publisher at Millstream Books.

First published in 2005 by Millstream Books, 18 The Tyning, Bath BA2 6AL

Set in Palatino and Times New Roman

Printed in Great Britain by Short Run Press Ltd, Exeter

© Frank Thorn, John Wroughton, Michael Bishop, Brenda J. Buchanan, Edward Yescombe, Holger Th. Gräf, William Evans, Angus Buchanan 2005

ISBN 0 948975 74 1

British Library Cataloguing-in-Publication Data:
a catalogue record for this book is available from The British Library

Contents

In the notes at the end of each article in this volume, the place of publication of books, so far as is known, is London unless otherwise stated.

A Celebration of *Bath History*: A Personal View

It may not seem entirely fitting that the editor of the last five volumes of Bath History should write a note of celebration for this journal, with which she has been closely concerned for many years. But I do so precisely because I know something of the history of this series since its inception in the mid-1980s, and have had the responsibility of editing the journal and bringing it to publication since the mid-1990s. Credit for the concept of *Bath History* must go to Simon Hunt, then of the Bath Museums Service. He secured the initial funding, and the support of the major archaeological and conservationist societies in Bath: the Bath Archaeological Trust, the Bath Preservation Trust, and the Bath Society, who all nominated the members of an editorial committee. But it was Sam (as Simon was more familiarly known) Hunt whose initial editing of the fledgling publication set the standard for form, design, and quality.

The early volumes were published by Alan Sutton of Gloucester, and a neat scheme for dividing the distribution between commercial outlets in the form of bookshops, and voluntary outlets in the form of supporting societies was devised. The latter, including for example the very-recently established History of Bath Research Group, were encouraged to make advance orders in bulk, to sell at a discount to members. Also participating in the scheme were the privately-funded museums such as the Holburne, and before Sam Hunt's career took him away from Bath, an arrangement had been made for substantial sales to an organization catering for the education of American students in the city.

By the time volume III was published in 1990, *Bath History* had a new editor, Trevor Fawcett, and a new officer from the Bath Museums Service on the editorial committee, Stephen Bird. Trevor's work on the history of Bath is well-known, and is attested by the many acknowledgements from later writers who have consulted him on matters about which he is almost uniquely able to give advice. He was the editor of volumes III (1990), IV (1992), and V (1994). The steady but unobtrusive support given by Stephen Bird is less well-known, and also deserves recognition. Not only does Stephen have a good eye for design and an instinct for an attractive cover, he is also an excellent negotiator, as we were to find when he persuaded the Bath Archaeological Trust, then in its heyday, to step in to underwrite the somewhat precarious finances of *Bath History*. This move rescued the journal from the threatening situation caused by the loss of support from societies, who no longer felt able to guarantee the purchase of a certain number of copies at a favourable price. From the mid-1990s these new financial arrangements, backed by a change of publisher to the Bath-based Millstream Books, together with the introduction of a new editor as I took over from Trevor Fawcett after his successful stint, have given a decade of stability to *Bath History*, during which a second set of five volumes has been published.

I must also mention particularly the publisher with whom I have worked on the last five volumes. Tim Graham is already well-known in the literary community for the many volumes of local interest that he has produced. In the publication of *Bath History* his work has been outstanding, not only for the strong commitment that has led him to combine the role of copy editor and illustration-advisor with that of publisher, but also for the sense of design that has contributed so much to the elegance of the finished volumes.

This accomplishment has I hope been matched by the high quality and broad range of the articles published – 40 of them on my watch in volumes VI to X. The cumulative index indicates the breadth of subjects presented, and the *Notes on Contributors* tell something about the authors. Some have been well-known to me already, whilst others have made contact to suggest a possible article. With regard to all the articles submitted, the advice of 'expert readers' has been a great help. The range of authors from within and beyond Bath shows that like the city that is its home, *Bath History* has the capacity to combine the unique quality of being both intensely local, yet at the same time of considerable international significance.

Now, after two decades, ten volumes, and some 80 contributors, we have reached the point where the financial underpinning by the Bath Archaeological Trust, which has been so much appreciated, has been lost. In an increasingly competitive archaeological world the Trust has been forced to step back from all its activities, including its exceptionally public-spirited support of *Bath History*. With no supporting organization and subscription list, but with plans for *Bath History X* well-advanced, it has seemed that the only way to keep faith with our contributors who had already worked hard on their articles, and with our readers keen for a tenth volume in the series, was for us to dig deep in our pockets and provide the funding ourselves, helped in large part by the sympathetic role played by our publisher. I can now only thank all who have played any part in the happy collaborations that have produced the ten attractive volumes at the high and interesting standard that has been the hallmark of *Bath History*.

Brenda Buchanan, 29 September 2005

Notes on Contributors

Dr.Frank Thorn was born and educated in Weston-super-Mare. He taught Latin at King Edward's School in Bath for 34 years, during which time he also lectured on Medieval Latin at the University of Bristol and helped to train teachers there. Between 1975 and 1986 he and his wife Caroline edited ten counties for the Phillimore edition of Domesday Book, and he is currently working on a possible revision of this edition for a fully searchable CD-Rom. He was maps and place-names editor for the Alecto facsimile edition of Great Domesday Book.

Dr John Wroughton was formerly Headmaster of King Edward's School, Bath. A Fellow of the Royal Historical Society, he now lectures extensively throughout the west country on seventeenth-century topics. A contributor to the *Oxford Dictionary of National Biography* (2005), he has written many books including *A Community at War: the Civil War in Bath and North Somerset* (1992); *The Stuart Age* (1997); *An Unhappy Civil War: the Experiences of Ordinary People in the Western Counties* (1999); and *Stuart Bath: Life in the Forgotten City* (2004).

Michael Bishop taught at Kingswood School, Bath, from 1950 to 1987, as Senior Classics Master and subsequently as Director of Studies. After retirement he remained at Kingswood until 2001 as Director of its Wesley Centre and School Archivist. Making models of (usually) vanished buildings has long been a major interest. He is married to Philippa Bishop, formerly Curator of the Holburne Museum and a contributor to *Bath History*.

Dr Brenda Buchanan, Visiting Fellow at the University of Bath, became in 1986 the first chair of the History of Bath Research Group. She has edited *Bath History* since 1994, and was invited to contribute biographies of figures of local interest to the *Oxford DNB* (2005). Currently chair of the UK Gunpowder and Explosives History Group, her recent publications include 'The Art and Mystery of Making Gunpowder' in Steele and Dorland (eds.), *The Heirs of Archimedes* (MIT Press, USA, 2005), and 'Making Fireworks' in Buchanan *et al.*, *Gunpowder Plots* (Penguin, 2005).

Edward Yescombe, a former banker, is now a consultant in project finance and public-private partnerships.

Dr Holger Th. Gräf is an Akademischer Rat (academic councillor) at the Hessisches Landesamt für geschichtliche Landeskunde, a research institute within the Hessian Ministry of Science and Culture. He has studied in Germany, the UK, and the US, and has published widely on the urban, diplomatic and cultural history of central and western Europe in the early modern period.

William Evans was secretary and solicitor to the University of the West of England, Bristol. He is honorary treasurer and membership secretary of the Avon Local History Association.

R.Angus Buchanan is now Emeritus Professor of the History of Technology at the University of Bath, which he joined in 1960. He is a Fellow of the Society of Antiquaries and of the Royal Historical Society. He is Honorary President of the Bristol Industrial Archaeological Society and of the National Association for Industrial Archaeology. His latest book is *Brunel: The Life and Times of I.K.Brunel* (Hambledon and London, 2002).

The Hundred of Bath in 1086 and Before

Frank Thorn

This article examines the evidence that Great Domesday Book (hereafter GDB) provides for the estates which lay in Bath Hundred,[1] and then works backwards in an attempt to understand their earlier history. Because no document simply speaks for itself, it is necessary to begin with a brief look at GDB. It is divided into counties and, within them, all the lands of each landholder are grouped together in chapters which represent their fiefs. For each estate, GDB sets out to give:

- The name of the estate, sometimes stating whether it was a manor or not
- Its 1066 holder, its 1086 holder and his subtenant if any
- Its assessment for geld, measured in hides at both dates[2]
- An estimate of the number of ploughs that would be needed for full exploitation of its arable potential, sometimes called 'plough-lands'
- Its actual resources in terms of ploughs, people (divided into various categories), pasture, meadow, woodland, mills, with occasional mention of other things such as churches and fisheries
- A valuation at 1066 and 1086 and sometimes at some intermediate date
- Additional information concerning disputed tenure or the fusion or fission of manors

The When? of the Domesday Survey is certain (begun, according to the *Anglo-Saxon Chronicle* (*ASC*), as a result of 'deep speech' in Gloucester at Christmas 1085); the Why? is never stated in any document that might have emanated from the king or his councillors; and the How? is the object of much research and speculation.

The repeated evidence of the entries in GDB is that they are a response to urgent questions about tenure and revenue. Who was the holder in 1066? From whom and in what way did he hold and had the estate, as constituted in 1086, passed wholly and legitimately to its then holder? As to revenue, the Book is obsessed with how much geld an estate should pay, what its exemptions were, whether it could pay more by exploiting its arable potential. The final value-clause seems to suggest an additional or alternative way of raising money. The indignant words of the Anglo-Saxon Chronicler,[3] and the list of questions found in the *Inquisitio Eliensis*[4] (which purport to be those that provided focus for the Enquiry) seem to affirm that these were the king's principal interests. It is not difficult to see that King William, faced with a shortage of revenue (the Tax Returns of 1084 illustrate the difficulty), pressed by the need to raise and support an army to face a possible invasion of England, troubled by the behaviour of some of his closest relatives and of his appointed officials,[5] uncertain of the loyalty of his magnates and perhaps unsure even as to who they were, and beset by petitions about the alienation and division of estates, concluded that increased knowledge was the way to assert power and proceeded with a survey unprecedented in detail and seemingly awesome in its authority. The English of a later age gave it the name 'Domesday' in reference to the Book of Judgement.[6]

As to the How?, it is clear that the process that produced GDB, though rapid, was not simple. I am inclined to think that GDB itself was not the intended outcome of the Enquiry, but was an abbreviation, ordered by the Conqueror when the size and unwieldy arrangement of the Survey became apparent. On this hypothesis, this preliminary stage would be represented by Little Domesday Book (LDB),[7] and the Exeter Domesday Book (Exon),[8] which correspond to two of the groups of counties (often called circuits which are generally reckoned as seven) into which England was divided for the purposes of the Survey.[9] If the king saw all seven of these putative volumes, he would probably have been shown about 3,000 folios in a variety of hands, probably unrubricated, unindexed and with somewhat rambling formulae. It is possible that the information derived from some at least of these 'circuit volumes' was available to him on 1st August 1086 when 'he came to Salisbury by Lammas, where he was met by his council and all the landholders who were of any account throughout England, no matter whose vassals they might be. All did him homage, and became his men and swore him oaths of allegiance that they would be faithful to him against all other men'. The information might also have assisted William in this next act: 'he did as he was wont, he levied very heavy taxes on his subjects, upon any pretext whether justly or unjustly' (*ASC*).

The abbreviation of this mass of documentation could have begun thereafter and it is estimated that the editing, writing and revising would have taken up to two years, before work ceased abruptly, leaving unincorporated the information for Essex, Norfolk and Suffolk contained in LDB. A very probable cause of this was the disgrace and exile of William de Saint-Calais, Bishop of Durham, who may have been 'the man behind the Survey'.[10]

The editorial process can be seen from Arnulf d'Hesdin's holding at Weston (near Bath) as reported first by Exon DB (fol.448b) and then by GDB:

Exon DB fol.448b

LAND OF ARNULF D'HESDIN IN SOMERSET[11]

Arnulfus [Arnulf] has one manor which is called *Westona* [WESTON near Bath] which *Eddricus* [Edric] held on the day when King Edward was alive and dead. And it paid geld for 5 hides; 7 ploughs can plough these. Of these [hides] Arnulf has 4 hides less ½ virgate and 3 acres in lordship and 2 ploughs and the villans have 1 hide and ½ virgate and 3 acres and 3 ploughs. Arnulf has there 6 villans and 1 bordar and 10 serfs and 6 cob-horses and 8 cattle and 16 pigs and 250 sheep and 1 mill which pays 20s and 30 acres of woodland and 13 acres of meadow and 60 acres of pasture and 3 houses in the borough of Bath which pay 2s and 3d each year and it is worth £8 a year and, when Arnulf received it, it was worth as much.

GDB ch.41,1

(LAND OF ARNULF D'HESDIN)

Ernulfus de Hesding [Arnulf d'Hesdin] holds *Westone* [WESTON near Bath] from the king. *Edric* [Edric] held it before 1066 and it paid geld for 5 hides. There is land for 7 ploughs. In lordship are 2 ploughs and 10 serfs and 6 villans and 1 bordar with 3 ploughs. There is a mill paying 20 shillings and 13 acres of meadow and 60 acres of pasture and 30 acres of woodland. In Bath 3 houses which pay 27d. The whole was worth £8 formerly and now.

The abbreviation into GDB has been achieved by the use of more compact formulae,[12] by the suppression of references to livestock, by not recording the hidages of the respective portions of lordship and villans' land on the estate,[13] and, in other entries, by the removal of bynames from the subtenants.[14] What is not so obvious in translation is that between Exon and GDB there has been considerable editorial intervention in changing the rules for the spelling of place-names, in altering the order in which information is entered and in substituting one Latin word for another.[15] What appears in GDB is not simply what was supplied in answers to the original questions.

It seems probable that Exon (like other circuit volumes) was preceded by a document that was written up after the hearing in the shire-court at which evidence was given 'by oath of the sheriff of the shire and of all the barons and of their Frenchmen and of the whole hundred (court) and of the priest, the reeve and of six villans of each and every vill'.[16] It is quite likely that such a document was drafted before the court-hearing and corrected at and after it and that it was itself the result of comparing and then merging (in as standard a format as possible) material (pre-conquest in origin but updated) relating to hundreds, vills, estates, hidage, tax and tenure drawn from existing records held by the shire and the hundred, with the same information asked of the predominantly Norman holders of the 1086 estates. To be of use to the court, this document would have needed to be arranged not as in Exon and GDB by county and within it by fief-holder and within his chapter by estate,[17] but by county, hundred, vill and constituent estates, as is the *Inquisitio Comitatus Cantabrigiensis* (*ICC*) which probably represents this stage of the enquiry. This would have allowed the members of each hundred and vill to succeed each other in court. For Weston (which was a vill divided between two landholders in 1086) such a document would have probably had this form:

> IN SOMERSETSHIRE ...
> In the Hundred of Bath these men swore (*list of the hundred jurors*).
> In this Hundred, Weston is assessed at 20 hides.
> Of these 20 hides, the Abbot of Bath holds 15 hides. Abbot Saewold held these before 1066. They paid tax for 15 hides (*The entry would then proceed as Exon fol.185b, abbreviated as GDB Somerset 7,5*)
> Of these 20 hides, Arnulf d'Hesdin holds 5 hides which Edric held before 1066. (*The entry would then proceed as Exon fol.448b, abbreviated as GDB Somerset 41,1 above*)

Exon would thus have been produced by rearranging material that was laid out by hundred, vill and estate into feudal chapters in which the estates, while generally remaining in hundredal groups,[18] have been taken away from their vills and divided between chapters. This process would have been greatly helped by the compilation of simplified conversion tables listing the old and new orders of which some may survive among the so-called Domesday satellites.[19]

This complex process, briefly outlined, has implications for understanding every entry in GDB. Not only has the initial material come from various sources, but it has been through processes of copying, revision, editing and abbreviation. Early errors and false claims never spotted nor contradicted may have become embedded. There will have been mishearings, misunderstandings, miscopyings, and lapses of attention. Minims will have fallen out, material will have been omitted accidentally as well as deliberately.[20] In particular, several individuals or groups (fief-holders, hundred-jurors, commissioners, various scribes including the main scribe of GDB) will have chosen particular forms of expression (for example, the assessment of woodland, the choice of population category) which may or may not have been unscrambled in the final product.[21]

If we recombine the vills that the Domesday process has splintered, the basic details of the estates in Bath Hundred can be tabulated as follows:[22]

Fig.1 Domesday Book, Somerset: Estates in Bath Hundred

Modern name	Exon/GDB References	1066 > 1086 Holders	Exon/GDB Place-names	Hides
Bath	114b/1,31	Queen Edith > King William	*Bade/Bade*	20h
	185a/7,1	Bath Church > Bath Church	*Bade/In burgo ipso*	–
Bathampton	186a/7,11	Two thanes from Bath Church > Hugh *the Interpreter* and Colgrim *an Englishman* from Bath Church	*Hamtona/Hantone*	3h+2h
Batheaston	114a/1,30	Queen Edith > King William	*Estona/Estone*	2h
	186a/7,10	Abbot Wulfward from Bath Church > Walter *Hussey* from Bath Church	*Estona/Estone*	1½h
	465a/45,10	Ingulf > Hugolin the Interpreter	*Estona/Estone*	3h
Bathford	185b/7,6	Bath Church > Bath Church	*Forda/Forde*	10h
Bathwick	144a/5,37	Aelfric > The Bishop of Coutances	*Wica/Wiche*	4h
Charlcombe	186a/7,8	A thane from Bath Church > William *Hussey* from Bath Church	*Cerlacuma/Cerlecume*	4h
Claverton	465a/45,11	Swein > Hugolin the Interpreter	*Claferttona/Claftertone*	5h
(Monkton) Combe	185b/7,7	Bath Church > Bath Church	*Cuma/Cume*	9h
Freshford	144a/5,35	Tovi > Roger Whiting from the Bishop of Coutances	*Firforda/Firford*	2½h
Langridge	144a/5,36	Alfsi > Azelin from the Bishop of Coutances	*Lancheris/Lancheris*	2½h
Lyncombe	186a/7,9	Bath Church > Bath Church	*LinCuma/Lincume*	10h
Swainswick	144b/5,38	Alfred > Nigel *de Gournai* from the Bishop of Coutances	*Wica/Wiche*	2h
	492b/47,18	Alfred (*of Wick*) > Alfred (*of Wick*)	*Wica/Wiche*	2h
Tadwick	464b/45,7	Three thanes > William Hussey	*Tateuuica/Tatewiche*	1½h
	465a/45,8	Godric > Ralph *brother of Roger* of Berkeley	*Tata Wica/Tatewiche*	½h
Warleigh	465a/45,9	Azor > Hugolin the Interpreter	*Heorleia/Herlei*	1h
Weston	185b/7,5	Bath Church > Bath Church	*Westona/Westone*	15h
	448b/41,1	Edric > Arnulf of Hesdin	*Westona/Westone*	5h
'Woodwick' [in Freshford]	186b/7,12	A monk from Bath Church > Ranulf Flambard from Bath Church	*Vudevuica/Vndewiche*	2½h
Woolley	144a/5.37	Aelfric > the Bishop of Coutances	*Wllega/Wilege*	1h

GDB references are to *GDB Somerset*, from which the identifications have been drawn. Personal names have been standardised. Italicised parts of personal names are derived from the fuller entries in Exon. Alfred of Wick is so identified by the Tax Return for Bath Hundred. Roger Whiting, tenant of the Bishop of Coutances at Freshford, appears to be the same man as Roger *de Courseulles*, a major tenant-in-chief in Somerset. The Tax Return identifies the tenant not as Roger, but as Robert Greno, either a subtenant of Roger or an immediate predecessor.

Somerset was dominated by about 40 landholders in 1086, Bath Hundred by the lands of its Benedictine Abbey (57 hides) and of three national figures, the king, the Bishop of Coutances[23] and Arnulf d'Hesdin.[24] It is likely that these three would have left reeves in charge of their estates and never visited them.[25] This was probably true of some of the 1086 subtenants such as Ranulf Flambard[26] and Hugo/Hugolin the interpreter,[27] but others, perhaps Nigel de Gournai[28] and the two Husseys, Walter and William, came and stayed. Very often the important tenurial pattern of Domesday is revealed by the way in which subtenants have acquired adjacent estates, where they settle and which pass down from generation to generation. Walter Hussey held Batheaston from Bath Abbey; William held Charlcombe from the abbey as well as Tadwick from the king.[29]

The Latin forms of the place-names show manglings such as *Lancheris* for Langridge[30] that took place before Exon was compiled, or those such as *Vudevuica/Vndewiche* for 'Woodwick'[31] that intervened between Exon and GDB.

As to the estates themselves, GDB does not even show whether the holding was a manor,[32] and no extant text produced by or for the Survey indicates the location or shape of any settlement nor the bounds of the estate. This was outside the Survey's concentrated and narrow remit. Yet while the shifting centres of estates are difficult to locate and put in sequence and the form of settlement may change over time between dispersal and nucleation, the extent of the estates can often be deduced from later evidence. Thus Batheaston stands for North End and St Catherine and included Bannerdown and Charmy Down. Weston, 20 hides in GDB, will have included Northstoke and part of Lansdown; Lyncombe spoke for Widcombe;[33] Monkton Combe for Combe Down (its chapelry) and possibly for South Stoke.[34] Walcot was probably included in the 20 hides of the borough of Bath (GDB Somerset 1,31).[35]

There is great correspondence between Domesday estates and the so-called ancient parishes, largely because in origin most parochial churches arose to serve the needs of manors or vills, after the monastic reforms of the tenth century meant that secular priests were no longer available to minister to the needs of people living within the *parochia* of their minster. This minster was itself usually the church of some extensive ancient estate from which the later manors were derived.[36] Where ancient parish and 1086 estate do not coincide, it is sometimes because the Domesday estate was very large and contained more than one church (for example, St Catherine was a chapelry of Batheaston), or because an estate had further subdivided. Thus Tadwick and Swainswick contain separate Domesday estates, two in each, but were probably in origin a single 'Wick', of 5 hides.

Domesday accounts by name or by silent inclusion for all the later administrative divisions of Bath Hundred except Kelston. There is no reason to doubt that Shaftesbury Abbey held land here in 1086, as later, but it does not appear in GDB or Exon for Somerset.[37]

The 1084 Tax Return for Bath Hundred allots it 95 hides; the total of estates that can plausibly be allocated to Bath Hundred from GDB is 108, but this includes the Borough of Bath notionally assessed as 20 hides, but which appears not to have paid tax via the hundred.[38] This reduces the GDB total to 88 hides, but 95 or so hides could be reached by assuming 7 or so hides at Kelston. Ninety-five hides itself is a tantalisingly close figure to 100 hides, and it is not implausible to assume that 5 hides were lost to the hundred when a triangle of land (its boundary starting from the Avon, then running between Freshford and Limpley Stoke as far as Midford and then back along the Midford Brook to the Avon) was granted to Shaftesbury Abbey as part of Bradford-on-Avon in 1001.[39]

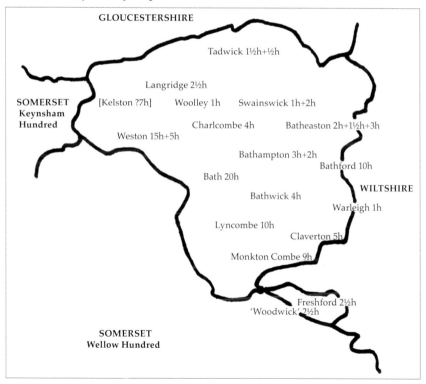

Fig.2 Estates in Bath Hundred in 1086 with Hidages (h=hide)

The estates of Bath Hundred in 1086 are of different sizes and often not assessed in round numbers, yet, with the restoration of Kelston and of the wedge of Wiltshire between Monkton Combe and Freshford, their total can plausibly be argued to have once been 100 hides. That many English hundreds once consisted of 100 hides is evident from Domesday Book, but they are mostly found in the areas which had been re-assessed or re-hidated after their recovery from the Danish invaders. In the shires of Wessex, the 1086 hundreds are often of very different sizes although the hidages of individual estates, as evidenced by charters from the ninth century onwards, have not been altered. Since the time of J.H. Round, it has been common to look for 5-hide units or multiples thereof,[40] and to assume that when hundreds were established as new units of taxation and law and order, they were either created by being drawn around estates which totalled 100 hides, or that an area was first rated as 100 hides and the burden then divided among its estates in multiples of 5 hides. Neither of these models works very well in Wessex where there are few 100-hide hundreds, and there is nothing universal about five and its multiples.

It is true that in Bath Hundred there are estates of 5 hides (e.g. Claverton), or of multiples of 5 (e.g. Weston). Other such units can be created: for example 'Woodwick' and Freshford (2½ hides each and sharing a mill), Tadwick and Swainswick, Charlcombe and Woolley, or Bathwick and Woolley, as suggested by DB itself, though the linkage may merely result from both having the same holder in 1066.[41] However, there are a number of hidages that impugn this pattern, especially around the edge of the hundred: 2½ at Langridge, 6½ (or 4½) at Batheaston,[42] 1 at Warleigh, 9 at Monkton Combe,[43] perhaps 7 at Kelston. Such odd hidages rather suggest that these estates have been granted out piecemeal from some large central core and that their size has been determined by the generosity of the giver or the merits of the recipient.

Another strand to the argument that the Domesday estates represent fragments of something larger comes from the place-names. Weston and (Bath)easton can only be the western and eastern *tunas* of Bath itself. North and South Stoke seem to be similarly linked by their relationship with Bath: the *stoc* element implies dependency. There are also a surprising number of 'Wicks', a name which, whatever its exact significance, also suggests dependency on other settlements. Charlcombe is 'combe of the *ceorls*, or free peasants', who no doubt occupied an outlying part of some greater estate, probably Bath itself. In a negative sense, within the whole of Bath Hundred, there seems to be no major settlement to rival the predominance of Bath itself. All were probably once subordinate to it.

In Somerset, as in many other counties, a significant proportion of the hundreds were named from major estates, mostly royal. Keynsham named a hundred as did Chewton (Mendip), while the royal manors of Frome, Bruton and Yeovil each stood at the head of three hundreds, probably representing their pre-hundredal territory.[44] In many cases, the antiquity of such estates is uncertain, but for Bath there is good evidence that the hundred of 1086 was the same size, if not necessarily with the same bounds, as an earlier royal estate from which it had evolved. By a charter ostensibly issued between 676 and 681 Osric, king or underking of the Hwicce and nephew of Wulfhere who had ruled Mercia between 657 and 674, is said to have granted to the Abbess Bertana *centum manentes* (one hundred homesteads, i.e. hides) which lay near the city called *Hat Bathu* for the building of a monastery of holy virgins.[45] The Hwicce, whose bishopric was established at Worcester, occupied lands that were later a part of Worcestershire and Gloucestershire. This people was ultimately incorporated into Greater Mercia whose royal centre was at Tamworth with a monastery at Repton and an episcopal seat at Lichfield (established in 664).[46]

This charter is suspect because of its dating, its format and the lack of synchrony between some of its witnesses. It is late, probably elaborated, and possibly forged, but such doubtful documents can nonetheless contain a core of authentic information.[47] The size of the grant was large but not unusual. The lands thus granted would not have been put together suddenly for the nunnery, nor emptied of their cultivators, but would probably have been the wholesale gift of the lands that then depended on Bath. Thus, they were probably the grant *en bloc* of a pre-existing royal estate that belonged at that time to the Hwiccian royal house, an estate which may or may not have had some continuity with the hinterland of Roman Bath.[48]

The nunnery itself did not survive for long, but that it existed seems guaranteed by two late seventh-century charters, the second of them sounder than the first. The first is a grant of 40 *manentes* at *Slaepi* [?Islip in Oxfordshire][49] and the second of 20 *manentes* next to the River Cherwell, possibly adjacent to the land at Islip.[50] The first is addressed to *Bernguidi* called a 'venerable abbess', the second to *Bernguidi* and *Folcburgi*, perhaps her deputy.[51] When next we hear of a religious house in Bath, in 757, it is occupied by monks, for in that year Cynewulf, King of the West Saxons (757-786), with the consent of Offa, King of the Mercians (757-796), granted to the brothers of St Peter's 'minster' in Bath, land at North Stoke which was in his jurisdiction.[52] This grant of North Stoke is not a foundation grant, but an isolated gift or restoration: it is likely that the monastery already possessed other lands, but there is a great gap in our knowledge. Moreover, it is not obvious why Cynewulf, a king of Wessex (757-786), held land at North Stoke unless he had purchased it or leased it from the Mercian king (who himself had pretensions to be *rex totius Anglorum patriae*: 'king of the whole fatherland of the English'), for Bath itself continued to be in Mercia.

In 781 at the Synod of Brentford, Bishop Heathured of Worcester (781-798 or 800), responding to a claim by King Offa of Mercia that he wrongly held the inheritance of his kinsman, King Ethelbald (716-757), restored to the same King Offa 90 hides at Bath and also returned to him the minster at Bath. Additionally, in exchange for land in Worcestershire and Warwickshire, he gave him 30 *cassati* of land south of the River Avon that he had bought from the same Cynewulf, King of the West Saxons.[53] It is perhaps significant that these 90 hides are close in number to the 100 hides[54] originally granted to the nunnery and that these evidently lay north of the Avon, in Offa's own territory of Mercia. That they were held by Heathured suggests perhaps that they had reverted to the see of Worcester when the nunnery ceased and that the bishop had either re-granted them to the monastery (of which he was perhaps patron) or kept them for his bishopric.

It is also significant that in 781 the Avon seems to have been the boundary between Mercia and Wessex and that the lands lying south of the Avon which were subsequently mentioned as being in the hands of the monastery (being recorded in later grants and/or in Domesday Book) totalled 29 hides. These were at Monkton Combe, Lyncombe (including Widcombe), Bathampton and 'Woodwick'-Freshford.[55]

One way of making sense of this fragmentary information is to suggest that a Mercian royal manor of 100 hides, which perhaps, with the exception of Bathwick, lay north and west of the Avon, was granted in its totality to a nunnery in the late seventh century and, that when that house closed, part or all of it went to a newly founded monastery. By 781 ninety hides were in the hands of Bishop Heathured of Worcester (among them possibly some of the monastic lands of which he was perhaps the overlord or which he had diverted to his own use). The effect of the transfer of the 90 hides to King Offa at the Synod of Brentford was perhaps that he became patron of the monastery in Bath, and certainly that Bath itself again became a royal estate. It is not certain that Offa gave or restored any of the 90 hides to the monastery, though he is credited with reforming it. As a result of the gift of a further 30 hides, the centre of gravity of the royal estate at Bath moved southwards. These 120 hides may well have been the 115 recorded in GDB plus the putative 5 hides of the wedge of land between Freshford and Monkton Combe that by 1086 had been granted to Shaftesbury Abbey.[56]

Thereafter, Bath itself and no doubt other dependent lands not yet granted out were in royal hands.[57] According to Domesday Book, 20 hides of Bath and land in Batheaston connected to it were still royal land in 1066 and in 1086.[58] By 1086, the major portion of the hundred was in the hands of the 'church' of Bath. The several charters which record grants of land in Bath Hundred are given below; all Domesday estates are listed, even if not the subject of a grant:

Estate	Charter and Date	Nature of Grant
Bath	S. 51 (676x681)	100 *manentes* granted by Osric, King of the Hwicce, to found a nunnery
	S. 1257 (781)	90 hides surrendered by Bishop Heathured to King Offa with the addition of 30 hides that Heathured had bought from Cynewulf, King of Wessex
Bathampton	S. 627 (955x959)	Granted by King Edwy to his faithful friend Hehelm who gave it to Bath Abbey
Batheaston	–	No pre-conquest history known, but associated with the royal revenue of Bath in 1066 and 1086
Bathford	S. 642 (957)	Granted by King Edwy to Bath Abbey
Bathwick	?S. 1484 (966x975)	Apart from the GDB entry, no pre-conquest history is known. Possibly the *Wickam* of the will of Ælfgifu
Charlcombe	–	Apart from the GDB entry, no pre-conquest history is known
Claverton	S. 1538 (984x1016)	Granted by the will of Wulfwaru to her son Wulfmær. It subsequently passed to Bath Abbey at an unknown date
(Monkton) Combe	–	Apart from the GDB entry, no pre-conquest history is known
Freshford	–	[See 'Woodwick' below]
[Kelston	–	Given at an unknown date, pre- or post-conquest, to Shaftesbury Abbey who held it in and after 1084]
Langridge	–	Apart from the GDB entry, no pre-conquest history is known
Lyncombe	S. 777 (970)	Granted (as *Cliftune*) by King Edgar to the monastery at Bath in exchange for *Cumtune*. Said to have been granted previously by King Athelstan (924-939); *BC*, ii. no.808. Included Widcombe and Holloway
(North) Stoke	S. 265 (758)	Granted to the monastery by King Cynewulf of Wessex with the consent of King Offa of Mercia. Confirmed by King Ethelred (865-871); *BC*, ii. no.808. Included in Weston in GDB
(South) Stoke	S. 694 (961)	Granted by King Edgar to the monastery at Bath. According to *BC*, ii. no.808, this was a re-grant of land already given by King Ethelred (865-871). Not named in GDB, but perhaps included in Monkton Combe
Swainswick	–	Apart from the GDB entry, no pre-conquest history is known
Tadwick	–	Apart from the GDB entry, no pre-conquest history is known
Warleigh	–	Not held by Bath Abbey in 1066 or 1086, but apparently in the abbey's hands in 1001
Weston	(1) S. 508 (946)	(1) Five hides given by King Edmund to Æthelhere, who gave them to Bath Abbey
	(2) S. 661 (956x961)	(2) A further five hides restored to the abbey by King Edwy. Bath Church held 15 hides here in 1066 and 1086 (GDB Somerset 7,5) of which five were no doubt at North Stoke. Arnulf d'Hesdin's 5 hides were given to the abbey after 1086
'Woodwick' [in Freshford]	S. 1538 (984x1016)	Probably the estate at Freshford granted to the abbey by the will of Wulfwaru
Woolley	–	Apart from the GDB entry, no pre-conquest history is known

Fig.3 Bath Hundred: Anglo-Saxon Charters Recording Grants of Land

These charters should not necessarily be taken at face value. A charter may be a restoration of something granted earlier for which no charter has survived. In particular, a re-grant may sometimes be only of an alienated part of a larger estate, whose original gift is undocumented but which continued to be held without interruption. No charters exist for some estates (e.g., Monkton Combe, Charlcombe) known to have been held by Bath Church before 1066. Moreover, in the absence of many charters, it is possible that Bath Abbey had once held more estates in Bath Hundred than Domesday Book allows. Monasteries found that a convenient way to manage some of their estates was to sub-infeudate them, often by granting them out to an individual for three lives. The land was supposed to return to the abbey after the death of his grandson or second heir, but estates often became alienated. By its minimalist recording of 1066 tenure, GDB defeats one of its objects. In what sense did Azor hold Warleigh or Tovi hold Freshford in 1066? Were they 'free to go with their lands where they would', or were they in fact holding abbey lands, for the abbey appears to have held both in 1001?[59]

Most of the material needed to produce a detailed and coherent account of the origins of Bath Hundred is missing, but there is perhaps enough to suggest some continuity from the '100 homesteads' granted at the end of the seventh century for the founding of a nunnery and the patchwork of apparently independent estates recorded by Domesday Book. These probably arose by grant, by alienation and by successive subdivision of portions of some greater whole which was an ancient royal estate, first of the Kings of Mercia, then of those of Wessex and England, and which may not have been entirely discontinuous with the land of Roman Bath.

Bibliography and abbreviations used in the notes

ASC: *Anglo-Saxon Chronicle*. Translations are from G.N. Garmonsway, *The Anglo-Saxon Chronicle* (Dent, 1960)

BC: W. Hunt (ed.), *Two Chartularies of the Priory of St. Peter at Bath*, Somerset Record Society, vol.8 (Taunton, 1894). Within this volume, the two cartularies are paginated separately; they are referred to as i. and ii. in the notes below.

Book of Fees: *Book of Fees* (*Testa de Nevill*), 3 vols. (HMSO, 1920-1931)

DB: Domesday Book

GDB: Great Domesday Book. References to individual counties followed by chapter and entry numbers are to the Phillimore edition: John Morris (gen. ed.), *Domesday Book* (History from the Sources), 40 vols. (Phillimore, Chichester, 1975-1992)

DB1-4: Domesday Book, associated texts, introduction and indices published by the Record Commission (1783-1816)

ECTV: M. Gelling (ed.), *The Early Charters of the Thames Valley* (Leicester University Press, Leicester, 1979)

ECW: H.P.R. Finberg (ed.), *The Early Charters of Wessex* (Leicester University Press, Leicester, 1964)

ECWM: H.P.R. Finberg (ed.), *The Early Charters of the West Midlands*, 2nd edn. (Leicester University Press, Leicester, 1972)

EHD: D. Whitelock (ed.), *English Historical Documents, i: c.500-1042* (Eyre & Spottiswoode, 1955)

EHR: English Historical Review

Exon DB: *Liber Exoniensis* in *Libri Censualis Vocati Domesday Book, Additamenta ex Codic. Antiquiss.*, in DB3 (4 in some bindings). Folio references are to recto (a) and verso (b).

Eyton: R.W. Eyton, *Domesday Studies: An Analysis and Digest of the Somerset Survey (according to the Exon Codex), and of the Somerset Gheld Inquest of A.D.1084*, 2 vols. (Reeves and Turner, London and Bristol, 1880)

FA: Inquisitions and Assessments relating to Feudal Aids with other analogous Documents preserved in the Public Records Office AD 1284-1431, 6 vols. (HMSO, 1899-1920)

Grundy: G.B. Grundy, *The Saxon Charters and Field Names of Somerset* (Somerset Archaeological & Natural History Society, Taunton, 1935). Also in *PSANHS* 73-80 (1927-1934), *passim*.

Hallam and Bates, *Domesday Book*: Elizabeth Hallam and David Bates (eds.), *Domesday Book* (Tempus Publishing, Stroud, 2001)

Hemming: Thomas Hearne (ed.), *Hemingi Chartularium Ecclesiae Wigorniensis*, 2 vols. (Oxford, 1723)

ICC: N.E.S.A. Hamilton (ed.), *Inquisitio Comitatus Cantabrigiensis ... subjicitur Inquisitio Eliensis* (1876)

Keats-Rohan, *DP*: K.S.B. Keats-Rohan, *Domesday People, A Prosopography of Persons Occurring in English Documents 1066-1166: I Domesday Book* (Boydell, Woodbridge, 1999)

OE: Old English

PBNHAFC: Proceedings of the Bath Natural History and Antiquarian Field Club

PSANHS:Proceedings of the Somerset Archaeological and Natural History Society

RH: Rotuli Hundredorum, 2 vols. (Record Commission, 1812-1818)

S.: P.H. Sawyer, *Anglo-Saxon Charters: An Annotated List and Bibliography*, Royal Historical Society Guides and Handbooks no.8 (1968). The abbreviation *S.* is followed by the number of the charter in Sawyer's list.

Shaftesbury Abbey Charters: S.E. Kelly (ed.), *Charters of Shaftesbury Abbey*, Anglo-Saxon Charters v (Oxford University Press for the British Academy, Oxford, 1996)

Somerset Domesday: A. Williams and R.W.H. Erskine (eds.), *The Somerset Domesday* (1989). This is part of the Alecto County Edition. The translations of each county have now been gathered together (not entirely satisfactorily) in: A. Williams and G.H. Martin (eds.), *Domesday Book, a Complete Translation* (Penguin, Harmondsworth, 2002)

Tax Returns 1084: Also known as Geld Rolls or Geld Accounts; those for Somerset are in Exon DB fols. 75a-82b, 526b-527a.

TBGAS: Transactions of the Bristol and Gloucestershire Archaeological Society

VCH: Victoria County History

Notes

1   Hundreds were administrative units dating from the mid-tenth century, responsible for taxation, policing and justice. On the Somerset Hundreds, see F.R. Thorn, 'The Hundreds of Somerset' in *The Somerset Domesday*, pp.32-41. On the immense bibliography of Domesday Book, see D. Bates, *Domesday Bibliography*, (Royal Historical Society, 1986), supplemented by the list in Hallam and Bates, *Domesday Book*, pp.191-98.

2   Geld was a tax paid to the Crown. The hide had once been a measure of area, sufficient to support a household or keep a plough occupied for a year. No doubt it had varied in extent according to the nature of the terrain and had probably once included woodland, meadow, pasture and rough grazing in addition to the arable to which it was later confined. Since each hide came to be liable for tax and various services, it also became a measure of liability.

3   'So very thoroughly did he have the enquiry carried out that there was not a single 'hide' not one virgate of land, not even – it is shameful to record it, but it did not seem shameful to him to do it – not even one ox, nor one cow nor one pig which escaped notice in the survey.' A virgate is a quarter of a hide. Animals are not recorded in GDB, but feature in predecessor documents.

4   In *ICC*, p.97.

5   For example, his half-brothers Robert of Mortain and Odo of Bayeux, his sheriffs Urso d'Abbetot (Worcs.) and Eustace (Hunts.).

6   Richard Fitz Nigel (ed. C. Johnson, revised by F.E.L. Carter and D.E. Greenway) *Dialogus de Scaccario* (Oxford University Press, Oxford, 1983), p.64.

7   See LDB in DB2. LDB contains a detailed survey of the counties of Essex, Norfolk and Suffolk.

8   See Exon in DB3. Exon is a large fragment of a survey of the five south-western counties (Cornwall, Devon, Dorset, Somerset, Wiltshire) containing fuller detail, including livestock. These additional details are included in *GDB Somerset* (etc.), either in smaller type in the translation or in appendices. For a fuller description of Exon and of the production of GDB, see *GDB Devon*, 'Exon. Extra Information and Discrepancies with DB', and Frank and Caroline Thorn, 'The Writing of Great Domesday Book' in Hallam and Bates, *Domesday Book*, pp.37-72.

9   The primary evidence comes from Hemming (pp.288, 296). The identification of circuits depends among other things on differences in the arrangement and choice of material and the formulae employed between groups of counties.

10 See Pierre Chaplais, 'William of Saint-Calais and the Domesday Survey' in J.C. Holt (ed.), *Domesday Studies* (Boydell, Woodbridge, 1987), pp.65-77.

11 Translations are by the author. There is a translation of Somerset without the Latin text in *VCH Somerset*, i. pp.434-526. There is also a translation in *GDB Somerset* and in *The Somerset Domesday*. The main differences between these translations lie in marking off the several paragraphs in an entry and in the handling of personal names and population categories. 'Village' and 'villager' in *GDB Somerset* may conjure up associations that mislead, whereas 'villan' and 'vill' do not. A vill is an administrative unit, a division of a hundred, and it may consist of one or more estates.

12 Exon calls the estate a manor (*mansio*), GDB uses no designation. Exon has *in burgo Badae*, GDB simply *in Bade*. Exon has *die qua rex Edwardus fuit vivus et mortuus* 'on

the day when King Edward was alive and dead', GDB simply has *T.R.E.* (*Tempore Regis Edwardi*) 'in the time of King Edward'. Exon has *reddidit gildum* 'rendered geld', while GDB has *geldabat* 'gelded'. Even the expression of money is tighter: GDB has '27d' for Exon's '2s and 3d'.

13 Lordship (or 'demesne') land was the portion of an estate worked directly for the lord, who received all the revenue and whose men were often serfs. The cultivators of the rest of the estate rendered various dues, tithes and services to the lord, but kept some profits for themselves.

14 For example, Nigel *de Gournai* who held part of Swainswick from the Bishop of Coutances (Exon fol.144 b) has been shortened to plain Nigel in *GDB Somerset* 5,38.

15 In the case of place-names, there was an attempt in Exon (subsequently reversed in GDB) to put many into the Latin first declension by giving them an –*a* termination, or spelling them in greater conformity with Latin norms. In terms of order, Exon has wood, meadow, pasture while GDB generally has meadow, pasture, wood. For the manorial population it has villans, bordars, serfs where GDB has serfs, villans, bordars. As to replacement words, for Exon's *ager, molendinum, nemus, pascua*, GDB substitutes *acra, molinum, silva, pastura*. More misleading is that Exon ties the first value of the estate to *quando Arnulfus* (etc.) *recepit* ('when Arnulf (etc.) received it'), for which GDB has the vague *olim* ('formerly') or simply the past tense.

16 *Inquisitio Eliensis* in *ICC*, p.97.

17 Exon, though feudal, shows a variation on this order, by making the county the first subdivision of material in the fief.

18 On the persistence of arrangement by hundred through subsequent re-orderings, the fundamental study is P.H. Sawyer 'The 'Original Returns' and Domesday Book', in *EHR 70* (1955), pp.177-97, now revised by F.R. Thorn, 'The Hundreds of Somerset' in *The Somerset Domesday*, pp.32-41, and in other 'Hundreds and Wapentakes' articles in that series.

19 For example the document known as Evesham K; see H.B. Clarke, 'The Domesday Satellites' in P.H. Sawyer (ed.), *Domesday Book: a Reassessment* (Arnold, 1985), pp.50-70.

20 In GDB no pasture is listed for any Batheaston holding, despite the presence of plough-oxen; this may have been an error by the jury of the hundred or the vill. There were vineyards at Lyncombe and Bath Abbey had salterns on the edge of the New Forest (*BC*, i. no.74), neither mentioned in GDB. There is not a single fishery mentioned on the Avon.

21 In Bath A, a document that probably dates from an early stage of the Domesday Enquiry, *coceti* are chosen to represent the middle group, but both Exon and GDB, which are derived from it or used its information, have *bordarii*; *BC*, i. pp.67-68; *GDB Somerset*, Appendix II.

22 A pioneering attempt to reconstruct the contents of Bath Hundred is T.W. Whale, 'Notes on the Borough of Bath and the Hundred of Bath Forinsecum', *PBNHAFC* 9 (1901), pp.128-49. S.C. Morland has published a reconstruction of the Tax Returns: 'The Somerset Hundreds in the Geld Inquest and their Domesday Manors', *PSANHS* 134 (1990), pp.95-140.

23 Geoffrey *de Montbrai* (Mowbray), Bishop of Coutances (Manche) 1049-1093. He was also (pluralist) Bishop of Saint-Lô. Newton St. Loe preserves the connection.

Geoffrey fought at Hastings and was an important administrative and judicial supporter of King William, but he also rebuilt the cathedral of Coutances and reformed its see; Keats-Rohan, *DP*, p.228. In DB his fief is a personal holding, not a holding of his Norman bishopric.

24 Arnulf held land in ten counties in 1086. He was from Hesdin in the Pas-de-Calais. His heirs were his daughters Matilda whose second husband was Patrick *de Caorces* (Chaworth) and Avelina, wife of Alan fitzFlaad and then of Robert fitzWalter. Arnulf was accused of involvement in a conspiracy led by Robert of Mowbray in 1093, but cleared himself by judicial combat. He died at Antioch on the first crusade. See *VCH Middlesex*, i. p.114; Keats-Rohan, *DP*, p.192. His holding at Weston was given to Bath Abbey by Patrick de Chaworth in 1100 (*BC*, i. no.41).

25 Saewine, steward of Arnulf of Hesdin, is mentioned in the Tax Return for Bath Hundred.

26 He was in the service of Maurice, the king's chancellor who was (from 1086) Bishop of London. Ranulf later became an important servant of William II. He controlled Chertsey Abbey from 1092-1100 and was Bishop of Durham 1099-1128. See *VCH Surrey* i. p.284; *VCH Middlesex*, i. p.105; Keats-Rohan, *DP*, p.354.

27 Hugh and Hugolin *Interpres* (the interpreter) appear to be the same person, Hugolin being a diminutive or pet form. He is identified as Hugolin *Legatus* (ambassador, envoy) by the Tax Return for Bath Hundred and Hugolin *cum barba* (with a beard) by *BC*, i. p.53. Hugh *Barbatus* (bearded) and Hugh *Latinarius* (Latinist) are also the same man. He held land at Dogmersfield in Hampshire and at *Ernemude* [?Keyhaven] in the New Forest (*GDB Hampshire*, 68,1. NF 10,3). His occupation suggests that he travelled widely in the service of the king and that the revenues from these estates, where he probably did not reside, were a reward for this.

28 As well as Swainswick, Nigel held Barrow (Gurney), Englishcombe and Twerton (*GDB Somerset* 5,32; 38; 44-45). His family appears to have later acquired Langridge (5,36) and Farrington Gurney (5,58), held by Azelin in 1086, unless Azelin was also *de Gournai*. All these lands were held from the Bishop of Coutances. For the several Gurney holdings in Somerset in the 13th and 14th centuries, see *Book of Fees* and *FA*, iv. *passim*.

29 In 1316 John Hussey had holdings in Tadwick and Swainswick (*FA*, iv. p.329). Members of the family held land from Bath Abbey throughout the Middle Ages and were involved in its affairs; see *BC*, *passim*.

30 The name is from OE *lang* and *hrycg* (long ridge); the GDB forms are erratic.

31 From OE *wudu* and *wic* (wooded *wic*). The Exon spelling is closer, the GDB form distorted.

32 Somerset and the other south-western counties appear to have been the last to be abbreviated into GDB, by which time the importance of the designation 'manor' seemed to have lessened, or the scribe intended only to indicate those pieces of land that were not manors. 'Manor' appears to have had a technical significance: it was a place with a hall or court where dues could be collected.

33 Included with Lyncombe in the bounds of *Cliftune* granted to Bath Abbey in 970 by King Edgar (*S. 777*).

34 It is possible that the 5 hides of South Stoke are omitted entirely from GDB. Whale (*op.cit.*, p.147) suggested that its 5 hides were included in the 20 hides allotted to

the Borough of Bath (*GDB Somerset* 1,31). But that was held by the king in 1086 and South Stoke was in the continuous possession of Bath Abbey. Eyton (i. p.103; ii. pp.13-14) argued that Freshford in GDB was too large to stand for Freshford alone and suggested that it included South Stoke. But this was based on the mistaken identification of GDB *Fescheforde* as Freshford. It is in fact Vexford (*GDB Somerset* 21,44-45). Freshford was not held by Bath Church in 1086; though 'Woodwick' was. G.S. Taylor, 'Bath, Mercian and West Saxon', *TBGAS* 23 (1900), p.155, perhaps influenced by Eyton, opted for 'Woodwick' as representing South Stoke, but the estate is too small at 2½ hides and the site has now been identified as lying in Freshford (note 59). I am inclined to think that it is included with the 9 hides of Monkton Combe with which it is associated in later records; for example *Suthstok cum Cumba* in *BC*, ii. no.327.

35 Walcot lay within the king's Barton, though there was an outlying portion on Lansdown where Woolley, Langridge, Charlcombe and Weston parishes met. This portion was probably original and gave Walcot woodland and upland pasture to balance its resources. The GDB entry for Bath contains no mention of land or agrarian resources, and the hidage could have been purely notional, as for certain other boroughs. However, it is very probable that some agricultural land was attached, but omitted. In GDB, Bath pays £60 per annum; at the end of the thirteenth century the Borough paid £20 and the Barton £30. The Borough was granted by William II to Bishop John of Wells on the transfer of his seat to Bath in 1088, confirmed by Henry I. Walcot was granted to it under King John; see *BC*, i. nos.39-40, ii. no.709; *RH*, ii. pp.132, 133, 135; A.J. Keevil, 'The Barton of Bath', *Bath History VI* (Millstream Books, Bath, 1996), pp.25-53.

36 On the association of minsters with large primitive estates, their decline and replacement by a network of manorial parish churches, see J. Blair (ed.), *Minsters and Parish Churches: the Local Church in Transition 950-1200* (Oxford Committee for Archaeology, Monograph no. 17, Oxford, 1988).

37 The 1084 Tax Return for Bath Hundred (Exon fol.76a) shows a remission of payment to the Abbess of St. Edmund's [Shaftesbury Abbey] on 3 hides of lordship land. I intend to argue elsewhere that Kelston does appear in GDB, as *Alvestone* a hitherto unidentified appurtenance of Bradford-on-Avon (*GDB Wiltshire* 12,4).

38 'Before 1066 it paid geld for 20 hides when the Shire paid geld'. There is no room for these hides in the 1084 Tax Return. Conversely, the 2 hides of Batheaston which are given no value in GDB because 'they were and are (part) of the lordship revenue of the Borough of Bath' can be identified in the Tax Return.

39 By King Ethelred (*S*. 899 = *Shaftesbury Abbey Charters*, no.29). This tongue of land has remained a part of Wiltshire, though west of the Avon, until the present.

40 J.H. Round, *Feudal England* (Swan Sonnenschein, 1895), pp.36-44.

41 Woolley has been added to Bathwick according to *GDB Somerset* 5,37. The details suggest that they were really separate estates and apart from the meagre woodland at Woolley, both appear to have had a full range of resources, so the linkage may have been quite recent. It lasted however, as in 1316 Bathwick and its hamlet Woolley were held by the Abbess of Wherwell Abbey (Hants.): *FA*, iv. p.329).

42 The fiscal size of Batheaston depends on how recently two of its hides (*GDB Somerset* 1,30) were joined to Bath for tax purposes. It may be a significant surviving linkage; see text below and note 38.

43 The part of Bathford ancient parish that contains Warleigh touches the corner of Monkton Combe parish. Together Warleigh and Monkton Combe make 10 hides, but Warleigh is across the Avon on the Wiltshire bank, and is continuous with Bathford, though that was a neat 10 hides in 1086.

44 See *GDB Somerset*, Appendix I, and F.R. Thorn 'The Hundreds of Somerset' in *The Somerset Domesday*, pp.32-41.

45 *BC*, i. no.7 (= *S*. 51). *Hat Bathu* means 'Hot Baths'. The wording of the charter is expressly against establishing joint houses for monks and nuns in the same place: *cenobialia etiam loca sparsim virorum sparsimque virginum deo famulantium erigenda statuimus* ('also we have decided that religious houses should be constructed separately for men and separately for virgins who are serving God').

46 See Bassett, 'In Search of the Origins of the Anglo-Saxon Kingdoms' in S. Bassett (ed.), *The Origins of Anglo-Saxon Kingdoms* (Leicester University Press, Leicester, 1989), pp.8-17, and N. Brooks, 'On the formation of the Mercian Kingdom', *ibidem*, pp.159-70.

47 The charter exists only in a later copy, see *S*. 51; Taylor (*op.cit.*), pp.136-37; *ECW*, no. 355, p.109; *ECWM*, pp.172-75. For a contrary view, see H. Edwards, *The Charters of the Early West Saxon Kingdom*, (BAR British Series 198, Oxford, 1988), pp.210-27.

48 The 100 hides of Bath and their relation, both to religious houses in Bath and to the Roman town, have been touched on many times. For recent examples, see M. Aston, 'The Bath Region from Late Prehistory to the Middle Ages', *Bath History I* (Alan Sutton, Gloucester, 1986), pp.61-89; Peter Davenport, 'Bath Abbey', *Bath History II* (Alan Sutton, Gloucester, 1988), pp.1-26; Jean Manco, 'Saxon Bath: the Legacy of Rome and the Saxon Rebirth', *Bath History VII* (Millstream Books, Bath, 1998), pp.27-54. The subject can only be mentioned here.

49 *BC*, i. no.6 (= *S*. 1168 = *ECTV*, no.258, p.123). This is a suspect grant by Wigheard with the consent of King Wulfhere of Mercia, dated 670-671, but possibly 681.

50 *BC*, i. no.8, (= *S*. 1167 = *ECTV*, no.259 p.123), a grant by Æthelhard with the consent of King Ethelred of Mercia, dated 681.

51 These names are OE *Beorngyth*; OE *Folcburh*.

52 *S*. 265. The monks of later times erroneously thought that the donor was the Mercian King Coenwulf (796-821), father of St Kenelm; *BC*, ii. no.808.

53 *VCH Somerset*, ii. p.69; Hemming, pp.224-27; Taylor, *op.cit.*, p.135. See *S*. 1257 = *ECWM*, no.228, p.95 = *EHD*, i. no.77, pp.466-67. Cynewulf's other grants in his own right were predominantly south of the Mendips (see *ECW*, nos.389-97, pp.117-18) but there is a tantalising grant (*S*. 262 = *ECW*, no.394, p.117) of 11 *manentes* by the River *Weluue* to the minster at Wells. Unfortunately the bounds have not been reconciled with any around Wellow (Grundy, pp.197-98). See *EHD*, i. no.70.

54 It is possible that 10 hides had already been granted or lost irretrievably. The monastery would already have possessed some lands, among them the 5 hides at North Stoke, but it is not certain if they were counted in the 90 hides. Bath Abbey also held Cold Ashton (*S*. 414, *S*. 664) which may have lain within the original 100 *manentes*, but was not in the later Bath Hundred.

55 The addition of 1 hide at Warleigh would make up the 30 hides.

56 This figure includes the 20 hides at which Bath itself was rated (*GDB Somerset* 1,30). For the grant to Shaftesbury Abbey, see note 39.

57 The death of Alfred, the reeve of Bath (the king's agent), is recorded in the *ASC* for 906.

58 The connection between the two recorded in *GDB Somerset* 1,30-31 may be the last surviving linkage of Bath with its former estates.
59 The boundary of the estate at Bradford-on-Avon, given to Shaftesbury Abbey by King Ethelred in 1001 (*S.* 899 = *Shaftesbury Abbey Charters*, no. 29), in part ran from the Avon at Freshford 'along the abbot's boundary to Midford' and later, after leaving the Avon, along 'the abbot's boundary to Warleigh'. Between Freshford and Midford the boundary would have run along the northern edge of Freshford, then of 'Woodwick', which lay in the western part of Freshford parish, centred on Peipards Farm (ST 7760). 'Woodwick' was held by Bath Abbey in 1086 and was probably the same estate that had been granted (as Freshford) to the abbey in the will of Wulfwaru (*S.* 1538 = *BC*, i. no.27 = *ECW*, no.524, p.148). But the bounds of the Bradford-on-Avon grant imply that Freshford was also then held by the abbey.

My wife Caroline has given help and support at every stage of the writing and revision of this article.

'At The Gates Of Hell':
The Seamy Side of Life
in Seventeenth-Century Bath

John Wroughton

[Bath] ... situated – or rather buried – in deep valleys in the middle of a
thick atmosphere and a sulphureous fog, is at the gates of Hell.
(*A French visitor to Bath in the late seventeenth century*)

The Attraction of Seventeenth-Century Bath

By the seventeenth century, Bath – a walled city of some two thousand
people surrounded by fields and meadows – was already gaining a fine
reputation as an attractive riverside resort.[1] Visitors and residents alike
lavished praise on its location and facilities. Tobias Venner, writing in 1628,
called it 'a little, well-compacted city; for goodness of air, nearness of a
sweet and delectable river, and fertility of soil, it is pleasant and happy
enough'; Henry Chapman, in 1673, admired its backdrop of 'pleasant and
fruitful hills full of excellent springs of water'; Thomas Dingley, in 1682,
noted that 'this city is besides, without doubt, the prettiest in the kingdom
– in a double construction, as it is little and handsome'; and Samuel Pepys,
in 1668, appreciated 'the pretty good market place and many good streets
and very fair stone houses'.[2]

In spite of a serious recession in the local cloth industry at the
beginning of the century, Bath still retained something of an air of
affluence. Indeed, the Corporation was exceedingly wealthy – thanks to
a rich endowment, granted by Edward VI in 1552, of property previously
owned by Bath Priory (dissolved in 1539). The Corporation used its assets
wisely to maintain the fabric of its buildings in good repair and to offer
generous support to the deserving poor through its management of four
hospitals (or almshouses) and its regular doles of bread, wood and coal.
Even during the harrowing years of the Civil War (1642-46), when vast
sums were spent on defence, the city's annual accounts always showed a
healthy credit balance. Furthermore, the charter, granted by Elizabeth I in
1590, conferred on the Corporation wide new powers of local government,
which enabled it to create a safe and secure environment for both residents
and visitors alike. Its medieval walls and gates were regularly repaired and
strengthened; its trained bands were always on hand to counter any threat

from outside; while its street patrols, courts and prison quickly took care of any disturbances from within. There was little crime.

Even by 1625, a visitor would find much to admire on a walk around the narrow streets of Bath – including the new Grammar School, which had been established in 1552 by Edward VI and was now housed in the nave of the disused church of St Mary by the North Gate; the fine new Abbey Church, which had finally been completed in 1617, after a nationwide appeal for funds; and the striking new Guildhall and Market, which, standing in the middle of the High Street, was opened in 1625. The star attraction, however, was undoubtedly the hot water spa, consisting of five baths – an attraction which drew visits from a succession of English monarchs, famous courtiers and distinguished generals.

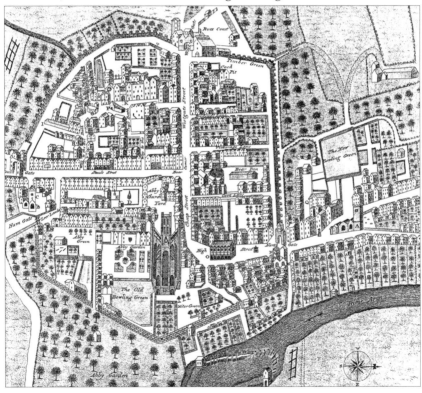

Fig.1 The central section of Joseph Gilmore's map of Bath (1717 edition), which illustrates the compact nature of a walled city surrounded by fields and meadows. Bath Common, on which the 'pest houses' were situated (see the section below on plague), lies off the top right-hand (or north-western) corner of the map. (*Author's collection*)

With the gradual transformation of the health resort into a leisure resort from 1660, an affluent consumer society was created which prompted the rapid expansion of inns, lodging houses, medical care and shops offering a wide range of luxury goods. A post office was opened for the first time in 1647/48; a theatre in 1705; a Pump Room in 1706; and the first Assembly Rooms in 1709. At the same time, recreational activities mushroomed to cater for the social needs of the visiting company. They included cock fighting, tennis, bowls, skittles, dice, formal walks, society balls and rides in sedan chairs. The arrival of

Fig.2 Visitors usually arrived at their inns or lodging houses in Bath by coach, often bringing with them a large amount of luggage. This sometimes even included bed curtains, tableware, furnishings and fuel for the fire. (*Drawing by Stephen Beck*)

Bath's first coffee house in about 1679 provided a rendezvous of a different kind from that already offered by the many alehouses and taverns. This frantic activity, masterminded at least in part by the Corporation, greatly increased the amount of employment available to local people and the general feeling of affluence which impressed visitors. Life, it would seem, was extremely good.

There was, however, another side to life in Stuart Bath, which visitors also noticed – for the city had long experienced a number of serious and intractable problems. The most worrying of these, especially in view of its image as a health resort, centred on beggars, sanitation and disease.

A Constant Threat: the Beggars of Bath

> You cannot be without peril at Bath, whither there is a daily
> resort from Bristol and specially of beggars and poor folks
> (*Letter to Lord Burleigh, 1552;*
> *Historical Manuscripts Commission, Salisbury Papers, 9/16, 1933*)

Even by the middle of the sixteenth century, Bath Corporation had been facing a major social and economic crisis with the steady influx of beggars on a daily basis. 'The Beggars of Bath' gained such national notoriety that the very reputation of the health resort was placed in jeopardy. In desperation, the Corporation decided to petition parliament for its urgent help in tackling this menace, which cast a heavy financial burden on the city's poor rates. The Poor Relief Act of 1572 (14 Eliz. I. c.5), therefore, gave recognition to Bath's unique problem (namely that 'a great number of poor and diseased people do resort to the City of Bath ... for some ease and relief of their diseases', resulting in the inhabitants being 'greatly overcharged'); and put forward a solution which forbade any 'diseased or impotent' person from visiting the city, unless he had been licensed to do so by two justices in his native county. The licence gave a guarantee that his own parish would eventually take him back and continue to support him financially. Failure to produce this licence at the city gates, however, would result in instant punishment as a vagabond – and, in 1572, this meant being branded on the chest with a 'V' and then handed over to a farmer for two years of slavery.

The Corporation tried hard to follow national policy on poverty throughout the seventeenth century. Nevertheless, its resources were often strained by the need to cater for its own resident poor, while at the same time dealing with the large number of beggars who flocked into the city from outside. Bath's affluence and its spa for well-heeled visitors, made it an obvious target for those in desperate need. The Corporation reacted to the need to get unemployed people off the streets by providing them with work. The Poor Law Act of 1601 (43 Eliz. I. c.2), had enabled local authorities to establish Houses of Correction (or Bridewells), so that the fit but jobless poor could be set to work in rather harsh surroundings. However, Bath Corporation did not respond to this opportunity until 1630 – the year which saw worrying food riots on the Midford Hill, just outside Bath. Spurred into action, it immediately called for voluntary subscriptions 'towards the building of a House of Correction', resolving two years later 'to set the poor of this city to work'.[3]

Suitable premises were found in the north-west corner of the city (in what was later known as Bridewell Lane), when Mr Chambers was paid £5 to vacate his barn, stable and backyard for conversion into a House of Correction. A committee was formed to receive and list contributions towards the vital task of transforming the existing fabric. The work was considered to be so urgent that, as contributions began to dry up towards the end of 1634, the Council resolved to charge a general rate on the whole town 'towards the finishing of the House of Correction'. Although little is known of its conditions, small clues appear in payments made for 'window bars' and 'wooden bars' (denoting its prison-like atmosphere); 'hooks and twists' (suggesting employment); and the loan of a rope by Goody Parker 'to dig the well at the House of Correction'. This centre continued in use for much of the century. Indeed, in 1664, the Council showed its determination to check any slackness which had crept into the system by passing this resolution: 'The house called the Bridewell, being built intentionally to be a place wherein to set the poor of this city to work, shall be put to that use'.

Although the House of Correction was chiefly intended to cater for Bath's own resident poor, its prison-like qualities also made it suitable for the temporary detention of rogues and vagabonds. No records have survived to indicate the extent to which it was used for this purpose, although there are occasional glimpses of the tough line taken by the authorities towards such undesirable elements. In 1613, for instance, the Council paid William Doulton, the metal smith, twelve pence 'for an iron to burn rogues with'. This indication of the sense of alarm felt by the authorities is surprising in view of the fact that the 1601 Poor Law Act had dispensed with the earlier practice of branding vagabonds. In most places they were now severely whipped, before being returned to their home parish.

Fig.3 The Poor Law Act of 1601 made provision for unemployed vagabonds to be whipped and sent back to their home parishes. (*By permission of the British Library: Bagford's Ballads, vol.III, 51*)

It was of course crucial to ensure that visiting beggars did not become a long-term charge on local people. They were therefore removed, if necessary, by force – such as the impoverished soldier who was manhandled out of town by two paid workers on the mayor's orders in 1699; or the woman and two children who were carried away 'after the regiment' on the mayor's instructions (her soldier husband having dumped them on the city). Nevertheless, in spite of the Corporation's active concern, the problem of aggressive begging was never entirely solved.

A Constant Eyesore: the State of the Streets

> The streets are no more than dung hills, slaughter houses and pig sties
> (*Dr Edward Jorden; A Discourse of Naturall Bathes and Minerall Waters, 1631*)

At the beginning of the century, the condition of the streets was appalling. Foul-smelling rubbish accumulated on every footpath to rot away slowly in the still and humid air of Bath. The open channel or culvert which ran down the centre of the main streets, was often blocked by ashes, rubble and other unpleasant debris, while horses, cattle and other animals (often on their way to market) left behind them a trail of manure and urine.

Fig.4 A contemporary drawing of a typical street scene. Note the piles of refuse, which the scavenger is loading into his cart; the central drainage channel, which has become an open sewer; the child using the street as a toilet; a pig wallowing in the dirt; and the chamber pot being emptied out of a first-floor window.
(*By permission of the British Library: Roxburghe Ballads, RAX.Rox.I, pt.2.547*)

Although the city's revised charter of 1590 had given the Corporation powers to make by-laws over such matters as street cleaning, it was not until 1646 that these were taken up. During the first half of the century, therefore, the streets were only cleaned at very irregular intervals. Payments were made occasionally by the chamberlain for 'shovelling up the dirt in Westgate Street', 'cleansing the way by the Bridge', or 'cleansing the way by the borough walls'. As late as 1654, John Evelyn was to describe the streets as 'narrow, uneven, and unpleasant' – for even after the publication of the by-laws the street-cleaning operation remained totally unsystematic. The Corporation only tended to respond either to a particular crisis of accumulated filth (e.g. 'cleansing Cox Lane and Vicarage Lane' in 1672; and 'shovelling at the Borough Walls' in 1682) or to a visit by a distinguished guest (e.g. 'cleaning Southgate when the Queen came' in 1687).[4]

Earlier, in 1602, the Corporation had found itself in a state of undisguised panic when rumours swept the city of an impending visit by Queen Elizabeth. The streets were in such a deplorable state that messengers were urgently dispatched to Tetbury, Cirencester, Frome, Bristol, Sodbury, Warminster and Chippenham 'to get paviours against the Queen's coming'. Emergency repairs were then quickly undertaken by these skilled workmen in both High Street and Westgate Street – although the rumours eventually proved to be false! Nevertheless, as the century progressed, the streets were increasingly well cobbled and kept in reasonable repair – a fact which undoubtedly aided the cleaning process. Sometimes it was only a matter of employing workmen 'for mending the highway at Holloway' or for 'pitching at Southgate', although occasionally whole stretches of road were completely remade. In 1648, for instance, the council resurfaced 268 yards of Westgate Street and 'under the gate', a task which required thirty-four loads of stone. Fourteen loads of 'rubbish stone' were carted away by the workers who spent a week in all on the job.

As early as 1633 the Corporation had tried to impose standards of behaviour on its citizens in relation to the streets, particularly over the matter of the drainage channels. Councillors ruled that 'everyone that doth sweep the street before their doors and put it [the dirt] into the channel shall pay 12d for each offence'. The measure met with limited success. However, the new by-laws which came into force in 1650 (having been first drafted in 1646), made a determined effort to tighten up on a number of abuses that had crept in over the course of time. The householder was henceforward strictly forbidden to throw 'any soil, dung or filth in or near any open street, which shall be offensive to such street'. He was also required 'to sweep and make clean the street before his house every Saturday morning' or face a one shilling fine for neglect. Fines were to be put towards the cost of repairing and cleansing the streets. Then, in order to reduce the amount of animal droppings, the city's first-ever 'parking' restriction was introduced. No-one from henceforth was 'to tie or feed, or suffer any kind of beast to stand in any of the said streets above the space of one quarter of an hour'.[5]

The activities of the butchers were also addressed by the new by-laws. A few years earlier (in 1631), Dr Edward Jorden had observed that 'the butchers dressed their meat at their own doors, while pigs wallow in the mire'.[6] Indeed, in the same year, after complaints about the problem of pigs, three councillors were detailed 'to view the annoyances in Mr Cox's garden next the [butchers'] shambles'. Two years later, when Cox was in the process of renewing his lease, the Corporation actually made it a condition that he was 'to remove his pigsties'. The by-laws therefore attempted to tackle the whole question of hygiene in the preparation of food, aiming to prevent butchers from adding to the filthy state of the streets and to ensure that only meat in good condition reached the market. Part of the problem was that cattle and sheep were often brought into Bath 'on the hoof' for slaughter by butchers in the spaces behind and around their shops. This practice not only contributed to the general stench, but also added to the whole question of waste disposal.

It was consequently stipulated in the new by-laws that 'no butcher should kill any calf, sheep, swine or any other cattle in any of the open streets, nor hang out any flesh newly killed so as to soil or annoy the said streets'. Furthermore, pig owners were strictly banned from allowing their animals to wander around the streets in search of discarded waste – a practice which had clearly been prevalent before. Fines for all these food offences were to be devoted to the care of the poor. Nevertheless, John Wood was to claim in 1765 that, even at the end of the seventeenth century, the streets were still the same as Jorden had described them with pigs foraging for scraps and horses being fed 'at almost every door from small racks or mangers'.[7]

The existing health regulations were somewhat strengthened by a resolution of the council in 1663, which also tackled the problem of children's behaviour in the streets. Anyone in future who did 'lay or deposit any manner of coal, ashes, dirt or soil whatsoever in any of the streets, lanes or ways within the city, or let forth their child or children to do their easement or ordure [excrement] in any of the streets' would be liable to a fine of 3s 4d (with half going to the informer and half to the poor). There is some evidence that this tougher line was implemented. In 1677, for instance, the Council ruled that Edward Taylor was to be prosecuted for establishing his own 'mixon' or rubbish dump 'in the highway'; while in 1683 the borough Quarter Sessions ordered Richard Edgill 'to carry away the soil and horse dung' that he had dumped in the Outer Bowling Green – or face a fine of ten shillings. Air quality was also important in a health resort – hence a decision by the Council in 1698 to prosecute Thomas Rosewell 'for the nuisance to this city' caused by his lime kiln; or an earlier ruling in 1646 that 'no inhabitant was to brew or dry malt by night between nine o'clock at night and four o'clock in the morning or light any fire' on pain of a five shilling fine. Pollution, however, remained a serious problem, thanks in part to the work of the tanners, chandlers and soap-boilers – in addition to the brewers and lime-kiln operators.

Nevertheless, in spite of the efforts of the Corporation to improve cleanliness within the city, corrective action still tended to be just as irregular and spasmodic at the end of the century as it had always been. Indeed, it was not until 1707 that the Corporation, after many complaints from visitors to the spa, gained an Act of Parliament giving them authority 'to pave, cleanse and light the streets and lanes of the town' in a systematic manner. In particular, the Act enabled the mayor and justices to appoint 'surveyors of the streets' in each parish 'to have the care of the cleansing of the said streets'. It required every householder to sweep the street in front of his house three times a week (on Tuesday, Thursday and Saturday) in readiness for a collection by the scavenger. In addition, the citizen was strictly forbidden to throw any filth, rubbish or dung into the streets, but to keep it inside his house or yard until the scavenger's visit. Of even greater significance was the stipulation that each householder would on occasions be directed 'to pitch or pave' the street in front of his house up to the middle of the road. Failure to comply with any of these regulations would result in a fine ranging from 3s 4d to 10s 0d.[8]

A Constant Stench: the Disposal of Sewage

[Bath] scarce gives the company any room to converse
out of the smell of their own excrements
(*Daniel Defoe; Tour of the Whole Island of Great Britain, 1927 edn., vol.2, p.168*)

The sanitary arrangements were primitive in the extreme. Some of the people living in Southgate Street had privies at the bottom of their gardens, which drained into Bum Ditch. These can clearly be seen on Joseph Gilmore's map of Bath in 1694. Most of the people who lived in the more cramped conditions inside the city walls would have been far less fortunate, being faced by a serious problem over waste disposal. If they had no space in a back garden or yard to site an earth closet and cesspit, they would be obliged to rely on the use of chamber pots and close stools. The servants would often dispose of the contents of these receptacles by emptying them into the channel in the middle of the street, where they were churned up with other refuse by passing traffic. The more idle servants would simply throw the contents out of an upper floor window – forcing pedestrians to walk as close as possible to the walls of houses seeking cover under the overhanging storeys. Samuel Pepys describes in his diary for 1664 how two men, 'jostling for the wall' in a London street, killed each other in a furious brawl over this issue.

In some houses sewage was stored in a vault in the basement. However, vaults such as these – and cess pits, too – needed to be cleared periodically by digging out the contents – an unpleasant task undertaken by 'night-soil men'. Failure to do so could often bring unfortunate consequences. Pepys, for instance, describes how the vault in his neighbour's cellar in London had not been emptied on a regular basis, with the result that the contents overflowed into his own basement. Going there one day, he stepped 'into a great heap of turds', which alerted him to the fact that 'Mr Turner's house of office is full'. It had been usual practice in many towns for this dung or 'night soil' to be dumped haphazardly outside the city or flung into the river, either by individuals or by the night-soil men themselves.[9]

Such behaviour was however banned by the Bath Council in 1613, when a scavenger was appointed to collect the refuse. Consequently, each citizen was ordered to 'send his dust [sewage] to the scavenger's cart ... in some vessel to be emptied into the said cart'. The scavenger then carried this refuse outside the city, where it was mainly deposited in mixons (or rubbish dumps) outside the South and West Gates – although there was also one outside both the East Gate in 1634 and the Ham Gate in 1615. This situation undoubtedly contributed to the stench which so upset visitors to the city in summer. In a determined effort to enforce this new order the Corporation instructed the beadle, and each tithingman within his tithing (or sector), to inspect each week 'the common annoyance of casting of soil over the town walls'. They were to present a list of offenders to the town clerk each Monday, for punishment in court.

As the century progressed, other locations were also used for the disposal of night soil. In 1632, for instance, the new 'scavenger of the common' (to give him his full title) was instructed 'to collect soil in the city and suburbs and to spread it on the common according to the overseers' orders'. Even so, no consistent policy seems to have prevailed. In 1689, for instance, the Council paid workmen for 'cleansing the soil abroad in the town'; and in 1685 for 'throwing soil over the borough walls'. At least they no longer threw it into the Avon, where water-borne diseases such as typhoid could thrive amid the pollution. It should also be remembered that the spread of germs from sewage was largely responsible for the high mortality rate in infancy, with possibly one in five babies dying in the first few months – many from diarrhoea.

In order to limit the scale of this problem, the Corporation had built 'a common privy' or public convenience in 1575, paying a labourer for 'digging a dyke [ditch]', constructing a timber frame and tiling the roof. In 1623, 'a house of office' (or public convenience) was built near the Ham Gate, situated over the stream which eventually ran into Bum Ditch.

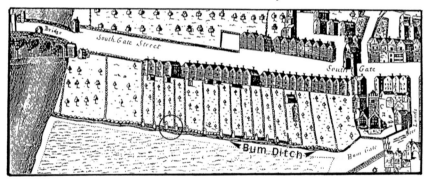

Fig.5 A section of Joseph Gilmore's map of 1694, which shows thirteen individual privies (two have been circled) situated at the bottom of gardens belonging to the houses in Southgate Street. These drained into Bum Ditch, which itself drained into the river. (*Author's collection*)

Payments were occasionally made thereafter for 'cleansing the Ham privy' – but whether this was abused by vandals or merely over-used by visitors, the chamberlain sealed its fate in 1636 by paying money for 'walling up the privy door and 2 sacks of lime'. However, other such conveniences were established from time to time – such as 'a house of ease' (also called 'the house of office') at the bowling green in 1681. Examples of these public privies found elsewhere suggest that they usually consisted of an oak bench with a row of holes (but with no partitions between) and a pit below. A great step forward was made in 1707 when a more elegant-sounding convenience – a 'pass house for the use of ladies frequenting this city' – was erected near the Abbey.[10]

The reality, however, was that Bath – like all other cities – suffered from a persistent and highly unpleasant stench, made worse by its high level of humidity and its location in a hollow. As noted earlier, one French visitor put it like this: 'Bath, situated – or rather buried – in deep valleys in the middle of a thick atmosphere and a sulphureous fog, is at the gates of Hell'. Even as late as 1716, the Duchess of Marlborough complained: 'I never saw any place abroad that had more stinks and dirt in it than Bath'. Daniel Defoe was much more specific after a visit to the city in 1722. Bath, he said, 'was more like a prison than a place of diversion ... where the city itself may be said to stink like a general common-shore'.[11] As a result, the Corporation – ever conscious of the city's reputation as a health resort – always did its best to ensure that a good stock of sweet-smelling herbs was available for the personal use of royal visitors (e.g. James II in 1686; his queen, Mary of Modena, in 1687; and Princess Anne in 1692).

A Constant Fear: the Terror of the Plague

*The contagious sickness did so much affright the inhabitants of
Widcombe that they were fearful to come into other people's company*
(*Local eyewitness, 1625*)

There is no doubt that Bath Corporation adopted a most responsible policy towards maintaining the health of the local community. It gradually set tight controls over the cleanliness of the city, the disposal of night soil and the purity of its water supply. With its public drinking fountains (and, indeed, many of its private houses) supplied with clear spring water from the neighbouring hills, Bath was spared many of the anxieties and problems over health which affected most cities at this time. Health hazards in Worcester, for instance, were alarming, with the river constantly polluted from the dyers' vats as well as refuse of all kinds. Outbreaks of bubonic plague – the scourge of most towns – were also frequent. Norwich suffered six epidemics between 1579 and 1665; Bristol lost a sixth of its population on three occasions between 1565 and 1603; Newcastle witnessed a mortality rate of a third during the epidemic of 1636-7; and over two thousand died in Chester during the attack of 1647.

The filthy streets and densely-packed houses of the large cities provided an ideal environment for the black rats on which the infection-bearing fleas bred. Although bubonic plague was in itself a disease of rats, when the host rat died the infected fleas attacked humans if another rat could not be found. As Roger Rolls has pointed out, the disease – indicated by swollen lymph glands (buboes) in the neck, groin and armpits, a high fever, delirium and red blotches all over the skin – was highly infectious.[12] Bath remained largely immune from threats of this kind within the community – its main problem being to ensure that a city, which actively encouraged visitors to flock in numbers to sample its healing waters, did not at the same time encourage the importation of plague. Precautions, however, did not always work. Sir Thomas Seymour, for instance, admitted in 1605 that, as the plague had struck down two people in his house in London, he had forsaken the capital and was living in Bath. In an attempt to counter this unwelcome form of intrusion, the Corporation had (as early as 1583) paid two watchmen, Oliver and Green, 'for seeing that none should come into the city from Paulton and other places which were infected with the plague'.

A much more serious crisis, however, arose in 1604 when the plague actually struck inside the city.[13] The extent of this is graphically described in a number of letters to Robert Cecil, James I's Secretary of State, who was planning a visit to the baths to gain relief from his chronic ailments. Dr John Sherwood, a leading and reputable physician at the spa, advised Cecil to delay his visit until the plague had passed its peak. By 21st July, he said, twenty-six people had died and seven or eight houses in various parts of the city had become infected. Revised figures were given in August by Captain John Winter of Dyrham in a further letter to Cecil. He reported that, although fifty people had died between 6th May (when the epidemic began) and 18th August, the disease was by then confined to four houses, including the *White Swan* in Westgate Street (where two people lay sick and a further six had already died). Winter, however, was forced to admit in September that a further three houses had become infected, although much of the city was by then completely clear.

Cecil decided to postpone his visit. Although Sherwood had given the Secretary of State an honest assessment of the situation at the end of August (seventy-two dead and twenty-four houses infected), many local people were furious with him for discouraging the visit of such an eminent person – someone who could have used his influence 'to renew their old charter with more immunities'. Sherwood was disgusted at such selfish attitudes, which failed to heed 'the health and safety of others' – especially when it later transpired that one of Cecil's own cooks, who would have been preparing his food in Bath, had been staying in one of the newly-infected houses. The prospect of this, commented Sherwood to Cecil later, was 'a thing of terror to those that truly love you'. On occasions, therefore, commercial interest could cloud the judgment of a city, even one so committed to the health of its community.

In human terms, the impact of this outbreak is vividly illustrated by a Bill of Mortality for the city dated 20th September. This revealed that no fewer than eighty-eight people had died within the city during the four months from the middle of May – including seventy-two 'of the plague', eleven 'by the ordinary visitation of God' and five whose deaths were 'uncertain'. These deaths were in stark contrast to the average *annual* death rate for Bath of just fifty-four during the period 1603-1620. The plague victims (who mostly lived in the parishes of the Abbey and St James) included eight people each from the houses of Goodwife Moore and John Adye; eight from the *Swan Inn*; five from the home of Dr Richard Bayly; and four from Walter Misam's house. In addition eight people, who had been 'carried from the town' in a sick condition, eventually died of the plague in the specially built 'pest house' on the common. Nevertheless, although Bath seems to have escaped quite lightly (unlike Bristol which lost over 2,000 victims during the same epidemic), such was the anxiety within the city that even many of the doctors had moved away in fear. Lord Zouche, in a letter to the Secretary of State (Lord Cecil) at the end of July, commented that he had been informed that 'the sickness is at the Bath dispersed so much as the physicians be fled from thence'. A week earlier, Dr John Sherwood had admitted in a letter that he was actually writing from Tockington 'where, for preventing the worst, I have for a time reposed my poor family'.[14]

Disturbing stories often reached the ears of the Corporation and terrified many local people as rumours abounded. In 1625 and 1626, plague once more threatened the area. It was at a time when cities throughout the country were again being devastated by the disease – thousands died in Exeter, while twenty per cent of the population were swept away in both Norwich and London. It was hardly surprising, therefore, that alarming news quickly spread from Frome of a man called Phillips, who had returned from London with his wife and child, having been exposed to the 'infection of the plague'. The authorities in Frome ordered them to be locked up in a house outside the town and placed under strong guard at the door. This remained in position until the family eventually died.

Bath did not escape completely from this outbreak, although the numbers affected never reached major epidemic proportions. Under the circumstances, the Corporation felt impelled to take decisive action by again isolating those who were ill, building three special houses 'for the sick folks' on the common – but also showing a little more compassion than was shown in Frome by ensuring that they were kept well supplied with food (at a cost of £13 1s 8d). When the crisis was over, workmen were paid for dismantling the temporary buildings and, in the words of the council minute, 'bringing the pest-houses home' (presumably for use on a future occasion). The burial registers show that, whereas the parish of St James remained largely unaffected, the parish of St Michael's took the brunt of the distress. In just four months (February to May, 1626) there were thirty-one burials (almost twice the annual average for that decade) – including those of Walter Robence and four of his children; and four sons of John Fowler. The Abbey parish (with thirty-three burials in 1625 as opposed to a normal average of twenty-three) also suffered greatly when Edmund Tucker lost his wife, his two sons and two daughters; and James Smith lost his five daughters and two sons. In all probability, the four families mentioned above were among those billeted in the 'pest-houses' on the common.

1635 witnessed another distressing outbreak of disease in Bath – which particularly affected children living in the parishes of St Michael's and the Abbey. A clue to the nature of this illness is given in Sir William Brereton's account of his visit to the city in July of that year where, he said, 'the smallpox had raged exceedingly'.[15] The problem was most acute in St Michael's where twenty-four children died in nine months from July 1635 to March 1636 – against an annual average for children *and* adults of just eighteen for that particular decade. The Allins lost three children, while the Sherstons, the Englands and the Lockwoods each lost two. Families living in the Abbey parish lost twenty-five children during a sixth-month peak period between June and November 1635 – a total which would normally have represented the number of all deaths (including adults) for a whole year.

As a result of this experience, the Corporation decided in October 1636 to look at the possibility of 'building of houses in the common for persons infected with the plague and for appointing of persons to attend them and for maintenance of them during their sickness'. The implication is that these would be held in readiness for future attacks. It has to be said, however, that most people – living, as they did, at a time when religion dominated every aspect of life – viewed sudden epidemics such as these as God's punishment upon a sinful community. For instance, John Taylor, writing in 1625, spoke of 'our heinous sins' which had provoked 'God's just indignation' and brought about 'this heavy visitation and mortality'. Furthermore, these outbreaks had become such regular events that they were generally accepted as part of the normal hazards of life, along with bad harvests, unemployment and inflation.

A much more alarming crisis hit the city in 1643 – quite apart from the Battle of Lansdown which was fought on its doorstep. The burial registers all recorded by far their largest total of deaths for any one year in the first half of the century – seventy-two for St James (compared with an annual average of twenty-two for the previous ten years), one hundred and nine for the Abbey (compared with an average of thirty-five) and about ninety-two for St Michael's (compared with an average of twenty-one).[16] Families again suffered terribly with at least seven of those living in St Michael's parish losing two or more of their members. It is highly unlikely that any of the people who died were casualties of the battle. Civil War soldiers killed in action were almost always buried speedily in great pits on the battlefield by local villagers in an attempt to prevent the spread of disease. Indeed, contemporary accounts refer to the royalist dead being loaded into carts and buried on Tog Hill and the wounded being carried away with the army in wagons as it retreated to Devizes. Commanders always tried hard to transport their sick and wounded to one of the war hospitals, which had been set up in various cities such as Bristol and Oxford.

Nevertheless, the soldiers were – in all probability – largely responsible for this outbreak. In 1643 the armies of both king and parliament were ravaged with what was known at the time as 'camp fever', 'gaol fever' or typhus – an illness which had already killed one-fifth of the population in the garrisoned city of Oxford. This virulent disease (the symptoms of which were a purple rash and a high fever) was transmitted by lice, which found a breeding ground in the bedding and clothing of soldiers crowded into insanitary billets. It was inevitable that large numbers of these troops were accommodated in the homes of local citizens whenever an army captured and garrisoned a city. Typhus speedily took root, therefore, among the civilian population. One eyewitness in Bristol, following the fall of the city to royalist forces in 1643, noted that twenty or thirty men were packed into quite ordinary houses, 'causing men, women and children to lay upon the boards, while the cavaliers possess their beds, *which they fill with lice*'. The disease rapidly spread throughout the entire place, a parliamentarian agent noting that 'there die a hundred a week of the new disease at Bristol'.

Bath had also suffered from a heavy military presence during the summer of 1643 in the weeks prior to the Battle of Lansdown, as parliamentarian forces waited to intercept the march of the royalist army from Cornwall. Many were billeted inside the city. Once Bath had been captured for the king in mid-July, a royalist garrison was installed – with soldiers from the Bristol garrison! It is perhaps not surprising, therefore, that the typhus outbreak in Bath was at its peak between August and November that year. It is also not surprising that when, two years later, the plague was again ravaging Bristol, the citizens of Bath objected strongly to a decision by Prince Rupert (the royalist governor of Bristol) to send a detachment of Welsh troops from that city to strengthen the Bath garrison. Local people turned out of their houses *en masse* to stage a noisy street demonstration, calling out to a man, 'No Welsh! No Welsh' – a cry which was really directed not against the Welsh, but against any potential carrier from plague-ridden Bristol.[17]

Further panic hit Bath in 1665, when the notorious Great Plague of London – carried over from Amsterdam – threatened to spread nationwide. It is estimated that, at one stage in the epidemic, a thousand people were dying each day in the capital – with the death toll eventually reaching 100,000. News was quickly circulated by travellers and merchants: of plague-stricken homes with red crosses daubed on doors as a sign of the plague within; of homes guarded by watchmen with halberds to prevent the escape of the family; of handcarts being wheeled through the streets to the cry of *Bring out your dead*; of corpses being thrown into great pits – some fifty at a time – and buried in haste.

The words of the Reverend Thomas Vincent also reverberated: 'Now death rides triumphant on his pale horse through our streets and breaks into every house where any inhabitants are to be found'.[18]

There was inevitably a great stampede out of London by citizens desperate to escape this threat to their lives – a stampede which brought terror to other places. During the earlier outbreak in 1625, John Taylor had described a similar situation in *The Fearful Summer*:

> The name of London now both far and near
> Strikes all the towns and villages with fear
> And to be thought a Londoner is worse
> Than one that breaks a house or takes a purse.[19]

The Council in Bath urgently debated the crisis and the worrying information that many people from London were daily attempting to reach Bath 'to the great danger of our city'. It was resolved that no citizen was to receive into his house any people from the plague-ridden areas on pain of a £10 fine. Furthermore, the night watchmen were instructed to prevent any strangers from entering the city between ten o'clock in the evening and five o'clock in the morning – or risk being fined £5 for each offence.[20] On this occasion at least – judging by the low number of burials – the city survived unscathed. The 1665 outbreak of plague turned out to be the last – partly because this disease (which was normally imported by black rats on board ships) was gradually contained through stricter

Fig.6 A contemporary wood-cut to illustrate the attempted flight from London by many fearful citizens during the Great Plague of 1665. Notice how Death waits to ambush them at every turn, indicating with his hourglass that, for them, the sands of time are running out. (*Author's collection*)

controls at the ports. As the black rats disappeared, they were replaced by brown rats, which may have been immune to the plague bacterium carried by fleas.

* * *

Despite the many attractions of Stuart Bath, the problems posed by the presence of beggars, insanitary conditions and disease, were not easily resolved. However, the seventeenth century marked an important but often neglected period of trans-ition from the medieval town locked within its walls, to the eighteenth-century city of space and elegance still admired by visitors today.

Notes

BRO = Bath Record Office

1   This article is based on research undertaken for the author's latest book – *Stuart Bath: Life in the Forgotten City, 1603-1714* (Lansdown Press, Bath, 2004). See this publication for fuller details of the following section. See also Trevor Fawcett and Marta Inskip, 'The Making of Orange Grove', *Bath History*, vol.V (Millstream Books, Bath, 1994), pp.24-50.

2   Tobias Venner, *The Baths of Bath* (William Oldys (ed.), Harleian Miscellany, vol.2, 1809), p.311; Henry Chapman, *Thermae Redivivae: the City of Bath Discovered* (1673), p.1; Thomas Dingley, *History from Marble* (Camden Society, vol.94, pt.1, 1867), p.58 of the facsimile; John Warrington (ed.), *The Diary of Samuel Pepys* (Dent, 1953 edn., vol.3), pp.244-47.

3   For references to the House of Correction see the Bath Chamberlain's Accounts (1613-1699) *passim* and the Bath Council Minute Books I (1630-34) and II (1644), BRO.

4   The source of all payments and resolutions by the Corporation throughout this article will be found in BRO – the Bath Chamberlain's Accounts (1646-1700) *passim* and the Bath Council Minute Books I (1631-49), II (1649-84) and III (1684-1715).

5   BRO – Bath Council Minute Books I (1646) and II (1650).

6   Edward Jorden, *A Discourse of Naturall Bathes and Minerall Waters* (1631).

7   John Wood, *Essay Towards a Description of Bath*, 3rd edn. (Bathoe and Lownds, 1765), p.217. For full details of the new by-laws, see Richard Warner, *History of Bath* (Cruttwell, Bath, 1801), pp.200-203.

8   Act for the Repair, Amending and Cleaning of the Highways, 1707, 6 Anne c.42, BRO.

9   Robert Latham (ed.), *The Shorter Pepys* (Unwin Hyman, 1990), 20th October 1660.

10 For all payments and resolutions by the Council see the Bath Chamberlain's Accounts and Council Minute Books for the relevant dates, BRO.

11 Daniel Defoe, *Tour of the Whole Island of Great Britain*, vol.2 (Peter Davies, 1927), p.168.

12 This information was provided by Roger Rolls from his unpublished lecture notes on the subject.

13 See Trevor Fawcett, 'Bubonic Plague at Bath in 1604' in *History of Bath Research Group Newsletter*, no.20 (Bath, January 1993).

14 For the Cecil correspondence in the preceding paragraphs and the Bill of Mortality see Historical Manuscripts Commission: *Salisbury Papers* (9 Salisbury, 16-17).

15 William Brereton, *Travels in Holland etc.* (Chatham Society, 1844).

16 Transcripts of the burial registers for the three Bath parishes can be found in the BRO. An allowance has been made in the figures relating to St Michael's parish to compensate for a missing page of additional entries, which has been torn out of the register. See also John Taylor, *The Fearful Summer: or London's Calamity* (1625) for a contemporary reaction to the plague.

17 For these and further details of events in 1643 and 1645 see John Wroughton, *An Unhappy Civil War: the Experiences of Ordinary People in Gloucestershire, Somerset and Wiltshire, 1642-1646* (Lansdown Press, Bath, 1999).

18 Roger Hart, *English Life in the Seventeenth Century* (Wayland, 1970), pp.103-111; Thomas Vincent, *God's Terrible Voice to the City* (1665).

19 Taylor, *The Fearful Summer* (1625), pp.1-4.

20 Bath Council Minute Book II (1665).

Bath's Second Guildhall
c.1630 to 1776

Michael Bishop

Bath has seen three Guildhalls. The first, medieval building stood in the courtyard behind today's Guildhall. The second, dating from the late 1620s, occupied the upper storey of the Tudor Market House in the middle of High Street. This 'Stuart Guildhall', enlarged in the 1720s, stood until 1776. By that time Baldwin's present building, the third Guildhall, was complete, and the old structure was demolished (Fig.1).

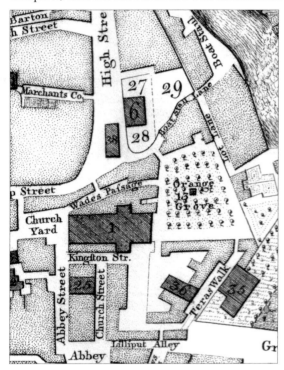

Little is known about the Stuart Guildhall, yet over a period of a century and a half its staircase echoed to the footsteps of mayors, city councillors, functionaries both high and lowly, Bathonians of all levels of society as, during the daylight hours, they climbed to the rooms above the arcaded market hall to attend their meetings and conduct their business; rooms which, in the evenings and with candles ablaze and the paraphernalia of administration cleared away, would be transformed into a setting

Fig.1 Detail from 'A New and Correct Plan of the City of Bath, printed by Frederick H. Leake and W. Taylor Booksellers in Bath', c.1776. It captures the moment when the Stuart Guildhall (no.38) still stood alongside Baldwin's new building (no.6). The site of the earliest Guildhall was just below no.29. Nos.27, 28 and 29 indicate respectively the Butter, Green and Meat Markets. (*Reproduced by courtesy of Bath Record Office*)

for balls and banqueting. By the 1770s, however, its structure had grown increasingly unsafe and was now considered unbefitting the kind of city which Bath had become; down it must come. Ruthless replanning of the city centre was overdue; so was a worthier Guildhall. But few records survive of what the earlier building looked like; and – model-making being one of my interests – I decided to go about things in three stages. First, having read what accounts I could find of the Stuart Guildhall, to marshal the evidence for its appearance; secondly, to make the model; thirdly, to go more closely into the documentary evidence for its history.[1]

Sources of information: the visual evidence

Visits to Bath Reference Library and the Victoria Art Gallery proved fruitful. In the end I had photocopies of seventeen different illustrations of my quarry: the two little drawings in the Gilmore map of the 1690s; the watercolour by Edward Eyre, and a crude copy improbably ascribed to G.P. Manners; eleven drawings of the north and west façades, undated, unsigned and hard to categorise, lying halfway between formal elevations and architectural sketches enlivened by little figures to add scale. Two recent views, a fanciful reconstruction by Paul Braddon (1864-1938) and one by R.W.M. Wright (c.1889-1963), were clearly of limited interest only. But what of the rest?

The Gilmore Map
    Familiar and frequently reproduced, this 'Mapp or topographical Description of the City of Bath ... exactly Surveyed by ... Joseph Gilmore Teacher of the Mathematicks in the City of Bristol', is best known in its 1731 version 'printed and sold by Thomas Bakewell, Map and printseller of Fleet Street'; but that was its sixth reissue since its initial appearance in 1694 'based on a draft drawn by Gilmore himself and engraved by John Savage'. It shows, from the east, a pictorial view of the city as it was in the early 1690s. Apart from its treasury of information (it includes a list of twenty-two inns) about a small spa town starting to expand, what distinguishes it particularly is its encircling border of thirty-five vignettes: thirty of these depict lodging houses, and of the remainder one shows 'the East Side of the Guild Hall'. This duplicates, though not precisely, what in the key to the map is called 'the Market House' in the High Street. Only the Abbey Church is similarly honoured by appearing twice.

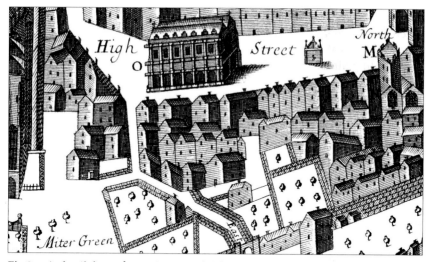

Fig.2a A detail from the main part of Gilmore's map of 1694 showing the Stuart Guildhall from the east. The northern side of the Abbey can be seen on the extreme left, flanked by houses. (*Reproduced by courtesy of Bath Record Office*)

Close scrutiny of the two versions (figs.2a and 2b) reveals variations, but both show the same basic features: a rectangular building arcaded at ground level, with six arches along the sides and two at the ends and, above the side arches, windows (given tripartite mullions in the more detailed version); buttresses stand at each corner, and at the northern end is a tall, rounded central window. There is a double roof, with twin gables at either end surmounted by finials, and further finials at the four corners; and a scallop decoration runs along the top of the east façade. Where the Gilmore versions differ most is in the pilasters flanking the arches below

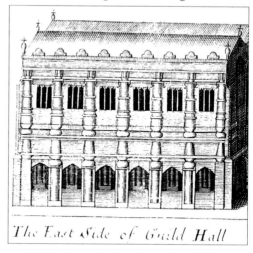

Fig.2b A vignette from the border of Gilmore's map showing a second picture of the 'East Side of Guild Hall'. (*Reproduced by courtesy of Bath Record Office*)

and the windows above; one version shows only five at ground level and seven (grotesquely bulbous) against the upper story, while the other has seven pilasters at both levels. But such evidence, crucial in what it tells us of a building already sixty years old, is of limited value to a model-maker.

The Eyre watercolour

One of three drawings by Edmund Eyre in the Victoria Art Gallery, this lively little watercolour (7½ins x 10ins) of *High Street, Bath, looking towards the old Guildhall* (Fig.3), presents certain problems: is this an on-the-spot contemporary view of the Stuart Guildhall before its demolition in 1776, or is this – more probably – the painting entitled *The Beginning of the New Town Hall at Bath, 1776* that was shown at the Royal Academy exhibition of 1786?[2] The purely fanciful classical portal (nothing like Baldwin's) visible to the left of the old Guildhall suggests that the painting is an imaginative reconstruction of what Eyre witnessed ten years earlier, perhaps based on sketches made at that time. An army officer, the artist

Fig.3 Edward Eyre's watercolour of the High Street, dated c.1776 but probably done some years later and showing the Stuart Guildhall shortly before demolition, with Baldwin's new Guildhall rising to its left (*Reproduced by courtesy of the Victoria Art Gallery, Bath and North East Somerset Council*)

is known to have visited Bath annually between 1772 and 1776 for the season, and might even have been in the city on the fateful November day in 1775 when Thomas Warr Atwood, the Chief Architect, fell to his death in a half-demolished building on the site. Atwood's death put an end to years of dilly-dallying, and his brilliant young associate Thomas Baldwin took his place.[3] All was set to go ahead with the new Guildhall, and the old building might well have been pulled down during Eyre's final visit in the winter of 1776/7. Certainly building materials saved from the demolition were auctioned off (for a mere £161) at the end of March 1777. In Thomas Malton's version of *The Town Hall at Bath* (c 1777) all trace of the Stuart Guildhall has gone: the street is clear.[4] Eyre's High Street, by contrast, is full of activity around the doomed old building. From the White Lion Inn on the left a horse emerges; workmen dig up cobblestones, carry a plank or push a barrow; three huts block the right-hand arch, huge doors are propped by the other arch near a parked cart; and in the meantime street life continues, as a coach rattles along and passers-by stroll or lounge. But is what we see less a snapshot than a scene recollected in tranquillity?

The Eleven Elevations

It was obvious that these would be crucial for my model; yet, as I compared the six views of the north end of the old Guildhall, and five views from the west, I found to my surprise that, though they were very nearly identical, each differed marginally from the rest. This was most evident when I scrutinised the little figures glimpsed through the arches: five women, eight men, and two dogs; and outside, a little hunchback apparently posting bills on the north-west buttress. Each version showed the same figures in the same places, but they differed so widely in dress and posture as to leave no doubt that none of my drawings was identical to any other, and that either the original lurked undetected among them or all were copies. All were undated and unsigned: one north elevation was attributed to Henry Venn Lansdown (1806-1860), one north and one west elevation jointly to J. Manners and J.C. Maggs (1819-1896), two announced themselves as the gift of G.H. Manners, one that of the architect Mowbray Green. But I was no nearer to who drew the originals, and when.

There was one straw to clutch at: a drawing of the west front presented to the Victoria Art Gallery in 1984 was recorded as being 'after George Vertue.' George Vertue (1684-1756) was the distinguished 'Engraver and Member of the Society of Antiquaries' who in 1750 published the noble engraving of a *Perspective View of the Abbey Church ... at Bath*,[5] after a drawing by his younger brother James, who dedicated the plate to Charles Fourth Duke of Beaufort. James Vertue (1686-1765) had moved from London to Bath for his health, and made his living as a painter, an 'instructor of Ladies and Gentlemen in the Arts of Drawing and Painting' and a seller not only of prints but, curiously, of snuffs and toys. Advertisements in the Bath newspapers show him living variously 'opposite Mr Morgan's Coffee-House in Wade's Passage' (1754), at Mr Page's, Pastry-Cook in Cheap Street (1758) and at West-Gate House (1760), all of them locations within a stone's throw of the Stuart Guildhall.[6] If the 1984 reference to 'George' Vertue reflects a pardonable confusion of the sibling with his better-known elder brother, it could perhaps be that during his sojourn in Bath James, by now an elderly invalid, emerged from his nearby lodgings to set up his easel and make a record of the perhaps-already-under-threat Guildhall. The dates fit; so too does the putative style of the original drawings.

The examples selected (figs.4 and 5), the cream of a mixed bunch, cannot be precisely dated but, if not themselves the originals, they are copies of originals done in the 1750s or 1760s. They constitute as good evidence as one could hope for, corroborating as they do not only Gilmore and Eyre but also, as we shall see, Wood the Elder. They do moreover furnish hints as to how the old Market House was used now that new markets were being established nearby. Of the thirteen figures with

Fig.4 The west side of the Stuart Guildhall, after an anonymous original, c.1750. (*Reproduced by courtesy of the Victoria Art Gallery, Bath and North East Somerset Council*)

Fig.5 The north façade of the Stuart Guildhall,
after an anonymous original, c.1750.
(*Reproduced by courtesy of the Victoria Art Gallery,
Bath and North East Somerset Council*)

which the scene has been enlivened, all but four either stroll at leisure or lounge about gossiping. Commercial activity beneath the arcades seems anything but lively: a tall woman in an apron chats with a youth and holds a bowl containing presumably something to sell; two men hold baskets perhaps of saleable produce, one seated on the kerb, the other leaning against a bollard, and a porter in the interior hurries along shouldering a heavy load. And there is a little old bill-poster with his brush and a water-pot filled from a rain-tank at his side. The impression created, perhaps fortuitously, is of a building no longer functioning as a market house; an impression confirmed by further details which are easily missed: the two northern arches have clearly been closed to wheeled traffic by barriers; and on the west, beneath every arch except the last, there is a substantial kerb. This last arch has no such obstruction but is blocked by a bollard, and might be where the internal staircase had its entrance. A curious feature of the drawings of the west façade, one meticulously reproduced in every version, is the bizarre irregularity of the east-facing arcade as glimpsed through the regularly-spaced western arches. Thanks to my model I was able to ascertain that the original artist had recorded exactly what he saw, and that the distortion (which, curiously, remained uncorrected) was due to his being inevitably over-close to his subject, a mere twenty feet back. This serves to underline the unsatisfactory location of the old Guildhall in the middle of the city's north-south artery; so closely hemmed in by adjacent buildings that only from the north was a reasonably long-distance view possible.

Scales, Measurements and the Model

A scale model cannot be made without a scale, and I was at once aware of a problem: none of my elevations gave any indication of scale except for the human figures under the arches. In them, I decided, lay my answer: I would suppose that the woman selling things in the left-hand arch of the north façade was five feet six inches tall. By that means I could calculate the height of the arches, and so work out a scale. But each version of the north façade gave a different answer, and it was only after much juggling of figures that I felt it reasonable to conclude that the arches were about twelve feet high. It was only later, with the model nearing completion, that I pursued a reference in Trevor Fawcett's first article, to the *Bath Advertiser* of 22 November 1755. I there found, to my delight, the true dimensions of the old Guildhall to the last quarter-inch. My calculations proved to be out by 14%: by my reckoning the building was 29 feet wide and 72 feet long; the true figures turned out to be 24 feet (and half an inch) wide, 62 feet (and three and three-quarter inches) long, while the arches were only 10 feet high. My discovery made no difference to the model itself; but it did mean that I had to change my scale from 72:1 to 60:1 (Fig.6).

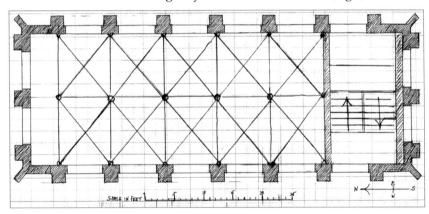

SCALE IN FEET

Fig.6 Plan of the Stuart Guildhall, including a hypothetical reconstruction of stairwell and vaulting. (*Drawing by the author*)

The North and South Fronts

By the 1750s the northern façade harked back to an earlier age, dominated by its large central window and embellished by stone shields (by Thomas Quilly c.1632) representing the royal arms to the left and those of the city to the right; and, high up, by two statues, each in its own

Figs.7a and b. The author's model of the Stuart Guildhall in 1750, (above) as from the north-east; (below) as from the south-east. There are no known views of its south façade, which is here therefore a hypothetical reconstruction (*Photographs by Peter Clulow*)

niche (Fig.7a). To the south, by contrast, we find the recent 1724 extension fronted by a façade in classical style and (presumably: we have no picture) containing the new entrance (Fig.7b). The reasons for this curious double frontage emerge from the history of the building; and that history, though based largely on documentary evidence considered in detail in Part 3, may conveniently be summarised visually at this juncture in order to clarify the main stages of the story (Fig.8). If – and the evidence points in that direction – the Guildhall of the late 1620s (Fig.8b) was a rebuilding on a grander scale of the arcaded Tudor Market House (Fig.8a), then a worthy approach to the new upper hall had to be incorporated into an area originally surrounded by arches on all four sides. Where, within the Market House, there had been a ladder or open staircase to the loft,[7] a new, secure stairwell was built, which occupied a fifth part of the groundfloor area,[8] blocking the arches at the southern end. These were left intact;[9] but with the prospect from the south now spoilt, and with generous open space to the north as far as the North Gate, the choice of the north front as the main one was natural for the 1620s builders.

As to the nature of the staircase itself, there are tantalisingly infrequent hints in the 1627/8 accounts: John Beacon is twice paid (a total of £1.16.0) for work on the 'stayers', and Nicholas Wilson receives thirteen pence for turning thirteen banisters. Dare we infer from this a wooden staircase with thirteen steps? Security, presumably at the foot and head of a stairwell walled off from the open market, was a consideration: John Gray receives

10/4d for 'door hinges' and five shillings for a lock 'for the door'; and there was an expenditure of ½d on a pair of hinges for the 'little dore'.

By 1750 (Fig.8d) the great window presented an awkward compromise between its pointed Gothic outline and its glazing bars. These, with their semi-circular-topped pattern, had been made to conform to a style ubiquitous in Georgian Bath's grander buildings, and had at some point replaced original casement windows,[10] perhaps when the other windows were sashed in 1718 (Fig.8c) or during the building of the annexe in 1724. It has been suggested that this admittedly ill-proportioned window (8ft 6in by 7ft) results from an enlargement thirty years after the Guildhall was built. That

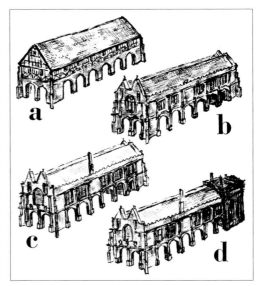

Fig.8. Drawings by the author which show stages in the evolution of the Stuart Guildhall.
(a) 1552: The new Tudor Market House. Owing to the lack of conclusive evidence this is only a hypothetical reconstruction.
(b) 1630: The new Stuart Guildhall. Note the staircase at the south end.
(c) 1720: Note the sashed windows and the extended chimney.
(d) 1750: The staircase has gone and the extension added.

in fact it was there from the start seems likely, not only from the mention in the 1627/8 Chamberlain's Accounts of a 'great window', but also from a reinterpretation of a Council Minute of 1657:[11] there it is agreed that a chimney be built on the east side of the Guildhall and that 'more light be added to the Counsell House'. Why, one wonders, the distinction in the same entry between 'Guildhall' and 'Counsell House' unless they were different locations? The answer lies in a description quoted by Elizabeth Holland, of rooms 'sometymes called the Councell House of the said Cittie'.[12] This refers to the medieval Guildhall, the north end of which was in process of conversion into a new butchers' Shambles: the old name had, it appears, stuck, and was still in use twelve years after the Guildhall had moved into the High Street. The room was still there as late as 1673; and it was surely this, rather than the new Guildhall, that was in need of more light.

Something of the High Street Guildhall that still survives can be seen in the square-topped niches which flank a first-floor window at the bottom of Bath Street opposite the Cross Bath (Fig.9).[13] Here, battered but still recognisable, are those same statues of King Coel and King Edgar which once adorned the Guildhall's northern façade, in a home now dwarfed by the new Royal Bath building. The choice of King Edgar was a natural one. It was in Bath's Abbey Church of St Peter that – fourteen years after his accession and only two before his death – Edgar was, on 11 May 973, crowned the first King of All England by the Archbishops of Canterbury and York. In the words of the *Winchester Chronicle*:

Fig.9 The figures of King Coel and King Edgar which originally adorned the north façade of the Stuart Guildhall and are now at the bottom of Bath Street, on the front of what was built as the House of Antiquities in 1797. (*Photograph by Peter Clulow*)

> Here was Edgar of Angles Lord
> With courtly pomp hallowed to King

The venue was chosen as lying within a prestigious monastery in a town on the borders of Mercia and Wessex, and the event was long celebrated every Whitsuntide.

The historical Edgar was accompanied by the mythical Coel because the latter – according to the legend as recorded by Geoffrey of Monmouth – was himself also, if briefly, king of all Britain before it came into Roman hands on the marriage to Constantius of his daughter Helena, mother of Constantine the Great. Popular mythology made him not only a merry old soul (and perhaps he was) but also the founder of Colchester (which he was not: Camulodunum's English name is derived from the river Colne). Not all, it seems, were pleased that Edgar and Coel should have displaced a figure even more deserving of such honour: Bath's legendary founder Bladud. Referring to an old, neglected statue of that Trojan prince which once stood at the North Gate, a satirist in the 1720s was moved to write:

Unhappy King, whose Glory thus depends,
Precarious on the Pleasure of false Friends:
Ungrateful City! whose unworthy care
Cannot afford King BLADUD Cloathes to wear!
Two upstart Princes of a modern Race,
That scarce in History deserve a Place,
Our entering street with dazzling Splendour grace:
One in Imperial Robes of Scarlet Hew,
Extends his Sceptre to the publick view;
The other dressed in shining Armour stands,
And with drawn sword the Market-Place commands.[14]

What, I wondered, was a model-maker to do about that unknown south frontage, towering above the narrow space between it and the north side of the Abbey? No picture survives; indeed, no artist could have been much tempted to set up his easel in so cramped and crowded a spot.

There are, to my knowledge, only two near-contemporary references to the architect of the southern extension, and they disagree. Richard Jones, Ralph Allen's devoted Clerk of Works from 1731 to 1764, made City Surveyor in 1767 at the age of sixty-four, writes in his memoir: 'I worked at the new end of the Council Room, built by one College, a Sidmouth Architect in Bath about the year 1725'.[15] Jones of course was recollecting what had happened four decades earlier. But the elder Wood, writing only eighteen years after the event, says of the Guildhall: 'At the opposite end [the south] there is a Heap of Ornamental Work well put together under the Direction of one William Killigrew, a Joiner who laid his Apron aside about the Year 1719; and I can only say this much of them (*sic*), that they incumber rather than adorn an handsome old Edifice.' This Killigrew was, alongside John Harvey, Thomas Greenway and John Strahan, one of Wood's chief competitors, and hence the recipient of what Mowl and Earnshaw call his 'heavy and ungenerous jocularity';[16] but, unless both architects were at work on the building together, Wood is likely to be the more trustworthy witness here than Jones.

Killigrew's works, like those of Harvey and Strahan, are gone, but Walter Ison illustrated two;[17] and given what can be seen in the west elevations of the old Guildhall (Fig.4) I felt there was justification for the south front I invented for my model. I almost left the south front blank; but I decided to be bold.

The Killigrew annexe has been criticised as incongruous, and certainly it could in no way be regarded as a sympathetic extension of what Wood described as a 'handsome old edifice'. It was on the other hand wholly in keeping with such other new buildings as 'General Wade's House' just round the corner in Abbey Church Yard, and one feels that Wood's might well have been a fairly lone voice of disapproval. The decision to pull down the old Guildhall a mere half-century after it had been extended was surely taken more because of its location than for stylistic reasons.

Sources of information: the historical evidence

In her important study 'The Earliest Bath Guildhall' (1988),[18] Elizabeth Holland adduces compelling historical evidence that the city's first Guildhall stood close to the Market House, but out of sight behind houses on the east side of the High Street. Here it continued its original function as the civic centre of the city until the first quarter of the seventeenth century. But in 1628/9 serious building work was undertaken at the site of the old Market House. Two basic questions arise: did this involve the demolition of the existing Market House and its replacement by a new building that was to serve as the Guildhall, or was it rather a refurbishing of the older one; and did Inigo Jones play a part in all this, as tradition suggests?

The first question can only be answered if we have some idea of the pre-1620s building. As to its age, documentary evidence unearthed by Elizabeth Holland in the Churchwardens' Roll of St Michael's church at the North Gate, shows that during the financial year 1551/2 forty shillings were paid, by consent of the parish, 'towards the building of the Market House'.[19] There is as yet no corroborative evidence, but such a date accords well with what we can deduce about the earlier building.

We may also consult four pictorial maps of Bath that survive from before 1625: William Smith's 'portraiture' of Bath, published in 1588 but thought by Stephen Bird[20] to have been made as early as 1568, when Smith published a map of Bristol; John Speed's map, published in 1610 as an inset to a map of Somerset and perhaps owing something both to Smith and to one of many lost 'engravings of English Cathedral Cities' listed in 1577 (Fig.10); a curious portrayal of some of the city's buildings with captions in French;[21] and fourthly the 'View of the City' reproduced by John Wood the Elder in his *Essay*, attributed in the first edition to a 1634 'Description' but in his second to a Dr Jones in 1572. Clearly the map is modelled on Speed; clearly, also, Wood's earlier date is belied by its inclusion of Bellot's Hospital, founded in 1609.

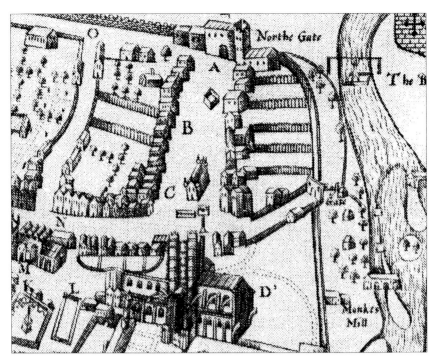

Fig.10 A detail of Speed's 1610 map of Bath showing (C) a stylised Market House in the High Street with stocks and pillory in front of it. (*Reproduced by courtesy of Bath Record Office*)

So here we have four 'aerial' plans of the city, none exactly datable, all of them depicting Bath at the end of the sixteenth and the start of the seventeenth centuries, and all – if different in detail – patently related to one another. But the information they reveal as to the Tudor Market House is scant indeed. All show, as from the south, a single-gabled building with steeply pitched roof and large central door. In Smith, a huge arched portal occupies most of the frontage; the other three reduce the size of the door, put two windows above and add, at either side of the gable, little protruding turrets. Can we trust this? I suspect that Smith's depiction is no more than the conventional representation of an important building seen in other maps of the period; that Speed, or his immediate source, determined to improve on Smith, made the proportions more credible, and that the other draughtsmen followed where Speed led. It is, I suggest, possible that the Tudor Market House – whether or not beneath a single gable – had from the start the twin arches incorporated into the Stuart

Fig.11 The Market House in Tetbury, dating from the mid-seventeenth century and still retaining features in common with Bath's Stuart Guildhall. (*Photograph by the author*)

Guildhall. We can perhaps get some idea of its appearance by looking at a comparable building that has survived, the Market House in Tetbury, some twenty miles north of Bath (Fig.11). Here, dating from the mid-seventeenth century, is a building which, despite subsequent alteration, bears at least a superficial resemblance to its Bath contemporary. It too lies in the centre of a bustling town; it too consists of a hall, approached by steps on its southern side, above an open colonnaded market with twin arches at its northern end.[22]

The second question to be faced is: what contribution, if any, did Inigo Jones make towards the creation of the Stuart Guildhall? Few recent histories fail to mention – if only to cast doubt on it – the 'tradition' that the Stuart Guildhall was built 'after a draft by Inigo Jones'. A few allow for its possibly resting in its predecessor's foundation; most presuppose that, whoever its architect, it was a new building. My own suggestion is that the Inigo Jones story be set aside, once and for all, as a red herring; and that the Stuart Guildhall, far from being a new building, be seen as a modifying, upgrading, and partial rebuilding of the earlier Market House.

As far as I know, the earliest reference to an Inigo Jones involvement is in the first edition of Wood's *Essay* of 1742; an assertion repeated, but not verbatim, in the 1749 and 1765 editions. Stating confidently that the Guildhall was 'rebuilt and finished in the Year 1625', he says it deserves special notice for its having been created 'after a Draught that was given to the Citizens by Inigo Jones.' On the occasion of an official visit to 'view the state of the Baths' (presumably in his capacity as Surveyor to the Prince of Wales), Jones, says Wood, was induced 'by a Natural Inclination to render all the Service in his Power'. This inclination sprang both from his own mother's being a Bathonian (daughter of a leading clothier) and from his being 'closely related' to the mother of George Trim, founder of Trim Street. None of these claims has, I believe, been substantiated from other sources. Wood himself, Bathonian though he was by birth, can adduce no stronger support for what he says than that he had learnt of Inigo's family connection with Bath from one Robert Cole, Lady Elizabeth Hastings' Steward at Bramham Park in Yorkshire. This conversation had taken place eighteen years before the first edition of Wood's *Essay*; the writer had clearly lost contact with Cole (he says of him 'if he is still living'), and his language suggests awareness that this might seem slender evidence for so bold an assertion. He therefore bolsters it with architectural evidence, leaning over backwards as a devoted disciple both of Jones himself and of Jones's own beloved Palladio, to prove to himself as well as to his readers, what he wants so urgently to be true. For example he writes, 'Nobody but Inigo Jones could cause the genuine Pattern of the Ionic Capital to be preserved in Opposition to that which was published by Scamozzi, and copied by People in general', contrasting with unconvincing hyperbole the 'genuine Pattern' of the capitals gracing the Guildhall's upper storey (where 'the Rim of the Volute runs straight along the face'), with the scandalous distortion promoted by Scamozzi, with its 'angular volutes springing out of a bowl'. Wood bolsters his case with further evidence which bears little scrutiny. In his first edition he goes so far as to liken Bath's Guildhall to the Town Hall of Delft, attributing that building to one Cornelius Danckerts, by whom Wood thinks Jones may have been influenced. In subsequent editions this passage is omitted, and it is easy to see why: the architect of the Delft Stadthuis (1618) was in fact Hendrik de Keyser. Cornelis Danckerts de Rij, City Mason of Amsterdam, is known to have worked with de Keyser on various projects in Amsterdam between 1603-20 and might well have been involved in the Delft Town Hall; but that building bears no resemblance whatever to the Bath Guildhall.

So much for that part of Wood's case: the rest is yet thinner in that he attempts to justify the wholly un-Palladian north and south fronts of the Guildhall, with their two arches and central pillar (described by Michael Forsyth as a 'solecism' in Palladian terms),[23] as having been suggested to Jones by the 'illustrious' five-columned examples of Moses' Tabernacle and 'the Porticoe of Jupiter Arbitrator in Rome'. What Wood glosses over is the extreme unlikelihood of Jones, if he started the design from scratch, opting for a layout so contrary to principles he applied elsewhere. If one bears in mind the preposterous 'prehistory' on which Wood based the ideas underlying his plan for Bath (how, immersed in Geoffrey of Monmouth's Britannic myths, he believed that Bladud was a Pythagorean, and ancient Bath a city dedicated to Apollo in a pre-Roman Britain that was in effect a pre-Hellenic Holy Land, peopled by Druids and Greeks), then one is bound to suspect here too a 'manipulation of data to support a preconceived notion', gently deplored by Mowl and Earnshaw, and suggestive of a self-educated man untrained in academic evaluation and debate. Wood would naturally rejoice if what was, in effect, Bath's first shot at a Palladian building could be shown to be the work of his idol, the great Inigo Jones himself; and one suspects that, in the absence of other evidence, he made up his own.

What is surprising is the speed with which, once promulgated, the story was accepted, though it was, of course, good publicity for a city whose fame was growing every year. A mere seven years after Wood's *Essay* first appeared, Boddeley's *Bath and Bristol Guide*, describing Bath's 'publick Edifices', confidently asserts: 'First, the Guildhall, which is situated in the Market Place, or High Street, was originally designed by Inigo Jones, Architect'. And that same year we find, as the leading article in Stephen Martin's *Bath Advertiser* of Saturday, November 22nd 1755, an unsigned letter (number VI in a series) purporting to be addressed to one Julian Alberti at Florence, and dated 'Bath, July 9th, 1753'. This date takes us back to a point only five years after Wood published his first *Essay*, and one year before his death. Mentioned briefly in connection with the scale of my model, the letter is here worth quoting at greater length.

Describing the impression made on a visitor to Bath as he passes through the North Gate (the 'grand and principal Entrance into the City'), the writer tells how he comes into:

> a spacious street called the High Street, near the Market-Place, that runs nearly South, [and] is about 57 feet broad and about 400 feet long. It was originally terminated with the North Front of the Abbey-Church, a front that exceeds all the Pieces of Gothic Architecture I ever saw, being, I

suppose the same with the South Front: but the Land on the North of the Church falling into private Hands, after the Dissolution of Monasteries, so little Regard was paid to the Beauty and Magnificence of the Building that they have blocked up this whole Front with erecting little, low, irregular Houses against it, quite from the East to the West: nay, they have gone so far, that I have seen a Necessary-house in one of the Buttresses of the Church, and an Oven in another ... Though the beauty of this Street is greatly eclipsed by hiding the Front of the Church: yet on entering it one is pleasingly struck with the Front of the Guildhall, which is now built in Middle, and near the Bottom of it; and the lofty and most simple, magnificent Tower of the Abbey rising directly behind it adds greatly to the Prospect. The Guildhall is very pleasing, and I may say in its original State, a magnificent Structure; it was built in the year 1625, after a Design, as I have great Reason to Believe, of that famous English Architect Inigo Jones. The building consisted originally of a Market House, and over it a Sessions-hall, or Court of Justice, and was formed on an Area of two Squares and a half ...

The writer goes on to describe in detail the building's half-columns, Doric supporting Ionic, with inter-columniations, six along the sides and two at the ends. Like Wood he finds a pattern for the unorthodox central-column façade in what he calls the Temple of Jupiter Arbitrator in Rome. He then proceeds to elaborate, maintaining that originally, at both ends, there were windows above each arch with a central column between a pair of flanking columns at either corner, below and above. He also claims that the north end was subsequently ruined by the introduction of a 'large, disproportionable Gothick Window', which destroyed the architect's design and so weakened the structure that the outermost pilasters were removed and replaced by diagonal buttresses. This dubious version of events is rendered more specious by what he says of the upper courtroom, maintaining that when the Mayor was enthroned between the two windows at the north end, this was

of great service to the Court of Justice. Everyone who is conversant with the Effects of Light and Shade, can only imagine how awful the Approach to the Tribunal must be, from the lower End of the Hall; and when the Culprit was plac'd at the Bar, the Light glaring full in his Face, was of great Assistance to the Magistrate, in forming a Judgment of his Guilt or Innocence'.

This is near-nonsense: light does not glare through north-facing windows, as testified by this same writer who, in his next letter deplores the 'very bad light' at the north end of the hall where, on each side of the great window, excellent pictures hang![24] But he cannot have it both ways.

Our writer seems not only a shaky witness but also an unscrupulous plagiarist, shamelessly lifting chunks of Wood's *Essay* verbatim. In both, for example, we read of 'Architects who fill the World with Whim and Caprice'; and in both, the 1724 annexe is condemned in identical terms as a 'Heap of ornamental Work by one Killigrew, a Joiner'. In other words, what we read in the *Advertiser* is not, as might at first appear, corroboration of Wood: it quotes him, no more; and Wood himself remains the sole source of the Inigo Jones story. Boldly dismissing that, therefore, one asks: what other evidence survives as to what was afoot in the High Street in or about the year 1625?

The Chamberlain's Accounts up to 1630

These, transcribed by the Reverend C.W. Shickle, Master of St. John's Hospital, are to the layman simultaneously marvellous and maddening: they provide precious detail not available elsewhere, yet tell us tantalisingly little. In the Stuart period, entries are in sequence of payments made, but impossible to date precisely. Furthermore, financial years begin on the second or third Friday in October and continue over the following twelve months.

What dare one deduce or surmise? First, 1625 is assuredly not the date of a 'new Guildhall'. Work had clearly been done eight years earlier: the year 1617/18 saw an overall expenditure on the Market House of £14.4.3d, a figure covering stone, timber, tiles, plumbing, ironwork and the services of carpenters and labourers; but that this was simply more-costly-than-usual maintenance of a sixty-year-old building buffeted by daily wear-and-tear is suggested by the fact that after 1617/18 the Market House disappears from the Accounts for seven years. Momentarily, hopes soared when I found that in 1625 a labourer was paid for 'carrying rubbell out of the Market House'. Demolition and site-clearance? No: it was a one-off payment of 3d, a morning's work.

Not until the following financial year, starting in October 1626, are there serious signs of activity: eleven loads of tiles cost 8/6d a load;

timber was bought, and eight loads of stone; and the services of Thomas Grymes were in demand for sawing, as were those of a plumber, a mason and two labourers. Work was clearly afoot: certainly on the roof, possibly on the upper floor. In the following year, between October 1627 and October 1628, the pace is stepped up: we find the names of no fewer than twenty workmen at the site, together with those of three carpenters, two glaziers (one of them a woman), paviers, a painter and a locksmith. Interestingly, the only building materials bought during this year are two consignments of floorboards; while the major recorded payment (apart from £8 on casual labour, representing somewhat under 200 man-hours) was for a glazier (£6.2.10d.). John Beacon, classified as 'labourer' but paid at a higher rate than the casual workman, was in much demand, earning (there are six separate entries) £4.10.10d, largely for work on the new building, though once for work at the 'old hall'. John Butler likewise figures six times, but is much more highly paid, receiving in total £15: surely a master-craftsman perhaps working alongside Walter Symons. Symons was someone of considerable standing: for work on the new Guildhall he receives payments of £5 on three occasions (the last, 'in full satisfaction for works about the Market Hall'); and on a final occasion, well into the year 1628/9, he is paid no less than £10 'towards the building of the New Shambles', the new market complex arising on the site of the now-abandoned original Guildhall. Could we perhaps identify him as a major player in the 'Palladianisation' of the new Guildhall?

Scant reference the following year 1628/9 to work on the new Guildhall suggests that it was nearing completion, an impression confirmed by the expenditure of £4.13.0d on twenty-four loads of cobblestones. The flooring of the arcaded 'market', now being found a new home elsewhere, must surely represent a last stage. These records, slender though they are, suggest that over this period work was concentrated more on the upper floor than the open market below; but that, hand-in-hand with this conversion of the original loft into an area capable of furnishing the space and services the old medieval Guildhall could no longer provide, there was a deliberate attempt to 'Palladianise' the resulting structure, to give it an up-to-date impressiveness worthy of a growing city.

The Council Minutes and the Stuart Guildhall's later years

It was from the Council Minutes that Trevor Fawcett had, from infrequent references to the fabric of the Stuart Guildhall, been able to piece together the story of its later years and sad decline. He generously shared his findings with me, and I was able to locate the minute of 28 December

1657, wherein it was agreed 'that a chimney be built on the east side of the Guildhall'. Later drawings do indeed show a chimney, but on the west side. Perhaps the secretary misheard, or plans changed. A half-century of silence on the Guildhall fabric follows, broken on 27 June 1710 when it was resolved that the Town Hall be sashed and wainscotted. Gilmore's illustrations (figs.2a and 2b) provide our only clue to the appearance of the original windows; were they perhaps lengthened to accommodate the new, fashionable style? As to the second part of the resolution, this must refer either to repairing or replacing existing wainscotting, since the Chamberlain's Accounts of 1627/8 refer to the payment of 5/- to John Bevill for 'colouring the wainscott'. At all events, the resolution was not immediately followed up; and it was not until 16 May 1718 that £100 was given 'towards the work' by Robert Gay of London (subsequently made Honorary Freeman of the City, and Member of Parliament for Bath), whose memory is enshrined in the street which bears his name. Within two years the wainscotting was done and, we learn from the Accounts of 7 September 1720, paid for.

And then on 1 December 1724, in the mayoralty of Thomas Atwood, the Council 'agreed that the Guildhall be added to, subject to such alteration as should be thought proper by this Corporation; all charges to be paid by the Chamber of this City'. Now it was that William Killigrew came to be employed as architect of the extension, work on which was clearly under way six months later when – 10 May 1725 – it was agreed that 'the sum of £200 shall be taken up on bond from this Corporation of Walter Estcourt, Esq., at 11% to pay the workmen employed to finish the additional buildings to the Guildhall'. This work included the demolition of the now superfluous staircase within the old market, which must have left unsightly scars; and within two years, on 11 April 1727, it was agreed that the 'remaining part of the ground under the Guildhall be vaulted in the same manner as the other is, at the charge of the Chamber of this City'. The term 'vaulting' provides important evidence, implying internal columns as at Tetbury.

In spite of improvements and additions, all was far from well with the older part of the building; by 1747 cast-iron props were needed. Eleven years later the roof required repair; and by 1760 the situation was such that on 19 May a decision was taken that the Town Hall 'be newly built in a more commodious place'. Yet progress was sluggish: three years later moves were afoot to purchase land, but it was not until 1764 that a committee of seven was appointed to consider proposals for a new Guildhall. Final plans had still not been decided when, somewhat prematurely, the Mayor laid a foundation stone on 11 February 1768. Uncertainty continued and when, seven years later, in July 1775, the plans of Warr Atwood (a member of the original committee) were at last adopted, a fierce public controversy erupted. Thomas Jelly and John Palmer put forward what they claimed to be a cheaper and better plan, and the dispute went before an arbitrator from Bristol. Matters were finally resolved only when Atwood's sudden death that same year put a stop to the wranglings, and within a year the new Baldwin building was rising resplendent on the High Street's eastern side. This is Bath's third and present Guildhall.

Such was the protracted sixteen-year finale to the story of the Stuart Guildhall. But before we leave it something should be said of its interior, by way of a postscript. The great hall had been handsomely extended when the 1724 annexe was built; but whether the whole of the floor space above the old market was now given over to a single hall, and just how the extension was laid out, we have no means of knowing. However, by comparing the limited space available in the old building with what the later Baldwin Guildhall provided (its great Banqueting Hall alone covered 3,200 square feet as opposed to its predecessor's 1,800), one sees why by the late eighteenth century the Stuart Guildhall, with its dilapidated older part and hardly capacious extension, was deemed ripe for replacement. In the new building the ground floor alone contained a separate Judiciary Court as well as an office for the Town Clerk, a Records Room, a Weighing House and rooms for jurymen and prisoners; while on the first floor was a separate Council Room. When one looks at its Stuart predecessor one can only marvel that so much was compressed into so small a space, and that from it was administered a city that had, during the building's lifetime, grown tenfold from two to twenty thousand.

One thing we do know of the Stuart building after 1724 is that it had begun to develop another role still played by today's Guildhall: acting not only as the city's civic heart, but also serving as a showplace for paintings and fine plate, and curiosities pertaining to the history of the city – an inchoate municipal art gallery and museum. We hear of portraits of Frederick, Princess of Wales and Princess Augusta on either side of the great window at the north end of the hall, and at the opposite end William Hoare's portrait of Beau Nash over the door, and by it that of General Wade. We hear too of portraits, presented by General Wade himself in 1728, of all the then Aldermen and Councillors. These last, commissioned from the artist Johann van Diest, must have presented a daunting spectacle: with Mayor, Aldermen, Constables, Bailiffs and other Councilmen, there could well have been up to thirty paintings on display. Eight survive, and each measures 4 feet by 3 feet 4 inches;[25] even if hung cheek by jowl they would have occupied much precious wall space in the new wing, for as the model makes clear, there would have been insufficient space between the great hall's windows.

Against this busy background other items also were on display, including not only Roman coins but also the famous Head of Minerva, thought initially to be of Apollo, doubtless to the delight of the elder Wood. In his 1735 *Survey of Bath* he singles out as the most noteworthy feature of the Guildhall, a 'curious Antique Head, supposed of Apollo, dug up in Staul Street in the year 1728'. Not until 1797 would the House of Antiquities be built opposite the Cross Bath to house such finds; the building where today, sole survivors and mute witnesses of the Stuart Guildhall's curious and largely forgotten history, the painted statues of King Coel and King Edgar still gaze out over the city as once they did above the High Street two and a half centuries ago.

Notes

1. I must acknowledge Trevor Fawcett's generous help and advice and his ground-breaking research into the Stuart Guildhall. See in particular the *History of Bath Research Group Newsletter* 17, January 1992 (now available on the Bath Past website) and *Bath Administer'd: Corporation Affairs at the 18th Century Spa* (Ruton, Bath, 2001), p.53.
2. I am indebted to Katharine Wall of the Victoria Art Gallery both for this information and much other help.
3. See Jane Root, 'Thomas Baldwin: His Public Career in Bath 1775-1793', *Bath History* vol.V (Millstream Books, Bath, 1994) pp.80-103.
4. A print of 1779 after Malton's watercolour, c.1777, may be seen in *Images of Bath* by James Lees-Milne and David Ford (Saint Helena Press, Richmond-on-Thames, 1982) no.661.
5. Susan Sloman, *Gainsborough in Bath* (Yale University Press, New Haven and London, 2002), illustrated on p.11.
6. I am grateful to Susan Sloman for her help here.
7. An entry in the Chamberlain's Accounts for 1612/13 records an expenditure of 8/2d on the 'Market Loft Windows'.
8. *Bath Advertiser* No.6, 22 November 1755. In Letter VI: 'stairs out of the Market House ... reduced [the area of] that Room [2 squares and a half] to a double Square'.
9. John Wood, Senior, *Essay towards a Description of Bath*, 3rd edn.(Bathoe and Lownds, 1765), p.317: 'each End [of the Guildhall] contained two of the like apertures'.
10. Chamberlain's Accounts 1627/8: 'to William Dalton for 2 cagements for the greate Window'.
11. Council Minutes for 28 December 1657.

12. Elizabeth Holland, 'The Earliest Bath Guildhall', *Bath History*, vol.II (Alan Sutton, Gloucester, 1988), p.170.
13. This was built by the Corporation in 1797 as the House of Antiquities, to house curiosities previously displayed in the Guildhall. Its architect was John Palmer (1738-1817), who succeeded Thomas Baldwin as City Architect.
14. Quoted in the *Bath and Bristol Guide*, 3rd edn. by Thomas Boddeley, 1755.
15. The memoir is available in Bath Reference Library, in both manuscript and typescript form.
16. T. Mowl and B. Earnshaw, *John Wood, Architect of Obsession* (Millstream Books, Bath, 1988), p.51.
17. Walter Ison, *The Georgian Buildings of Bath* (Faber and Faber, 1948), pp.99, 122.
18. Elizabeth Holland, *op.cit.*, pp.163-179.
19. *ibid.*, p.168.
20. Stephen Bird, 'The Earliest Map of Bath', *Bath History*, vol. I (Alan Sutton, Gloucester, 1986), p.130 and *passim*. The whole article is of great interest in this connection.
21. Barry Cunliffe, *The City of Bath* (Alan Sutton, Gloucester, 1986), p.80 illustrates this.
22. David Verey, *Gloucestershire: The Cotswolds*, 2nd edn. (Buildings of England, Penguin Books, Harmondsworth, 1986), p.450.
23. Michael Forsyth, *Bath* (Pevsner Architectural Guides, Yale University Press, New Haven and London, 2003), p.174 where the centre of Eveleigh's Camden Crescent is described as 'committing the solecism of having five columns, i.e. an even number of bays'.
24. *Bath Advertiser* No.7, November 29th 1755, Letter VII.
25. One of these (the portrait of Henry Atwood) was included in the exhibition 'Pickpocketing the Rich', Holburne Museum of Art, Bath, 2002, cat. no.1, p.31.

Bath's Forgotten Gunpowder History: The Powder Mills at Woolley in the Eighteenth Century

Brenda J. Buchanan

The manufacture of gunpowder was of major significance in Britain for four centuries, until chemical explosives began to assume a greater role from the 1870s. Gunpowder had first been seen in the western world as an agent of progress, along with the printing press and the compass, but by the mid-seventeenth century it had lost its early promise as it became obvious that despite its awesome power in battle it was not going to deter conflict and end all wars.[1] It remained however of civil importance as its use in mining, quarrying and road building developed, and its continuing significance in British trading and imperial history deserves recognition. Yet until some twenty-five years ago this subject was neglected by historians.[2]

My own 'discovery' of gunpowder came as I studied the papers of North Somerset gentry families for a thesis on investment in the region in the eighteenth century, and saw how much the Stracheys in particular had profited from their involvement in this business. But for background information on this mystifying industry, especially on the ingredients and process of manufacture, I had to go to books written by explosives engineers at the beginning of the twentieth century.[3] There was one exception to this generalisation, and that was a charming short article in *The Countryman* (1971) by Robin Atthill, who wrote as well on this subject as he did on the Mendips in his major work.[4] A problem remained, for as a relative newcomer I did not realise that the Woolley powder mills were so close to Bath, a circumstance which must also have surprised visitors to Bath in the eighteenth century when they learnt of this. The question of location was solved by meeting Malcolm Tucker, whose father had converted a former mill building at the site into a family home. With my documentary evidence and my co-author's practical knowledge, we were able to undertake an exploration of the surviving and hidden features in a study that was published in a national journal in 1981.[5]

Soon, interest was found to be developing in other regions, and a group began to meet at the national level, with international contacts quickly following.[6] My own research is now concerned with this more comprehensive approach to the subject, but the initial focus still intrigues. This has led to the publication of an article on the technology of gunpowder making in the Bristol region in the *Transactions of the Newcomen Society* (1995-6), and another on the role of gunpowder as a barter good in the Bristol slave trade in the *Transactions of the Bristol and Gloucestershire Archaeological Society* (2000).[7] But nothing has yet appeared in a local publication on this still largely forgotten local industry, and so it seemed appropriate to remedy this by an article in *Bath History*, which I have had the honour of editing for five volumes, through ten years.

Early History, and Bath's Saltpetre Bed

It is likely that gunpowder was first made in China in the ninth century, as alchemists experimented with many ingredients in their search for the recipe that would give longevity through an 'elixir of life'. At some point, saltpetre, sulphur and charcoal were mixed together with explosive results, and so was born the 'fire-drug' or *huo yao*. This knowledge spread through Arab intermediaries to scholars of western Europe like Roger Bacon, the Ilchester-born Franciscan friar who in the 1260s wrote down the recipe for gunpowder in code, so conscious was he of its dreadful power.[8] This code was not cracked until the early twentieth century, although by then the forbidden knowledge had long become known through others. However, the difficulty of procuring the seemingly simple ingredients imposed a limit upon gunpowder's availability, and it was in the matter of saltpetre production in particular that Bath first entered the national gunpowder records.

Saltpetre (potassium nitrate) is the most important ingredient in two respects: first in terms of bulk, rising from the 41% of Bacon's recipe to the 75% of the later standard military mix; and secondly of significance, for it introduced oxygen to the mix, thus promoting its combustion.[9] Saltpetre's unwholesome origins lie in decaying nitrogenous waste. This 'black earth' must be heaped up in beds, layered with ashes and shells, and watered, preferably with the urine of beer-drinking men and wine-bibbers, in a closely regulated way. The liquids sprinkled on the beds leached out the nitre as they trickled through the mix, falling into pans beneath before being boiled until crystals of saltpetre were formed. But much of the saltpetre used in England in the early years was imported from northern Europe, with which there were close trading links, and until the Armada in the second half of the sixteenth century there was no sense that this dependence might be dangerous. An effort had already been made in 1561 to learn from a German expert the particular skills needed to operate a saltpetre or nitre bed,[10] and now a nation-wide system was introduced for the collection of 'black earth': dung and detritus, the riper the better. Patents were issued by the Crown, dividing the country into separate districts and authorising the appointment of saltpetremen to gather in the ordure and process it in the way described above. The operation of this system prompted many complaints, often recorded in the State Papers Domestic of the time.[11] The activities of the saltpetremen were greatly resented as they dug out the rich earth from dovecots, stables (the floors of which owners were forbidden to tile), and animal sheds; and gathered in human detritus near to and inside houses. When the men went too far complaints were made to the Star Chamber, as in June 1631 when it was claimed that Thomas Hilliard, who operated chiefly in Wiltshire, had 'dug for saltpetre under the beds of persons who were sick therein'. Perhaps Hilliard was too good a supplier to rein in, for only three months later he was reported again, this time for selling the King's saltpetre to some of Bristol's illicit powdermakers. Having 'some private foreknowledge' of the charge they managed to slip away: Hilliard continued at work.[12]

The saltpetre bed at Bath comes to our notice as a result of a boundary dispute. John Giffard had been appointed to collect and 'work' the nitrogenous waste to be found in Bristol and ten miles around, but in 1634 he became the subject of a complaint by Thomas Thornhill, the saltpetreman for 'the greatest part of Co. Somerset'. Perhaps from a failure to estimate the distance from Bristol correctly, or more likely because the 'city excrements' of Bath offered a rich source of 'black earth', Giffard set up one of his nitre beds there. The judgement of the Commissioners for Saltpetre was that he could continue 'his works' for that season, but when the time to 'work the same grounds' came round again, that is when a sufficient amount of ordure had built up, Thornhill was to have the working of it.[13]

What would the nitre bed in Bath have looked like? I am aware of only two items of visual evidence for the whole country: a sketch of a saltpetre works on a grant of land of 1593 to an Ipswich powdermaker (reproduced by courtesy of the Suffolk Heritage Department in the Newcomen *Transactions* already mentioned), and an archaeological drawing of the surviving earthworks from a nitre bed at Ashurst in Hampshire. Both are rectangular in shape, and enclosed on the pattern indicated by the surviving banks shown in Fig.1, some 300ft by 150ft overall. To this may be added a feature shown on the Ipswich sketch of 1593 that would also

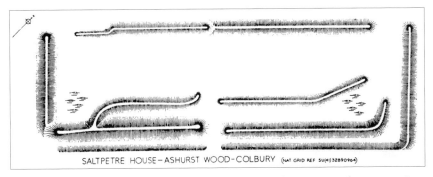

SALTPETRE HOUSE – ASHURST WOOD – COLBURY (NAT GRID REF SU(41)32890964)

Fig.1 Surviving earthworks of the Saltpetre House at Ashurst, Hampshire, *Proceedings of the Hampshire Field Club*, vol.18 (1953), p.335.

have been seen at Bath, namely a simple arcade around the sides, covering the beds and offering protection against indiscriminate watering by rain. The Ipswich sketch also shows steam rising from the boilers which were an integral part of the process. Although perhaps on a smaller scale, there would have been boilers at Bath, to provide for a preliminary crystallization before the 'grough' saltpetre was carried off in carts commandeered by the saltpetreman, for further refinement at a larger works. We know from the State Papers that John Giffard had such a depot at Thornbury north of Bristol, because he complained in December 1634 that people were refusing to carry coal from nearby pits to his 'boiling-house' there.[14] Lastly, the nitre bed at Bath would have announced its presence in a way that cannot be conveyed by an archaeological drawing, for as the Ipswich sketch shows, it would have been surrounded by 'Colde Donghills' – heaps of manure, rotting and steaming until sufficiently broken down to be lifted into the regularly aerated and watered beds. Such a feature at Bath must surely have been outside the walls of the town, perhaps between the south gate and the river where the pervasive smell of the latter may have nullified somewhat the pungency of the saltpetre bed.

Despite the efforts to establish a national system, it was clear that the saltpetre industry was not only a potent cause of civil unrest, it could not meet demand. There were therefore renewed attempts to look overseas, a challenge that was met with growing success in the course of the seventeenth century by the trade in this commodity developed by the East India Company. Again, this is a neglected aspect of our history, but by the 1620s the Company was sending home small quantities of saltpetre (finding it useful to tip it into the holds of ships as ballast), and by the 1650s it was establishing itself in Bengal, the part of India most productive of saltpetre, where the pressures of people and their animals generated the waste that could be processed exactly as described here. Saltpetre was thus indeed a 'Commodity of Empire', and countries such as France and Sweden that lacked this connection were forced to rely on a domestic supply until at least the early nineteenth century.[15]

Bristol Craftsmen Powdermakers: an Urban Industry

Although a failure in terms of supply, the establishment of the saltpetre industry in the provinces led to an unexpected success in terms of the growth of the gunpowder industry outside the metropolis. The illicit purchase of saltpetre by Bristol powdermakers, already mentioned, enabled these domestic manufacturers to develop their skills and their businesses beyond the control of the Crown and its patentees. An engraving of 1630 (Fig.2) shows the small scale on which the rogue powdermakers would have operated, allowing them to move on to escape detection. It also enables us to describe the process of manufacture, which was to grow in scale as procedures were mechanised, but which did not change in the

Fig.2 Workmen making gunpowder by hand. Engraving from Hanzelet's *Pyrotechnie* of 1630, reproduced by Oscar Guttmann, *Monumenta Pulveris Pyrii* (1906), Fig.22.

fundamentals. The raw materials (saltpetre, sulphur and charcoal) were assembled in the required proportions and crushed to remove lumps and stones or other foreign bodies (see the scales and sieve hanging on the wall). The workman on the left holds a pestle, but he does not just stir the ingredients in the mortar, he pounds and mixes them so that they are 'incorporated' under pressure. A little water was added to produce a paste that would be transferred to the large sieve held by the workman on the right. He must rest this on the tub, because he needs both hands to use the 'rolling pins' to force the paste through the holes punched in the leather base of the sieve. This procedure, introduced in the early fifteenth century, was known as 'corning', presumably because the grains of powder thus formed resembled grains of corn. It was a step of great importance because in transit, the previously uncorned or 'serpentine' powder would separate out into its original ingredients. The sieve was also the way by which the size of the grain, as required for different purposes, could be regulated. Sometimes these holes would become clogged, and the advice in some instructions of the 1660s, that a twig should then be used to clear the blockage, perhaps explains the small branch on the corner of the table. Having been kept moist for safety and ease of handling, the grains were then dried slowly on open trays. It remained for the powder to be tested, and this may have been the purpose of the open-lidded receptacle on the table. Some of the finished product would be packed into the 'powder tester', the lid closed, and a match applied through a hole in the container. The force of the explosion would cause the lid to spring up. This was a rough and ready version of what was still being demonstrated to the Royal Society in the 1660s.

The provincial powdermakers' move to respectability began when, despite having been harassed and banned by the authorities, they responded to the Royalist call for gunpowder expertise at the beginning of the English Civil War. William Baber and some of his family moved from Bristol to Oxford, where the King had established his military headquarters in what was fast becoming a munitions-making town. Here Baber made a significant contribution to the Royalist cause, starved as it was of gunpowder because most of the powder mills, and the Tower where supplies were stored, were in and around London and so under Parliamentary control.[16] William Baber returned to Bristol, held by the Royalists between 1643 and 1645, to resume gunpowder making there. It is likely he remained active for some years, because in 1668 he was still campaigning for payment by the King for powder made at Bristol and Oxford, and his later works are shown on Jacob Millerd's plan of Bristol of the early 1670s. In the 1673 version they are drawn more elaborately than in 1671, and named as 'Baber's Tower', suggesting the owner had requested more detail from the mapmaker. The location of the works on the eastern edge of the city, south of Lawford's Gate, is significant, because having earlier been well clear of dwelling houses, they were now about to become engulfed as the town expanded. The industry itself was also facing change, from the small, often domestic scale, to the larger works needed to meet the increasing demands of Bristol, second city and thriving port.

Bristol Merchant Powdermakers: The Move to the Countryside

The pressures of encroaching dwellings and city regulations, combined with the attractions of the security and seclusion of the wooded valleys of north Somerset, offering water power and charcoal, must have made a move into the countryside seem a very attractive proposition to the Bristol gunpowder makers. The first powder mills were established at Woolley in the 1720s, nearly three miles north of the city of Bath; then came the Littleton mills in the Chew Valley south of Bristol, in the 1740s; followed by other mills nearby in the 1760s; and a further one at Moreton, now under the Chew Valley lake.[17] As part of this move to the countryside we should also note the transfer in the mid-eighteenth century of the main magazine from Tower Harratz, a fortified tower in the old city wall, near the present Temple Meads Station, to a new site down river on an isolated bend of the Avon. The new location was both secure and convenient, for here surplus powder could be removed from ships coming into Bristol harbour, and cargoes of powder for the outgoing vessels could be loaded on board. These sites are worth mentioning, even briefly, because they show that the Woolley powder mills did not exist in isolation but were part of a larger network.

The new powder works were substantial complexes of buildings and water courses. There is no record of the Babers or other craftsman families taking part in this move to the countryside, perhaps because the financing of it would have been beyond them. Indeed, with heavy capital costs and revenue requirements, a new type of powdermaker now entered the industry. These were usually Bristol merchants and Somerset gentry with an eye for an opportunity, funds to invest, and good contacts within the credit network through which the port operated. They formed partnerships, with a managing partner and an office in Bristol, and a technical manager living at the site.

Partners, Managers and Workers at the Woolley Powder Mills

The Woolley Powder Mills were founded in 1722 by four partners, well-established Bristol merchants, members and officers of the Society of Merchant Venturers, shipowners, and traders in linen, iron and sugar. Three (Abraham Hooke, John Parkin, Edmund Baugh) were also engaged in the slave trade, in the operation of which gunpowder was to play an important role as a much-coveted barter good. The fourth, Harrington Gibb(e)s, had gained experience in the sugar plantations of Jamaica, returning home to become the agent of planters such as William Beckford.[18] The merchant network extended to London, especially in relation to the leasing of the site, secured by arrangement with the landowner William Parkin, brother of John and himself a partner in the 1730s. The Parkins were a geographically and socially mobile family. From their base in Sheffield, John moved to Bristol where he continued as a merchant in the family iron trade, and William went to London where he was already by 1722, in the lease of the land at Woolley to the partners, described as an 'esquire' of Foster Lane. John Parkin died in 1743 and his share of the partnership was divided between his daughters, Elizabeth and Ann. Although continuing to live near Sheffield, where she bought the Ravenfield estate near Rotherham, the unmarried Elizabeth retained her interest in the gunpowder firm until her death in 1766 at the age of 63.[19] Ann meanwhile had married into the Strachey family to whom her share then passed, being held by them until the early nineteenth century.[20]

The London connections of the Stracheys were of great importance to the partners. As a young man the later Sir Henry Strachey lobbied there for contracts on their behalf, reporting in 1762 that he had as a result suffered a great deal of 'tongue and foot fatigue'. He went to India as secretary to Robert Clive, returning to become a Member of Parliament from 1770 to 1804. He held many public offices during that time and was created a baronet in 1801.[21] The Dyers also offered useful connections in the capital. The Woolley partners had an account with James Dyer of London from 1764 until the turn of the century, probably for saltpetre traded there by the East India Company. George Dyer, a London broker, provided insurance cover in the 1780s, and became a partner in the 1790s. Robert Dyer of Bristol had become a partner in 1780, taking charge of the firm's accounts.[22] But a family network was not essential for influential work in London. William Wansey, for example, a Woolley partner from 1753 to 1767, was active in the interest of all the Bristol merchants engaged in the Africa or slave trade. In 1749 he was admitted to the Merchant

Venturers in recognition of this service, 'having given a long attendance in London about the Africa trade'.[23]

The Woolley partners also had useful connections with the local Members of Parliament. Robert Nugent, later Earl Nugent, a Bristol Member from 1754 to 1774, presented a petition to Parliament in 1756, seeking to overturn a wartime ban on the export of gunpowder on the grounds of its importance for the Africa trade 'which is of very great consequence to this port'.[24] Field Marshal Sir John Ligonier, later Lord Ligonier, one of Bath's Members of Parliament from 1748 to 1763, was particularly well-placed to give advice as he was closely connected to the Board of Ordnance for all that time. When consulted by the partners during the Seven Years War (1756-63), he was so absorbed by the problems of military supply that he delegated his response to Sir Charles Frederick, the Surveyor General at the Board. This was a wise move because Sir Charles was experienced in the problems of gunpowder making, and gave the partners sound technical advice.[25]

The works were managed by the Worgan family: by John from at least 1740 when he became a partner with responsibility for the 'inspection and superintendancy of the works', until his death in 1747; then by his son Matthew until his death in 1793. Matthew was the nephew of Elizabeth Parkin, and on her death in 1766 he inherited her share in the works. Like many early industrialists he continued to live at the site, despite becoming a man of such substance that in Benjamin Donn's map of 1769 (Fig.3) his house assumes equal significance to the powder mill, here demoted to a single mark.[26] Worgan's will shows that the terms of his inheritance were not simple, for the deeds of properties at Ravenfield and York (but not Woolley) were, under the will of Mrs Elizabeth Parkins (sic), spinster, to be sent to Wm Parkins Bosville Esq, her next heir. Local names amongst the Worgan legatees include the Gunnings, neighbours with whom there was an early business connection through the purchase of timber for charcoal. The bequest of £5,000 to John Gunning of Old Burlington Street, London, with the pictures by 'Zuccarelli he bought for me', suggests that a later friendship still had a useful business element. The partners in the 'Gunpowder Comp. at Woolley' were each to receive a mourning ring, James Willmington [the name is not clear], his clerk, was to have £40, and the men at the works one guinea each.[27]

With this last reference we come to the anonymous workforce – named only if death or injury at the mills was recorded in parish registers or newspaper reports. The numbers employed would never have been very large, for this was not a labour-intensive industry. A memorandum of 1747/9 notes that twelve men were then employed, and even if the number doubled in the course of the eighteenth century with the doubling of the capital invested in buildings and equipment, this would not have been a large proportion of those living in the Swainswick Valley – a total of 348 in 1801 according to the Census that year (Woolley 80; Langridge 86; Swainswick 182).[28] But there were personal tragedies and the first, noted in the *British Gazette* of 23 January 1724/5, was reportedly of a scale to suggest there may have been a dangerous unfamiliarity with this hazardous industry established so recently. A night-time explosion was recorded at the powder mills near Bath, 'by which sad accident four persons were killed outright and two others very dangerously wounded. 'Twas remarkable, that two of the deceased persons arms were torn off by the force of the powder'. The Swainswick parish registers record the burial on 7 January of Edward Roberts and Daniell Workman, both killed at the powder mills. It may be that with the complicated parochial arrangements of the valley, the names of the other victims must be sought elsewhere. Of the two already named, the latter must have had the greater family responsibilities, for a note in the Poor Rate Accounts for 17 January 1724/5 records that for a year Elizabeth Workman was to receive 4 shillings per week, her husband having been blown up at the powder mills; and a memorandum of 1727 states that 8 guineas was placed in the hands of Mr Scudamore, churchwarden, by 'ye gentlemen of the Powder Mills towards Apprenticing Widdow Workman's Children'. A decade later Thomas Sandall was killed at the mills, and his burial on 26 June 1734 was recorded in the Swainswick parish register. The Sandall children, like the Workman's, were apprenticed to trade.[29]

By the mid-eighteenth century the workforce may have become more skilled, or luckier, for danger was twice averted. The *Bath Journal* of 29 July 1745 reported that, 'Last Friday Evening the Powder-Mills at Woolley near this City were blown up; but as the Men employ'd there had just left off Work, it happily did no other Damage'. Five years later it was reported in the same journal that on 18 June 1750, 'A Beam at the Powder-Mills at Woolley, this week, by some Means or other, took Fire, and burnt for some Time, but was happily extinguish'd, without doing any Damage; had it not been stop'd, near three Tons of Powder must have been blown up'. The dangers were real but most of the workforce survived, and of these James Skrine of the parish of Walcot deserves recognition for he was buried on 19 March 1797 in his 80th year, having been 'a workman in the gunpowder mills upwards of 50 years'.[30]

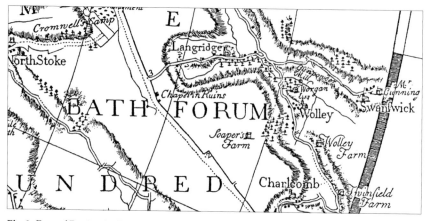

Fig.3 Part of Benjamin Donn's *Map of the Country 11 Miles round the City of Bristol* (1769).

The Manufacture Of Gunpowder At Woolley

In Donn's map (Fig.3), we see what a challenge the establishment of gunpowder mills at Woolley must have been. Here were woods in abundance for charcoal and an adequate supply of water for power, but the map shows a steep-sided valley and gives a sense of restriction, that was conveyed also by the Rev. John Collinson in his *History of Somerset* of 1791. He notes the narrowness of the meadows watered by the small brook that runs into the Avon below Lambridge, and observes that here '... are the gunpowder mills of Matthew Worgan Esq., situated in a deep picturesque spot, and almost environed with wood'.[31] The limitations of the valley bottom meant that the layout of the works could not follow the more advantageous scheme seen in the 1839 tithe map of Littleton Powder Mill and at other less-restricted sites, where water was drawn from a long mill pond to power a linear series of buildings.[32] Instead, at Woolley, some ingenuity had to be shown to make the best use of the site: probably by converting to gunpowder use the two corn mills (with a history going back to the Domesday Book) on the lower site, with their long narrow mill pond; and by creating a further supply of water and more workshops on the slopes above. This had the additional advantage of isolating the new main works from the valley floods to which streams in the catchment area of the Bristol Avon were liable, especially important as gunpowder is very susceptible to damp. This solution may be seen in the Woolley Tithe Map of 1839, which indicates a substantial upper mill pond supplied by water brought in by a long leat, with a scatter of buildings close by.

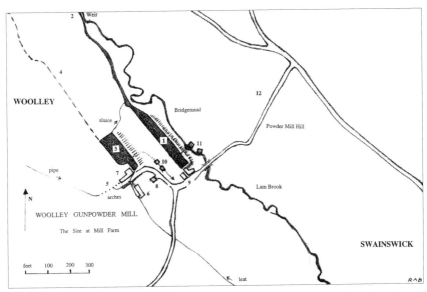

Fig.4 Plan of the Woolley Gunpowder Mills from documentary and physical evidence, drawn by Angus Buchanan. See the text for an explanation of the numbers shown here.

In pursuit of a fuller understanding of the layout of the site, a sketch map has been drawn (Fig.4). The process of interpretation is helped by the survival of the Strachey documents already noted, although since these relate chiefly to the business and financial aspects of the undertaking it is not easy to detect the often incidental information on the making of gunpowder that they also contain. It must also be explained that those buildings shown on the sketch that do still survive are now put to domestic or agricultural use, and although signs of earlier architectural features and subsequent adaptations were examined and drawn in an article already mentioned,[33] their former industrial function must remain a matter of speculation.

A glance at Fig.4 will show at once the extraordinary measures taken to bring water to the site. There is the lower mill pond (no.1 on the map), supplied by a leat that can be traced back to a weir (2); and a substantial upper mill pond (3), supplied by a leat (4) which ran for about ¾ mile to a dam at Lower Langridge (ST 743695). This leat is now largely grassed over, but it can be traced in part along the 200ft contour. It is likely that this was the new cut mentioned in a lease of 1729. This renewed the term of the first lease of 1722 and referred to a '... Cutt lately made at Woolley ... running down to the new Powder Mills there lately erected'.[34] It is likely that the imposing upper millpond was built between the granting of the lease and its renewal, perhaps in 1724 when a further agreement was signed for the conveyance of water to the site.[35] Lastly, fresh spring water was brought into the western edge of the site by pipes and an aqueduct (5). Taken together, these arrangements were elaborate, but they are put into perspective by the comment of the managing partner in March 1801, that the annual stock taking took place in June because then '... our Mills usually stand still for want of Water'.[36]

We know from the archival evidence that the manager lived on the site, and it is likely that the Mill House (6) or some earlier version of it served as the home of the Worgan family. We also know, from the annual statements of account, that saltpetre and sulphur were each stored on site in both a rough and a refined state. So there must have been storage sheds, and workshops in which boiling, crystallization, and distillation took place, probably in the buildings (7) near the Mill House, because although noxious the refining was the least dangerous part of the work, and therefore the most appropriate to house near the manager's home. There may also have been practical reasons, for the aqueduct mentioned previously would have brought fresh spring water, suitable for the refining processes, to these buildings. Not only do the foundations of the aqueduct survive, we also have a drawing of it, sketched in 1826 by a visitor, Dulcibella Chester, and copied here (Fig.5).[37] The powder mill would have been out of use some twenty years by that time, but the aqueduct survived as a conduit for spring drinking water The water tower would have been associated with its industrial function. A little downhill is a building (8), later a

Fig.5 Sketch of the pipe-carrying aqueduct (no.5 on Fig.4) and water tower at the Woolley Gunpowder Mills, drawn in November 1826 by Dulcibella Chester and reproduced in the *Bath & Wilts Chronicle & Herald*, 19 September 1932.

stable, that lies below the level of the upper mill pond and might therefore have been supplied by it. It has undergone much alteration, but bears evidence of having housed a waterwheel. Traces of charcoal suggest that this may have been a crushing mill, a structure found at other powder mills such as those at Chilworth in Surrey where one is shown on a plan dated 1728, and so a close chronological match.[38] Shown at (9) are the corn mills which probably, like the stable, had at some time a gunpowder function.

After their preparation the ingredients were incorporated. The mills in which this most important stage was carried out have not yet been located on the ground, possibly because these dangerous buildings with their residue of gunpowder were dismantled when production ceased, but a possible site (10) will be suggested later. From the Memorandum of 1747/9 we learn that at Woolley there were four mills, each capable of grinding 25lbs in two hours, using water that was 'worked twice over'. This information is scrappy but telling. To receive water from the purpose-built upper mill pond, the 'grinding' mills must have been on the slopes leading away from it, and if the water was used 'twice over' there must have been two buildings, in sequence, each accommodating two incorporating mills, making four mills in all. This arrangement is shown in drawings of the late 1790s (Fig.6): in the upper sketch a central water wheel works a mill on either side, and the used water flows away in a central channel; in the lower, the upright runners are shown on the beds around which they would trundle, grinding and mixing the raw materials under pressure. At Woolley the water, having worked both sets of mills, would have drained away into the lower millpond or to the stream leading from the site.

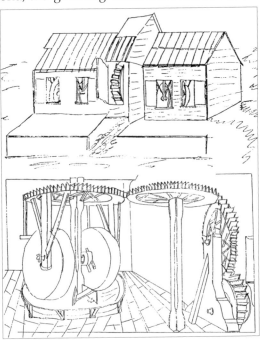

Fig.6 Water-powered incorporating mills like those at Woolley. The external view above shows the central water wheel with a mill either side; the internal view below shows the edge runners and bed. The complicated and possibly unworkable gearing suggest these may have been apprentice sketches, from John Ticking's Notebook of the later 1790s. (*Reproduced from E.A. Brayley Hodgetts (ed.), The Rise and Progress of the British Explosives Industry, Whittaker, 1909*)

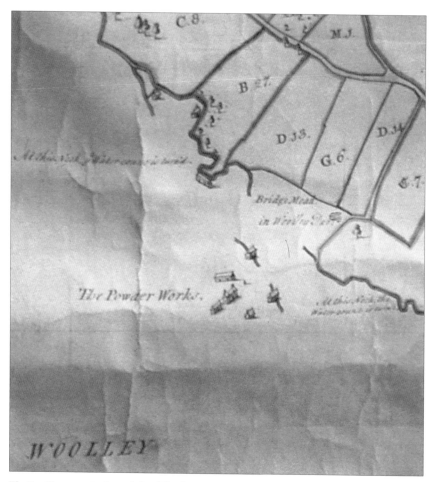

Fig.7a Representation of the Woolley Powder Mills by Robert Whittlesey, looking beyond the boundaries of the parishes of Swainswick and Batheaston, the estate of Oriel College, Oxford, which he surveyed in March 1729. (*Reproduced by kind permission of the Provost and Fellows of Oriel College, Oxford*)

This speculation may prove helpful in interpreting what is so far the earliest known representation of the site. We are fortunate that 'The Powder Works' are shown on an estate map drawn by Robert Whittlesey, in a survey of parts of the manors of Swainswick and Batheaston for Oriel College, Oxford, 1729. The gunpowder works were not part of this surveyor's remit, but may have been sketched in as an interesting after-

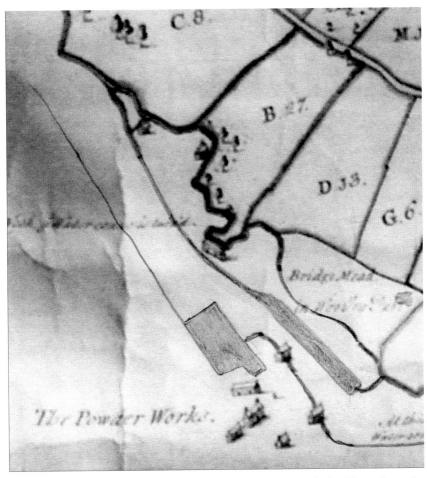

Fig.7b Conjectural interpretation of the Woolley site, placing the buildings drawn by Whittlesey within the context of the known features at the gunpowder mills.

thought, or because of some possible future significance in relation to water rights.[39] The layout shown in Fig.7a is very disjointed, with disrupted watercourses redeemed only by the three-dimensional aspects of the buildings. But if in Fig.7b we join up the arms of the Lam Brook as it flows through Bridge Mead, and add the two mill ponds and their leats known to have been there, we can then link in the two buildings drawn by Whittlesey, shown most significantly astride a watercourse which must at this level have issued from the upper millpond. The buildings

Fig.8 Thomas Thorpe's Map of Five Miles around the City of Bath (1742).

given authenticity by Whittlesey's map of 1729 are very probably the incorporating mills mentioned in the early documents, and discussed above. They have been added to Fig.4, as item (10). We can also add the two buildings (11), shown across the Lam or 'Wolley' Brook on Thomas Thorpe's map of 1742 (Fig.8), which may have been built as magazines away from the main site and close to the lane up Powdermill Hill (12). Based on an informed interpretation of the documentary and physical evidence, we now have in Fig.4 an acceptable representation of the site in its active years.

The ingenuity shown in using the site to its best advantage was also noticeable in the equipment introduced here, especially as this was in several cases ahead of the general practice. The system of incorporation by pounding with a single pestle (seen in Fig.1) had by then been mechanised, with rows of pestles (known also as stamps), being raised and dropped by water power. But the Woolley partners took advantage of the move to a greenfield site in the 1720s to introduce a new and efficient system of incorporation that was ahead of its time in gunpowder making. This involved the use of edge runners, the upright stones revolving on fixed horizontal beds that may be glimpsed in Fig.6. Perhaps the partners were influenced by their familiarity with Bristol's port industries – for in the production of oil for soap, and dyewoods for cloth manufacture, as well as the snuff, glass, and sugar industries, vertical edge runners were used to crush materials. By the mid-eighteenth century most mills in the London area, where much of the military powder was produced, had followed suit, although at some of these works stamps or pestles continued in use. Concern about the danger of the over-heating of stamps and the associated explosions, led the government to introduce an Act of Parliament in 1772 (12 Geo.III c.61) outlawing this procedure, except for the production of fine shooting powders.

The partners were also innovative in the introduction of cast-iron machinery, especially edge runners and beds. These goods were all purchased from the Coalbrookdale works of Abraham Darby, through their resident agent in Bristol, Thomas Goldney. In 1759 a bed of 1½ tons and runners of 2½ tons were bought, followed in 1764 by a bed of 4 tons and runners of 5 tons. The latter purchase may have been occasioned by the failure of the partners to secure a government contract in the early 1760s. They were assured by Sir Charles Frederick of the Board of Ordnance that their runners were adequate in weight, but they suspected that those of their competitors at Faversham were more effective, being they believed of the order of 5 to 6 tons. They may have ordered this 'heavyweight' from Coalbrookdale in an effort to match them.

After incorporation the dampened 'mill cake' would be sent to a workshop with a hand-operated screw press, to increase its specific gravity and explosive power. Then it was corned, not by hand as shown previously, but in a water-powered shaking frame, before being glazed in revolving barrels to further compact and round-off the grains. The dust caused by these processes was removed by screening, which was also mechanized, taking place in gauze-covered revolving cylinders. The powder was then ready to be dried. The evidence here is particularly interesting because this was done in special dry houses, heated by stoves that were attached to an outside wall and thus separate from the main structure. The drying capacity at Woolley was already considerable when

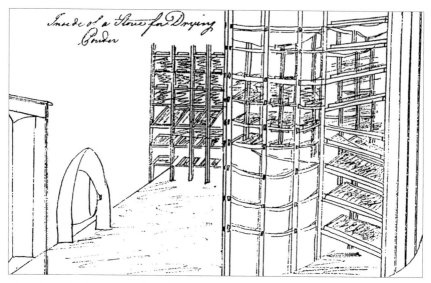

Inside of a Stove for Drying Powder

Fig.9 A Drying House, in which heat was conveyed from an adjoining stove, through a cast-iron dome or 'cockle', into a semi-circular room holding racks of powder. From Ticking's Notebook (late 1790s), in Brayley-Hodgetts (see Fig.6).

in 1750 another 'Gun Powder Stove' was ordered from Coalbrookdale, with another in 1751. The second weighed one ton, the first rather less. It is likely a third was delivered in 1763. The term 'cockle' stove appears in Goldney's Account Book to describe these deliveries, and those at the Littleton works. The term was unknown to me, but research suggested it referred to a dome through which the heat could pass safely and effectively to dry the gunpowder on racks, see Fig.9. There the matter may have rested had not my report on these features come to the attention of historians of central heating, who had previously thought that cockle stoves dated only from the early nineteenth century. The evidence from Woolley has taken the history of these stoves back by 50 years.[40]

Lastly came the storage of the powder in a safe magazine before its sale through the Bristol merchants. It had seemed likely that a vault set into the hillside behind the putative refining workshops (no.7 in Fig.4) might have fulfilled this function, though it now seems possible that this could have been a 'cooling magazine' such as may be found elsewhere to house materials between processes.[41] But the need for safe storage had to be met, and there is evidence from both the partners' accounts and those of Mrs Elizabeth Parkin in Sheffield, that in 1750, £500 was 'laid out upon a new magazine'. Its location is a puzzle, but a possibility has already been noted, across the Lam Brook on what is shown on Fig.4 as Powdermill Hill, leading up and away from the works. Here we enter upon the last conundrum – how were the raw materials brought in to Woolley and the barrels of powder carried out? This was a time when river facilities were being improved in this region, but the evidence from the partners' accounts of expenditure on 'road carriers' and 'hauliers', suggests that goods went by the turnpike roads rather than the Avon Navigation. One noteworthy payment in 1764 was to Mr Wiltshire 'for carriage of Petre'.[42] The road through Tadwick to Tog Hill and so into Bristol would probably have been the route followed by these waggons, the barrels of powder covered by leather hides to reduce the effect of any explosion and blast.

The Profitability of the Woolley Gunpowder Mills

In the earlier years, whilst the works were being established and extended, the dividends were not as handsome as they were later to become. However, as the century went on, and especially in its closing decades, the large dividends due to the partners became a matter of great concern because of the difficulty of making payments in a financial system that was not as well developed as it was to become in the nineteenth century. In 1796 for example, Henry Strachey was sent £513 from Bristol in seven bills (which would each have carried a promise to pay), with a note that 'it is a matter of the greatest difficulty to secure any sort of London paper here'. The problems were worse the following year, when there had been 'very considerable sales of Gunpowder at Liverpool' (reached coastwise, and a port through which the partners sold powder in addition to Bristol), but these had been met by 'Bills at a long date'. The partners were offered interest until these became due. These high returns caused some unease – discretion was urged in 1795, for 'the dividend is so great that the utmost secrecy is necessary'. The rate in these later years was some 30%, and over the period of 60 years for which the information is available, the returns averaged 15%.[43] Here was a profitable cycle as merchant capital, and the revenues derived from trade (especially the Africa trade, but also general commerce such as that to be found in the trans-Atlantic markets), merchant shipping, war-time privateering, and mining, were invested in an industry whose sales enhanced those profits still further. These profits confirm that although the production of gunpowder at Woolley might seem highly localised – operating in a fairly remote valley near

Bath, some 13 difficult miles by road from Bristol, with a provincial workforce and manager living on site – yet this was also the centre of a business that operated successfully within a prosperous network of sea-borne trade. For most of the eighteenth century it must have seemed that this prosperity was unassailable, especially with the growth of mining both locally and in western regions like Cornwall, made accessible by coastal shipping and a subject requiring a separate essay, but this was not to be the case.

The End of Gunpowder Making at Woolley

Because of its reliance on international trade for most of its raw materials and markets, gunpowder making in the Bristol region was profoundly affected by changes in the world economy, especially the abolition of the slave trade in 1807. The significance of gunpowder as a barter good in this sorry trade cannot be over-emphasised: a study of the *Bristol Presentments* has revealed not only the consignments going to Ireland and beyond to the New World, but also those on the slave ships, with an average of 6000 barrels a year (each full barrel holding a 'short hundredweight' of 100 lbs) on ships bound for the west coast of Africa in the mid-1770s.[44] The largest consignment recorded was on the *Hector*, which sailed for this region in 1792 with 26,100 kegs on board. Holding one-sixteenth of a barrel or 6.25lbs, kegs were more easily handled as part-payment in this human trafficking. Perhaps this extraordinary voyage was made in anticipation of what was seen by Bristol merchants as the end of the trade, due to the forthcoming legislation. At the same time, the trans-Atlantic market was also threatened by the new powder works being set up in the United States, such as those established by the du Pont family in Delaware in 1802. The Woolley partners began to discuss a 'consolidation' with Littleton, with whom they had long had a commercial understanding for the sale of gunpowder through an office in the Bristol Exchange. A memorandum of 1802 revealed that after the expansion of the middle decades, the two firms were now together only producing as much as Woolley had done alone some 50 years earlier, which was less than 4,000 barrels per year. The firms recognized they now had a productive capacity greatly in excess of their market. The downturn was in the merchant trade rather than the military market (which after a failed attempt in the 1760s the partners never again felt the need to or tried to enter), although the expansion of the du Pont works showed that there was no lack of potential in that part of the industry. But the Bristol merchants seem to have lost their entrepreneurial spirit. The Woolley mills closed, and those at Littleton did not survive long into the nineteenth century. They were taken over by a large firm of powdermakers from the London area, Curtis's and Harvey, and then closed down as part of a policy of rationalization. Curtis's and Harvey were themselves later taken over by I.C.I.

And so these once-flourishing manufacturing sites reverted to an agricultural use, but their historical significance deserves to be recognized and remembered. They were an unusual outpost of Bristol's industrial life, operating out in the countryside and yet fundamentally a port industry, dependent on merchants and sea routes for raw materials and markets. The Woolley Powder Mills are indeed Bath's forgotten industry, on a site that is difficult to interpret but for which we are fortunate to have some important surviving documentary and physical evidence.

Notes

1 Roy S. Wolper, 'The Rhetoric of Gunpowder and the Idea of Progress', *Journal of History of Ideas*, vol.31 (1970), pp.589-598.

2 The two most important books of the middle decades of the 20th century were by a chemist and a bio-chemist: see J.R. Partington, *A History of Greek Fire and Gunpowder* (Heffer, Cambridge, 1960) and Joseph Needham *et al.*, *Science and Civilisation in China*, vol.5, part 7, *Military Technology: the Gunpowder Epic* (Cambridge University Press, Cambridge, 1986).

3 For example, Oscar Guttmann, *The Manufacture of Explosives*, 2 vols (Whittaker, 1895).

4 Robin Atthill, 'The Gunpowder Mills of North Somerset', *The Countryman* (1971), pp.134-139; *Old Mendip* (David & Charles, Newton Abbot, 1964).

5 B.J. Buchanan and M.T. Tucker, 'The Manufacture of Gunpowder: A Study of the Documentary and Physical Evidence Relating to the Woolley Powder Works near Bath', *Industrial Archaeology Review*, vol.5 (1981), pp.185-202.

6 The Gunpowder and Explosives History Group is the national society; the International Committee for the History of Technology is the international body. Please contact the author for information.

7 Brenda J. Buchanan, 'The Technology of Gunpowder Making in the Eighteenth Century: Evidence from the Bristol Region', *Transactions of the Newcomen Society*, vol.67 (1995-96), pp.125-159; and 'The Africa Trade and the Bristol Gunpowder Industry', *Transactions of the Bristol and Gloucestershire Archaeological Society*, vol.118 (2000), pp.133-156.

8 Roger Bacon's *Letter on the Secret Workings of Art and Nature, and on the Vanity of Magic* was published c.1267.

9 The proportions prescribed by Bacon were: saltpetre 7 parts (41.2%); sulphur 5 parts (29.4%); charcoal 5 parts (29.4%). In the closing decades of the 18th century the standard military mix came to be: 75-10-15. For mining the saltpetre proportion was usually lower, so as to shake but not shatter the rocks.

10 See A.R. Williams, 'The Production of Saltpetre in the Middle Ages', *Ambix*, vol.22 (1975), pp.125-133, for an account of Gerrard Honrick's recipe.

11 The State Papers Domestic (SPD), Charles I, vol.ccclxi, no.8, 1637, Public Record Office (PRO), for example, contain a complaint by Dean Christopher Wren, father of the architect and rector of Knoyle Magna or Episcopi, Wiltshire, that saltpetremen digging in his pigeon house had so weakened the foundations that one of the 'massy stone walls' twenty feet high had fallen in.

12 PRO, SPD, Charles I, vol.cxciii, no.83, 14 June 1631 and vol.cc, no.26, 24 September 1631.

13 PRO, SPD, Charles I, vol.ccxcii, f.222, 17 July 1634.

14 PRO, SPD, Charles I, vol.cclxxviii, no.4, 2 December 1634.

15 A chapter by the present author entitled 'Saltpetre: A Commodity of Empire', in Brenda J. Buchanan (ed.), *Gunpowder, Explosives and the State: A Technological History*, is now in press with Ashgate Publishing Company.

16 A chapter by the present author entitled ' "The Art and Mystery of Making Gunpowder": The English Experience in the 17th and 18th Centuries', in Brett D. Steele and Tamara L. Dorland (eds.), *The Heirs of Archimedes: Science and the Art of War through the Age of Enlightenment* (MIT Press, Cambridge, Mass., 2005), includes an account of Baber's activities.

17 For accounts of Woolley, Littleton and the new magazine at Shirehampton see B.J. Buchanan, 'The Technology of Gunpowder Making ... in the Bristol Region' (1995-6) and 'The Africa Trade' (2000), n.7 above. The site at Moreton was excavated before being flooded, but the opportunity to investigate the gunpowder site was lost because it was decided that, 'the chief interest of the site lies in the plan of the mediaeval house', P.A. Rahtz and E. Greenfield, *Excavations at Chew Valley Lake, Somerset* (H.M.S.O., 1977), p.114. It has been suggested there was a powder mill at Dead Mill, a mile downstream of the Woolley works, but there is so far no evidence of this.

18 Information on these and other Bristol merchants mentioned later comes from documents relating to their business interests, chiefly in the Somerset Record Office and Bristol Record Office, or from printed sources including: G.H. Cave, *A History of Banking in Bristol* (privately published, Bristol, 1899); John Latimer, *The Annals of Bristol in the Eighteenth Century* (privately published, Bristol, 1893; Kingsmead Reprints, Bath, 1970); Patrick McGrath, *The Merchant Venturers of Bristol* (Society of Merchant Venturers of the City of Bristol, Bristol, 1975); W.E. Minchinton, *The Trade of Bristol in the Eighteenth Century* (Bristol Record Society [BRS], vol.20, 1957) and *Politics and the Port of Bristol in the Eighteenth Century* (BRS, vol.23, 1963); David Richardson, *Bristol, Africa and the Eighteenth-Century Slave Trade to America*, 4 vols. (BRS, vol.38, 1986; vol.39, 1987; vol.42, 1991; vol.47, 1996).

19 For Elizabeth Parkin's business activities in the Sheffield area see B.A. Holderness, 'Elizabeth Parkin and Her Investments, 1733-66. Aspects of the Sheffield Money Market in the Eighteenth Century', *Transactions of the Hunter Archaeological Society* (1973), pp.81-87.

20 For the history of the family into which Ann married see C.R. Sanders, *The Strachey Family, 1588-1932* (Duke University Press, Durham, North Carolina, 1953) and Barbara Strachey, *The Strachey Line, An English Family in America, in India and at Home* (Gollancz, 1985). Neither refers to their gunpowder interests.

21 Information on the Strachey family's involvement with the gunpowder industry comes from papers deposited in the Somerset Record Office (Strachey Papers, DD/SH, Boxes 22, 27 & 33, not catalogued when studied). As a long-term plan these are

being prepared by the author for publication by the Somerset Record Society, and as part of a history of the north Somerset powder mills.

22 The Dyers have not been found in the Bristol printed sources, and may have been a London professional family.

23 The award of an honorary freedom of the city of Bristol to William Wansey places him in the select company of distinguished visitors and suggests he was not a Bristolian by birth.

24 Minchinton, *Politics and the Port of Bristol*, p.85. For a portrait of Nugent, who came to live in Bath, see Susan Sloman, *Gainsborough in Bath* (Yale University Press, New Haven and London, 2002), p.81.

25 See Brenda J. Buchanan on 'Sir John (later Lord) Ligonier (1680-1770), Military Commander and MP for Bath', *Bath History*, vol.VIII (Millstream Books, Bath, 2000); and on Sir Charles Frederick, 'Art and Mystery' in *The Heirs of Archimedes*, see n.16 above.

26 A note added to the Indenture of Co-partnership at the Woolley Mills of June 1747 (SRO, DD/SH, Loose Deeds), records that 'whilst Matthew Worgan has management of concern at Woolly, shall have use of messuage he lived in and grounds belonging rent free as he has for some time past enjoyed same' – that is, in his father's lifetime.

27 Bath Podium Library, Shickle Notebook no.20, copy of probate of will of Matthew Worgan Esq., 5 February 1794.

28 *Victoria History of the Counties of England, Somerset*, vol.2 (Constable, 1911), pp.340-352.

29 I should like to thank the following for helpful information : Bridgett Jones of London; David Whittock of Lower Swainswick; Marta Inskip of Bath.

30 I am grateful to Bath colleagues for helpful information: Trevor Fawcett, Marek Lewcun, Marta Inskip, Susan Sloman. See the Register Book of the Parish of Swainswick, 1557-1812, and that of Woolley which, 'being decayed and almost obliterated', was transcribed by Matthew Worgan for the period 1749-1760. It is recorded that in 1757 Mrs Elizabeth Parkin, Lady of the Manor, gave a silver flagon and plate to the chapel for the communion service, together with linen, surplice and bible, and in 1761 she had a new chapel built at her own expense. Also R.E.M. Peach, *The Annals of the Parish of Swainswick with Abstracts of the Register, the Church Accounts and the Overseer's Books* (Sampson Low, 1890).

31 Rev. John Collinson, *The History and Antiquities of the County of Somerset*, 3 vols. (Cruttwell, 1791), vol.1, pp.167-8.

32 See also for example Brenda J.Buchanan, 'Waltham Abbey Royal Gunpowder Mills: "The Old Establishment" ', *Transactions of the Newcomen Society*, vol.70 (1998-99), pp.221-250.

33 Buchanan and Tucker, 'The Manufacture of Gunpowder ... Woolley Powder Works', note 5 above.

34 *Ibid.*, p.188

35 I thank Marek Lewcun for the reference to the agreement of 1724.

36 Buchanan and Tucker, 'The Manufacture of Gunpowder ... Woolley Powder Works', pp.189, 201.

37 The *Bath & Wilts Chronicle & Herald* of September 1932 records the sad history of this sketch which was taken into the offices of the paper, reproduced in an issue, but subsequently lost.

38 For a copy of the Chilworth plan see Buchanan, 'The Technology of Gunpowder ... Bristol Region', p.144, note 7 above.

39 I would like to thank Oriel College, Oxford, for allowing me to study the maps relating to the Manor of Swainswick and the notes on the same. These show that the estate was purchased in 1521 by Dr. Richard Dudley, Fellow and sometime Senior Tutor, and later presented to the college. A special word of thanks to Mary Stacey for alerting me to the existence of this map.

40 For a fuller account of the technological innovations at Woolley see Buchanan, 'The Technology of Gunpowder ... the Bristol Region', note 7 above.

41 George W. Rains, *History of the Confederate Powder Works* (Augusta, Georgia, 1882), p.21.

42 See B.J.Buchanan, 'The Great Bath Road, 1700-1830', *Bath History*, vol.IV (Millstream Books, Bath, 1992) and 'The Avon Navigation and the Inland Port of Bath', *Bath History*, vol.VI (Millstream Books, Bath, 1996).

43 Buchanan, 'The Africa Trade', p.149, note 7 above.

44 *Ibid.*, pp.133-137. The *Bristol Presentments* in Bristol Central Library carry information on ships leaving Bristol for a number of years.

'Hazardous and Scanty Securitys'
The Career of William Yescombe, Bath Attorney, 1760-1774

Edward Yescombe

The decade following the death of Beau Nash in 1761 was one of growth and prosperity for Bath, epitomised by the building of John Wood's Royal Crescent (1767-1774) and New Assembly Rooms (1768-1771), and the granting of a Royal Patent to the Theatre Royal (1768). Thomas Gainsborough and William Hoare painted portraits of the residents and fashionable visitors, and musical figures included the composer Thomas Chilcot at Bath Abbey and William Herschel (later famous as an astronomer) as organist of the new Octagon Chapel. These personalities and events touched the career of William Yescombe, who set up his plate as an attorney in 1760. Despite coming from a family with no connection with Bath he rapidly made his name, and rode a wave of speculation on Bath's prosperity until financial disaster struck. His career can be reconstructed from a variety of scattered sources – newspapers, court cases, property records – and parallels the fortunes of the city over that decade.

The Yescombe Family

The Yescombe family came from the village of Blackford, near Wedmore in Somerset. Judicious marriages raised them above yeomen status by the early eighteenth century, by which time the family owned a number of farms around Wedmore, producing rentals of some £350 *per annum*, an adequate income for a country gentleman. Reflecting this improvement in fortune, Robert Yescombe (1706-1750) moved to Bristol and set up in practice as an attorney. At this time the country attorney's role was mainly one of a general man of business, managing his clients' estates. He would not have done property conveyancing, which was carried out by scriveners, nor would he have dealt with complex legal matters, which would have been referred to counsel.[1]

Robert married Anne Daniel (d. 1777), the daughter of a Bristol brewer. They had three sons – Robert (1737-1815), William (1738-1774) – the subject of this essay – and Edward (1740-1772), as well as three daughters. Robert

Senr appears to have had a successful career, which was cut short by his sudden death in 1750. In 1755, following in their father's footsteps, Robert Junr was apprenticed to John Weston, an attorney in Olveston, Gloucestershire,[2] and William to Thomas Nash, an attorney in Bath.[3] Their brother Edward was sent to Oxford University and went into the church. After the statutory five-year apprenticeship, Robert and William were enrolled as attorneys in the Court of King's Bench on the same day in November 1760 (and probably also – like their father – as solicitors in the Courts of Exchequer and Chancery).[4] Thereafter they set up their plates in Bristol and Bath respectively. However, Robert, who had inherited most of the family estate from his father, seems to have lived mainly on this inheritance rather than his profession.

William had received an inheritance of only some £400 from his father. But in September 1760 he transformed his position by marrying Sarah Collin,[5] described in a *Bath Journal* announcement as 'an agreeable young Lady, with a fortune of £6000'.[6] This was no doubt intended to improve his credit in the city, but Sarah's family, with prescient prudence, took care to ensure that a substantial portion of this fortune did not fall under William's control: £3,300 was transferred to the trustees of her marriage settlement.[7] They rented a house in Kingsmead Street, from where William carried on his practice. They had no children, and little is known of William's personal life,[8] except that as his business improved he moved house in 1764,[9] purchasing (for £600) a house at 21 Monmouth Street.[10] He advertised it for sale in 1770,[11] but was still living there at his death in 1774.

William's Practice

Apart from his basic 'estate management' work – property conveyancing, trusts and wills – William also acted as an estate agent. His first advertisement appeared in August 1761:[12]

> To be Lett *And Enter'd upon at MICHAELMAS next*, (READY FURNISHED) The LANTHORN HOUSE At the *CROSS BATH*, now in the Possession of Mrs. ROBINSON. For further Particulars, enquire of Mr. WILLIAM YESCOMBE, Attorney, in BATH; or of Mr. ROBERT YESCOMBE, Attorney at Law, in BRISTOL.

He was sufficiently uncertain of himself to add his brother's name to the advertisement, which he only did again when they jointly advertised their brother Rev^d. Edward Yescombe's vicarage to let in 1765.[13] Thereafter, William regularly advertised properties, mainly in Bath, to let and for sale. He also dealt with more complex property cases, such as that of the Highfield estate at Bitton in Gloucestershire, of which William's client Benjamin Perrott was tenant for life under an entail. William organised a private Act of Parliament in 1772 to break the entail so it could be sold.[14] He made full use of his connections to move the process on – his brother Edward's father-in-law, Sir Edward Bayntun (M.P. for Chippenham), saw the Act through the House of Commons.[15]

Around 1765 the firm of Jenkins & Bray, attorneys of New Inn (near Lincoln's Inn Fields), became William's agents, handling work on his behalf when he could not get to London. They worked, *inter alia*, on the Highfield Act.[16] Abel Jenkins had links with Bristol, which is where this connection may have originated. He was later attorney for Matthew Brickdale, the Bristol M.P. who was famously defeated by Edmund Burke in 1774, and with whom William's mother's family, the Daniels, had a connection.[17] His partner William Bray (1736-1832) was later Treasurer of the Society of Antiquaries, and co-author of a history of Surrey (published 1804-1814); he was also the first editor and publisher of the diaries of John Evelyn (in 1817).[18]

William regularly represented builders of new houses who put them up for sale after they had found tenants. In 1763, for example, he advertised an auction of five houses (three of them in Orchard Street) belonging to James Townsend, a builder from Warminster.[19] The housing boom which developed in Bath in the 1760s resulted in a great growth in this business,[20] and led over time to William raising loans for his clients, then lending money himself, and eventually becoming a direct investor in building houses. It is not surprising, therefore, to find the most important developer in Bath at that time, John Wood the Younger (1728-82), crossing William's path. William's client Thomas Clement appears to have been the builder of No.5 Royal Crescent,[21] and as will be seen William built three houses in Wood's development of Queen's Parade. Wood's attorney (and banker) was John Jefferys, who had been in practice since the 1750s and later became Town Clerk.[22] Jefferys crossed swords several times with William – we will shortly see the roles he played in the Westgate Theatre scheme and the Chilcot estate.

Another project in which Jefferys and Wood were on the opposite side to William was that of the New Assembly Rooms, which Wood completed in 1771, having raised funds through a public subscription. William acted for Cam Gyde, the lessee of Simpson's Rooms (the Old

Assembly Rooms), when he tried to expand his facilities in 1771 to meet this competition, but was hindered by Wood having an agreement with his landlord, the Duke of Kingston, which prevented further building.[23] Gyde's Rooms eventually succumbed to the competition.[24]

The Nash Estate

Richard 'Beau' Nash, the godfather of fashionable Bath, died in February 1761 at the age of 86. He was a lawyer by training, and was Treasurer of the Inner Temple before he moved to Bath in 1705, but there is no obvious connection with the Thomas Nash to whom William was apprenticed. Beau Nash maintained his position of Master of the Ceremonies in the Assembly Rooms until the end, but became very frail, relying on charitable handouts from the city corporation and others, mainly disguised as subscriptions to a history of Bath and Tunbridge which everyone knew he would never write. He left no will, and although he had had a series of mistresses (the last of whom, a Mrs Hill, was living with him when he died), he never married and had no children. His heir was his nephew Charles Young. It was clear that Nash's liabilities exceeded the value of his estate, and the main concern of Nash's family was for an orderly settlement of his affairs. Young (who lived in Devon, and only visited Bath briefly after Nash's death) therefore asked George Scott (1719-1780) to help in dealing with the creditors. Scott, who lived in Essex, was a regular visitor to Bath for the sake of his wife's health, and knew Nash personally as he had served with him on the board of the Bath Hospital.[25]

Possibly on Scott's recommendation – although he later denied this – Young appointed William Yescombe as his attorney. So in March 1761 William achieved a considerable publicity coup for one so early in his career by placing the standard advertisements in the Bath and London papers, calling for 'All Persons who have any Demands on the Estate of Richard Nash, late of the City of Bath, Esq. deceased' to contact him.[26] Scott in the meantime was dealing with the creditors, writing to one correspondent in April:

> ...I have been for this month last past engaged in settling our late Governour's Affairs, which has been truly fatiguing; but no one else would undertake this laborious Task; and had an Execution (which was threatened) taken Place, some Hundreds must have been lost; to the great Prejudice of many Inhabitants of this City ...

William obviously flattered Scott's not inconsiderable ego, as Scott wrote to Young in May: 'M^r: Yescombe (who deserves great Praise) has been frequently visited by me since you left us, and has very politely paid all the Regard I could wish to what I have submitted to his Consideration.'

An auction of Nash's effects did not succeed in selling his collection of crayon portraits of Bath celebrities by William Hoare (whose portrait of Nash still hangs in the Pump Room). William therefore did his best to ensure a stream of fashionable visitors to his office by further advertising in the Bath papers that 'All the Family Pictures that were in the Possession of RICHARD NASH, Esq. at the Time of his Decease, may be had, at FIVE GUINEAS each' by applying to him,[27] but again with little success. This created problems with Mrs Hill, to whom Nash had given a bond for £250, and then colluded in her obtaining a court judgement for it, as a way of ensuring she had a claim on his estate. She remained dissatisfied with the way matters were progressing – Scott wrote to Young in May that he

> ... went to M^r: Yescombe's ... to consult with him on your Business; but he was not at home; his Lady was, and with her I staid until M^{rs}: Hill accidentally came in, & appeared in full Character; from such a Tongue may I ever be delivered. She used me very cruelly, and I must beg leave to concern myself no further with these matters, for I would not go through the same kind of Treatment again upon any Consideration. She abused me for having an Auction instead of a Sale. I told her, & indeed proved to her, nothing but an Auction would have been deemed legal, as there will not probably be enough to pay off the Debts, and the Creditors ought to be satisfied the Effects were fairly and honestly disposed of ... I am very certain Mr: Yescombe will act clearly & honestly. He had all your Law Papers, Bills and Receipts of me some Time ago ...

As Scott grew increasingly impatient with Mrs Hill – 'poor Nash had no small Degree of Punishment living with this termagant Woman, Solomon could not describe a worse' – he also began to hint to Young that he was not entirely happy with the service provided by William, 'who I am certain acts very uprightly in the Trust, tho' his ill State of Health, and hurry with his own and his Clients business in this City prevents your hearing from him so often as you may wish.' Finally Scott had had enough of Mrs Hill, and Young's own behaviour – in particular taking away items of Nash's effects which should have been sold for the benefit of the creditors – and refused to have any more to do with the matter, but William's continued neglect caused Young to try to drag him back in. Scott wrote to Young in December 1761:

> I really was extremely sorry to receive a Letter from your Friend in your name about any matter relating to M^{rs}: Hill, or your Uncle's Affairs, when I had desired you to excuse me from acting farther in a Business, wherein I have been so cruelly used by the Principal Parties ... M^r: Y. has been to blame in not writing to you, as I have often desired him to do; but he has heavily and justly complained to me of the indecent manner you came to his House, and of your going from hence without leaving an Account of the Money and Things you carried away with you, I assure you, I have already taken some Pains to make the Creditors easy on this Head, otherwise you would have heard from them in a way which would have been disagreeable to you. I am far from being ashamed of what I have said on M^r: Y. since I have known him, but I hope you will not say, that I recommended him to you ...

This withdrawal did not prevent Scott complaining to William about the way he had sold off the last of the Hoare portraits:

> M^r: Scott's compliments to M^r: Yescombe, and he is extremely sorry he is obliged to trouble him on so disagreeable a Subject, which he cannot help doing after the Professions of Friendship he has made to M^r: Yescombe. M^r: Scott was then greatly surprized yesterday to hear M^r: Yescombe declare, that he had sold the five last Portraits for 6 Guineas, after M^r: Yescombe had told M^r: Scott he had refused more for them from the Upper Waiter at Simpson's, and after M^r: Yescombe had assured M^r: Scott that they should not be sold for any such Price. M^r: Scott could have got more for them, and nothing could justify the selling them even for a Guinea and an half each, (if the Glasses were whole,) but another Dividend's being immediately to be made. M^r: Scott would have expressed himself fully in this Subject yesterday, but it was of too delicate a Nature to speak to before M^{rs}: Yescombe. M^r: Scott hopes M^r: Yescombe will take this Note as it is meant, for he can truly say, no one is more sincerely and warmly M^r: Yescombe's Friend than he is, and as such he now begs leave to observe, that nothing hurts

a Man of Business more, than not keeping strictly to his Word. M^r: Scott is likely to suffer himself for publicly declaring, these Portraits would not be sold for the Price they have late gone off at, and which he fears will occasion some unfavourable reports.

    Bath. March 22, 1762

P.S.

M^r: Scott is sure M^r: Yescombe upon Recollection will remember, that he said the Portraits should be given to the Creditors rather than sold for a small sum.

He noted in his letter book, however, that this was not sent, as he met William the following day.

    Scott's main role thereafter was to collect materials which were used by Oliver Goldsmith in writing his *Life of Richard Nash*, published in October 1762. The book sold well, prompting Young to get his son, Richard Nash Young, to write to Scott in September 1763 demanding a share of the profits. Scott replied indignantly denying he had received anything from the publication, and told him to apply to William if he wished to have this confirmed. A couple of days later, after meeting William in a bookshop at Charing Cross in London (near where Sarah's family lived), Scott had breakfast with him and read him this correspondence – according to Scott, William agreed that he was in the right.

    The end result for Nash's creditors can be judged from the fate of a £100 promissory note from Nash which Ralph Allen donated to the Bath Hospital – presumably not expecting to recover much from it. The Hospital was paid a dividend of £25 in January 1762, and a final £12/10/- the following December,[28] at which time William's involvement with the Nash estate must have come to an end.

    William later dealt with Thomas Joye, who had been one of Nash's partners in introducing the game of 'E.O.' (Evens and Odds – an early version of roulette)[29] into the assembly rooms of Tunbridge Wells and Bath in the 1740s, after public gambling with cards and dice were made illegal. Nash was an undercover partner, because as Master of the Ceremonies in both cities he could not be seen to be profiting from this activity (which was in fact his main means of support), although he later sued his partners, and the assembly-room proprietors in Bath, for not paying over his share of the takings.[30] In 1762 Scott mentioned that Joye was 'starving' in Bath; in 1767 William advertised in the *Bath Chronicle* for claims against his estate,[31] presumably another one with more liabilities than assets.

The Westgate Theatre Scheme

Bath was the leading theatrical town outside London, but had only one theatre, in Orchard Street. In the mid-1760s William became involved in a complex legal case resulting from a failed attempt to build a second theatre.[32]

In July 1765 John Walker, a hosier, died, having appointed William as executor under his will,[33] and trustee of his estate together with Roger Hereford, an apothecary. Jointly with John Cottell, a tailor, Walker owned a piece of land known as Webb's Gardens just outside the Borough walls at the Westgate. The City Corporation agreed to rent them 369 feet of the walls at 1/- per foot, and to allow them to remove the walls to get good access to the site.[34] Shortly after Walker's death, Cottell and the Walker family agreed to lease part of this land to a consortium led by a comic actor, John Lee (1725-1781), best known to posterity for playing Sir Lucius O'Trigger at the disastrous first night of Sheridan's *The Rivals* at Drury Lane in 1775.[35] Lee was in partnership with John Pritchard, a silk-mercer, and Charles Davis, a scene- and house-painter. The Lee consortium intended to use the land to build a new theatre, with Davis having found the deal, Pritchard probably putting up the initial cost, and Lee managing the theatre. Under their lease they were to spend not less than £2,500 to build 'one or more substantial Houses or other Buildings' on the land, paying a rent of £37 p.a. The lessors agreed to demonstrate they had a good freehold title to the land, and to deliver full access to it, by December 1766. The consortium planned to raise funding through a public subscription, but failed to do so. They claimed that uncertainty on the lessors' title to the site had caused this failure, while the lessors claimed that the consortium were just trying to find an excuse to get out of the contract because their scheme had failed. They also suggested that Lee had spent too much time 'in that part of Great Britain called Scotland and in other remote places to delay or avoid carrying the ... Contract into execution'. (Lee had been occupied trying to secure a Royal Patent for a theatre in Edinburgh.) The contract was not financially viable if the land could not be used for a theatre.

The pivotal point – the title to the site – revolved around William Yescombe. Because he and Hereford were trustees under Walker's will, he insisted that they had to be parties to the signing of the final lease. However the lessors' attorney, John Jefferys, differed violently, and would not even allow them to endorse it with their consent – according to Lee, Jefferys said that 'he would himself rather give £10,000 security to [Cottell and the Walkers] against any Molestation of the s^d. Trustees than suffer them to be made parties [to the lease]'. There is no obvious reason for these strong views by Jefferys – as the consortium pointed out, it could have done no harm to have William and Hereford sign as well as Cottell and the Walkers, which suggests some personal as well as legal antagonism by Jefferys. In fact, Cottell eventually agreed that William and Hereford could sign the lease, but by then the deadline date had passed and the Lee consortium refused to proceed.

In November 1767 Cottell and the Walkers brought a Chancery suit against Lee and his partners, calling for their contract to be implemented. In 1770 the Court ruled that the contract should be performed so long as the plaintiffs had a good title, thus overruling William's views on his position as a trustee. Commenting on this, the *Bath Chronicle*, in what appears to be editorial comment but was probably a paid insertion, called it a 'great and much contested cause', and said that the Court had treated William's objection

> ... as it really deserved, with contempt, as being not founded in reason or law; and that those who had invented it, as it was one of the principal causes that gave rise to the present suit, or at least, those who attempted to shelter themselves under it, and to avail themselves thereby of not carrying the contract into execution, must now pay for it.

The actual court judgement does not support these comments, as it does not even refer to William's objections. Lee responded in the *Bath Journal* that the decision was not a final one, since they could show that the title was defective. 'Veritas' – who from his use of legal phraseology was probably Jefferys himself – wrote a lengthy refutation in the *Bath Chronicle*, claiming that Lee could not prove a bad title, and had made several offers to settle the case.[36]

The death-blow to the plan was the grant of a Royal Patent to the Orchard Street Theatre (which then became the Theatre Royal, the first outside London) in the spring of 1768. Lee became its actor-manager shortly afterwards. But the case continued, and in 1772 Davis, claiming that he had only been acting as a trustee for Lee, won a suit at Wells Assizes for all the expenses he had incurred; Lee lost an appeal and found himself in the King's Bench debtors' prison.[37] Meanwhile, in 1771, a new case was brought against Cottell and the Walkers by Edward and Margaret Williams.[38] The latter was the daughter of William Webb, whom, she claimed, had been unjustly deprived of a reversionary interest in the Westgate land by his parents. Cottell and the Walkers not surprisingly argued that this intervention was a put-up job funded by Lee and his fellow defendants, but it had the desired effect – this case dragged on into 1775, when it was referred to the Somerset assizes for a decision on the truth of the Williams' story. But by then William Yescombe had ceased to have any involvement in the affair.

Thomas Chilcot's Estate

Joseph Tylee was the Deputy Organist at Bath Abbey, and gave music lessons, sold music and hired out harpsichords and other instruments from a shop in Queen Square. Tylee also invested in property – William acted for him in the purchase of some land in Walcot in 1762,[39] and in letting two houses on Lansdown Road in 1763-4.[40]

It was thus perhaps through Tylee that William met Thomas Chilcot, who had been the Organist at the Abbey since 1726. Like Tylee, Chilcot ran a music business, from his house in Wood Street. He was a frequent performer of organ and harpsichord music, and conducted public concerts (including the first concert of Handel's music in Bath in 1749).[41] He was well-known for his settings of Shakespeare's songs, and is also now recognised as one of the leading English composers of keyboard concertos in his time.[42] The composer and musician Thomas Linley Sen[r] was his pupil. Chilcot made William executor and trustee of his will,[43] drawn up shortly before his death in November 1766.[44] Most of the estate was to be used to purchase property, with the income divided between Chilcot's three surviving children – Elizabeth (the wife of David Walker of St Martin-in-the-Fields, London, a cabinet maker), Thomas (a yeoman in Walcot) and Fanny (who had been keeping house for her father). After their deaths, the estate was to be divided between their children.[45] The funeral took place in Tawstock, Devon (where Chilcot's first wife was buried) on 3 December, and after discussion with Fanny, William commissioned a monument to Chilcot for erection in Bath Abbey.

A week after Chilcot's death, William published advertisements calling for claims against the estate.[46] Amongst the smaller debts due to Chilcot's estate which William collected was £1/6/- from Thomas Gainsborough for music lessons. Gainsborough moved to Bath from Suffolk in 1759 and became the leading portrait painter in the city. In

1763 he rented a house on Lansdown Road for the sake of his health, but retained his studio in the city. He moved back to a house at The Circus in late 1766.[47] William advertised the Lansdown Road house for sale (as 'late in the Possession of Mr Gainsborough' – i.e. he was selling it for the owner rather than Gainsborough himself) in the summer of 1767.[48] William's relationship with Gainsborough dates from before Chilcot's death, as Gainsborough's London bank account records a payment to him of £100 in July 1765. The pattern of payments in the bank ledger suggests this could have been repayment of a loan in anticipation of Mrs Gainsborough's half-yearly annuity payment from the Duke of Beaufort's estate (she was the illegitimate daughter of a former Duke).[49]

William's relationship with Chilcot's family soon deteriorated, because they complained that he was selling some of Chilcot's possessions cheaply to his clients and friends. Some allegations were rather petty – for example, William sold Chilcot's horse for six guineas to a friend of his, George Tyndale; the Chilcot family claimed that the livery stable owner would have given £10 for it; William responded that the horse was 'accustomed to Stumble Extreamly Old and almost worn out,' and Tyndale had sold it for less than he had paid. The family also claimed that William sold Chilcot's harpsichords and spinets – which he kept for hire – to Tylee (who succeeded Chilcot as the Organist at Bath Abbey) below their true value. William said that he had used 'Mr Seed of the City of Bristol … an Organ Harpsichord and Spinett maker and … a proper and Skillful Judge of the Value of such Instruments' to value them,[50] and that Seede told him 'that the … Harpsichords and Spinetts were all of them very much out of repair and the Spinetts so broken to pieces as to be of very little Value.' William was also said to have kept a manuscript book with unpublished compositions by Chilcot, 'merely on purpose to oblige his Friends and Acquaintances with such Book and to permit them to take Extracts or Copies of some part or parts thereof whereby the Sale of such Book was totally prejudiced and such Book rendered of little value.' William's response to this was that 'in a Conversation which [I] had with [Chilcot] some short time before his Death touching his music [Chilcot] told [me] that he had an Inclination to give all his Musical Books to the Musick School at Oxford for that in case such Books were sold for the benefit of his Estate they would not fetch above Twenty pounds.' He did agree that he held various Chilcot manuscripts, though no one book of unpublished compositions, but denied that he allowed his friends to take copies. He had asked two of the leading musicians in Bath, William Herschel (1738-1822, then organist of the newly-built Octagon Chapel but later to become far more famous as an astronomer) and Dr Henry Harington (1727-1816, well-known in Bath both as a doctor and as a composer; his memorial is in Bath Abbey), to examine Chilcot's music library. They agreed it was of little value. Because of this dispute Chilcot's musical books and manuscripts were withdrawn from the sale of his effects which took place in January 1767.[51] William later paid Herschel 1½ guineas to produce a complete catalogue of Chilcot's music library, but then did nothing more with it. This library, which contained early Handel manuscripts and unpublished Chilcot pieces which are now lost, was sold (mistakenly) in the sale of William's own effects in 1774.[52]

William also dealt with Chilcot's *Opera Secunda*, a volume of six harpsichord concertos, of which the first volume had been published in 1756. Chilcot advertised for subscribers between April 1761 and June 1762.[53] Despite the later advertisements promising that the volume 'speedily will be published', in 1764 he made an apology for its non-appearance.[54] This delay probably arose because Chilcot was publishing the book himself rather than through London and Bath booksellers, as with his previous works. Based on the final list of subscribers he had only disposed of 79 copies, compared to over 100 for his previous volume, and over 300 for his *Twelve English Songs*, published in 1744. He had some 200 sets of engravings of the music printed in 1765, but at his death the final volume had still not been published, so William had the engravings bound up with a list of subscribers, adding a note that 'It is humbly requested that no Subscriber will take it ill whose name is not inserted, as Mr. CHILCOTT's death was so sudden'. He arranged for the surplus to be disposed of by the Bath bookseller Frederick, who advertised them weekly for nearly nine months in 1768-9.[55] William paid him half a guinea for his trouble: no money received from sales was paid into the estate.

Because of the disputes with the family, William stopped paying for the work on the planned Abbey memorial to Chilcot, which was never erected. He also presumably refused to pay for the inscription of his monument in Tawstock church, so that the space intended for Chilcot's details beside his wife's remains blank to this day. The net value of Chilcot's estate was £2,159, his house in Wood Street and a mortgage over some farmland in Somerset being his main assets. William made some payments of interest to Elizabeth Walker and Thomas Chilcot Jun[r], but nothing to Fanny. The family claimed that they asked him to explain what he was doing with the money, without success. William however said that he had shown the accounts to the portrait painter William Hoare on Fanny's behalf, and the latter had been satisfied with them. Moreover, he offered to pay the money over to Hoare to manage, if he was indemnified for doing so. Then a more formidable opponent came into the picture. The family signed a letter of attorney giving John Jefferys and another Bath attorney the authority to demand an account of the administration of the estate from William. As in the Westgate Theatre affair, Jefferys' actions in the Chilcot case suggest a desire to cause William the maximum difficulty. Initially William took a robust attitude to Jefferys' arrival on the scene. The Chilcots claimed that William made them revoke the letter of attorney by refusing to make any interest payments to them, thus 'taking Advantage of their extream Poverty' – Thomas Chilcot Junr at that time being on parish relief in Walcot – and by suggesting that these attorneys would just 'draw them into a Law Suit and that the Expense thereof would be after the Rate of ten Pounds a Day and would come out of the ... Estate'. But Jefferys and his colleague were then given authority to continue the suit at their own expense, William claiming that they had gone to Thomas and threatened him with prison if he did not agree to this. As a result, in May 1769 the family filed a suit in the Court of Chancery, in which they asked, *inter alia*, for William to give an account of his administration, and to pay the funds in his hands into court.

Apart from the various grievances set out above, the plaintiffs also claimed that William had called in Chilcot's £1,500 Somerset mortgage,

merely with a View to have an Opportunity of applying the same in Hazardous Building Schemes and in Payment of his own Debts ... And in Particular [we] Charge that ... William Yescombe being very much Concerned as a Builder of new Houses in or about the City of Bath and especially in three or more Houses in a certain Place called the Queens Parade in Bath and which he had mortgaged to one Mr Fisher for securing the Principal Sum of Three Thousand Four Hundred Pounds thereon and being in great want of Moneys called in [Chilcot's] Moneys which was out on ... good real Securities of Interest meerly and alone to supply his own Wants and to apply ... the same in such Hazardous Buildings and the money so applied of ... Chilcotts thereon with the Mortgage due to Mr Fisher greatly exceeded the real Value of such Houses Whereby such Moneys was in Danger of being lost.

They argued that

> [Yescombe] being but in low Circumstances there is great Danger
> of the Clear Surplus of [Chilcot's] Estate being lost or embezzled if
> the same is not forthwith secured And ... there is at Present a great
> many new Buildings or Houses now Carrying on and Building
> at Bath and ... many Necessitous or Poor Persons are Concerned
> as Principals in such Buildings several of whom are Clients or
> become Clients to ... William Yescombe on Account of his having
> so large a Sum of Money in his Hands arising from the Estate
> of...Thomas Chilcott to lend or play with ... [and that he has made
> loans] at the rate of five Pounds per Cent or some other very
> large rate of Interest in Order to gain some Advantage to himself
> by Accounting to [us] for a less rate of Interest than he made of
> such Money And ... such Securitys are all Hazardous and Scanty
> Securitys whereby the Moneys arisen from the Estate and Effects
> of ... Thomas Chilcott is in danger of being lost or Misapplied.

William made no attempt to deny these claims. He said that he was
crediting the £2,159 which he held from the estate with interest at 4%,
admitting

> that from time to time as [I] received any Moneys on Account
> of [Chilcot's] Estate and effects ... [I] did Intermix the same with
> [my] own Moneys and did not keep the same Separate or distinct
> And ... having frequently since the death of [Chilcot] Sent divers
> Sums of Money to divers Persons upon Securitys taken in [my]
> name ... and also laid out divers other Large Sums in Building and
> purchasing Buildings [I] cannot therefore distinguish what part
> thereof belongs to [Chilcot's estate]

but stating his willingness to pay this amount over at such rate of interest
as the Court might direct. In fact his behaviour was quite normal for
country attorneys at this period – as the Bank of England had a monopoly
on joint-stock banking in England, the development of country banks
was relatively slow. So people with money had no convenient way of
investing it short-term, nor could loans easily be obtained. As a natural
development of their business, therefore, attorneys took money on
deposit and lent it out in their own name or on behalf of their clients; a
deposit rate of 4% and loan rate of 5% were quite reasonable.[56]

In July 1770 William was ordered to pay the £2,159 into the Court (which he duly did in November), with the interest on these funds used to make payments to the Chilcots. Thereafter, the case of *Walker v Yescombe* went into hibernation: the Chilcot children had little incentive to take further action as they were being paid their income from the estate by the court; Jefferys had presumably lost interest once he had made William pay over the money. Little happened until 1793, when Fanny's son Hiern Croome revived the case against Robert Yescombe, as William's heir-at-law, and his cousin Edward Daniel, as his executor, claiming that they still held funds from the Chilcot estate.[57] Evidence was taken from Daniel, from which it was clear that no other funds existed. And so in July 1796, nearly 30 years after Chilcot's death, the Court of Chancery agreed a final settlement of the estate.

The Creaser Bankruptcy

After raising funds to pay back Chilcot's £2,159, William's position must have become increasingly precarious. It is clear from what he said in his evidence that he had numbers of investments or loans beside his three houses in Queen's Parade on which he had borrowed £3,400. These were part of a development by John Wood of 12 houses off Queen Square, mentioned earlier. William advertised the '1st house' in Queen's Parade to let in 1770, and the '2nd house' – rented to the Countess of Warwick – for sale in 1773. By May 1772, when William made his final response in the Chilcot case to the Court of Chancery, he admitted that he 'hath sustained and is likely to sustain considerable Losses by other Moneys which he hath lent' during the time the case had been going on.

William was therefore ill-prepared for the financial crisis which affected the whole country in 1772, caused by over-expansion of credit, especially to the American colonies after the repeal of the Stamp Act led to the ending of the colonial boycott on British imports, and by speculation in the West Indian colonies taken from the French after the war of 1756-1763. This led to a heavy circulation of short-term bills of exchange as a way of raising credit, which was very vulnerable to a collapse in confidence. The crisis began with the failure in June of the London banking firm of Neal, James, Fordyce and Down, caused by speculation in East India Company stock. A run developed on all the major banks in London as depositors withdrew their money and short-term bills were no longer renewed.[58] The ensuing panic was described by the *Gentleman's Magazine*:[59]

It is beyond the power of words to describe the general consternation of the metropolis at this instant. No event for 50 years past [i.e. since the collapse of the South Sea Bubble] has been remembered to have given so fatal a blow to both trade and public credit. An universal bankruptcy was expected, the stoppage of almost every banker's house in London was looked for. The whole city was in an uproar; many of the first families in tears…

This credit crisis spread throughout the country. Although triggered by speculation it was primarily caused by a loss of confidence in the credit market, and in this sense it was the first 'modern' financial crisis; the novelty of the situation explains the panic which ensued. It brought the Bath housing boom to an end,[60] and caused a devastating blow to William's position with the bankruptcy in August 1772 of Thomas Creaser.[61] Creaser had begun business as a draper in 1762;[62] in 1770 he joined William's client Cam Gyde in constructing a grandstand at Claverton Down for the horse races.[63] But he also ran a banking business – like attorneys, drapers were commonly bankers before separate country banks were established, as they dealt with suppliers of cloth all over the country and therefore had a good network of contacts for discounting bills.[64]

Creaser's bankruptcy caused considerable bitterness in Bath – so much so that in October 1772 the Bath newspapers refused to publish an advertisement from his creditors demanding another examination of his affairs: they had to resort to circulating hand-bills, and publishing their advertisement in Bristol.[65] In June 1773 Creaser claimed in an advertisement in the *Bath Chronicle* that his creditors would have all their debts repaid; in response his bankruptcy assignees (i.e. the administrators of his estate, appointed by the bankruptcy commissioners) published a statement of his affairs.[66] According to this, claims against Creaser totalled at least £31,000. His assets had a notional value of around £30,000, but the assignees gave them a real value of around £10,000. The notional assets included a claim of more than £10,000 on the firm of Beynon & Dibbs (described as ribbon weavers, but given the scale of the claim they must also have been bankers) who had gone bankrupt shortly before him,[67] as well as other bad debts. In fact his only real assets related to his draper's business, with some £3,000 of debts due to this business, and stock valued at £5,000.

Advertisements for the sale of this massive stock ran for several months from the Spring of 1773:[68]

A Real SALE *of* Woollen Drapery, *&c.*
This Day began SELLING OFF

THE ENTIRE STOCK (late Mr CREASER's) in the Abbey Church
Yard; consisting of a Large and Fashionable Assortment of
Superfines, and other Cloths of all Qualities, Ratteens, Cassimeres,
Bath Bevers, Napp's Duffels, Coatings, and every other Article
in the Woollen Trade; together with a great Variety of Men's
Mercery, Manchester Goods, Men's Hats, Ladies Riding ditto,
Silk Waistcoat and Breeches Pieces, in plain Colours, Stripes and
Figures, Gold and Silver Lace and Buttons, &c. – A great Variety
of Tambour and Brocaded Shapes for Waistcoats, in Gold, Silver
and Colours.

N.B. As this Stock must be disposed of for Ready Money, on account
of Mr. CREASER's present Situation, he assures the Public, that
each Article will be sold at Prime Cost, (the Price being marked
on the Goods) and also that a Discount of FIVE PERCENT. will be
allowed on every Sum to the Amount of Twenty Shillings, except
on SUPERFINE CLOTHS, which will be sold for Fifteen Shillings
per Yard.

William's involvement with him became public with an advertisement
in the *Bath Journal* in February 1773:[69]

To be SOLD
A DEBT of £.550 due from the Estate of THOMAS CREASER,
a Bankrupt, for eight Shillings in the Pound. – For further
Particulars enquire of Mr. Yescombe, in Bath

This prompted a vitriolic response from Creaser in the next *Bath
Chronicle*:[70]

A CAUTION to the PUBLIC

ON reading the PIOUS Attorney's Advertisement in Keene's last
Journal, for selling the Debt due from the Estate of a Bankrupt, I
was led to enquire of one of the Assignees, whether such a Debt was
really due to him; when the Assignee assured me, the Advertiser
had not proved ANY Debt upon the said Estate, therefore he can
have no debt to sell. – Let the candid Public judge then of this
upright Attorney's Intentions! – But what may not be expected from
Men who are Strangers to Truth and every Feeling of Humanity!

Which not surprisingly produced a strong response from William in the next *Journal*:[71]

> WHEREAS Mr. YESCOMBE caused an Advertisement to be inserted in Keene's Bath Journal of the 15th Instant, for the sale of a Debt of 550l. due from the Estate of THOMAS CREASER, a Bankrupt, for 8 Shillings in the Pound. And whereas in the Bath Chronicle of the 18th Instant, a Scandalous Paragraph appeared under the Title of "A CAUTION TO THE PUBLIC," (inserted by the *Just* Bankrupt, or some *Honest* Person connected with him) Infamously reflecting on the Character of the said Mr. YESCOMBE, and intimating that as he had not proved any Debt against the Bankrupt's Estate, he could have no Debt to sell: – Mr. YESCOMBE, with a view to clear himself from such reflections, and to convince the Public of the propriety of such Advertisement, declares that tho' he has not proved any Debt upon the Bankrupt's Estate, he has a very large Demand thereon, which he now offers to dispose of upon the above Terms, and engages to sell several Thousand Pounds of the Bankrupt's Debts as the same Rate.
>
> N.B. Any Gentleman of Character and Property inclinable to become Purchasers, shall meet with great Encouragement; and for Ready Money considerable Abatements will be made.

A public admission that he held 'a very large Demand', from which he was willing to sell 'several Thousand Pounds' of debt on which his asking price was no more than 8/– in the £ shows how serious William's financial situation must have become. In fact by the end of 1773 only 4/6d in the £ had been paid out to Creaser's creditors.[72]

The Final Crash

The first to suffer from William's problems was his own wife's family, as can be seen from a rather pathetic action brought against him in the Court of Chancery by his wife's aunts in February 1773.[73] Apart from the £3,300 transferred to trustees at the time of her marriage, most of the rest of Sarah's £6,000 fortune consisted of an estate at Belton, Rutland, left to her by her uncle John Collin.[74] His will transferred the estate to trustees and charged it with paying annuities of £20 each *per annum* to John Collin's two sisters, and after their deaths with the payment of a legacy of £500 each to their daughters. When William and Sarah's marriage settlement was drawn up its trustees agreed to take over the liability to pay the £500 legacies, and the Belton estate was thus released from the trust. But no provision was made to secure the payment of the £20 annuities to the aunts, which William and Sarah stopped paying in 1771, claiming both that there was not enough money in the Belton estate and that it was not charged with the annuity. William never replied to the aunts' writ and the case petered out.

Meanwhile William had to deal with larger and more persistent creditors as writs for debt were issued against him in the Court of King's Bench[75] – the Court in which he was an attorney. The first claim for £100 came from Frances Jacques, a Bristol baker, the endorsee of a promissory note issued by William to John Powell in December 1772, in return for the latter advancing cash on a draft drawn by Creaser which William endorsed. Obviously this was renewing an earlier draft from before Creaser's bankruptcy. Jacques obtained judgement against William in May 1773, although William then attempted a delaying action in the Court of Chancery by claiming that he had endorsed the original draft 'as an act of friendship' to Creaser, and was now facing two £100 claims, one on the original draft and one on the promissory note.[76] This attempt at confusing the issue did not succeed, but it did delay a final judgement until December. The fact that William had to take so much trouble to delay payment of a debt of only £100 speaks for itself. The pleas in the case also mention claims for a further £600 by Jacques. Another writ for £300, also relating to William's guarantee of sums due by Creaser, was issued at the same time as Jacques'.

By late 1773 William could no longer hold off his creditors by himself, and turned to his brother Robert. In November Robert guaranteed a promissory note of £450 issued by William (which was also endorsed by Edward Daniel) to the Bristol Exchange Bank.[77] The note was not paid, and Robert took over liability for it in January 1774. This was clearly part of a much larger support action – their mother Ann Yescombe's will, drawn up in December,[78] stated that Robert had 'advanced and paid and entered into many Securities for payment of divers Sums of Money' for William, and therefore left William nothing, dividing her estate between Robert and her orphaned grandson Edward Bayntun Yescombe (1765-1803). However Robert's support was not enough. Early in 1774 Roger Hereford, who had been involved with William in the Westgate Theatre scheme, sued on a debt of £244 owing since 1770. The final blow came from Jenkins & Bray. William had borrowed £300 from William Bray in 1771,[79] as well as further sums from Abel Jenkins, or the partnership as a whole. In January 1774 Bray went to visit William in Bath over the weekend. Bray's journal records that he spent Saturday afternoon with him, dined with him on Sunday after church, and spent the whole of Monday with him.[80] This was obviously a last-ditch way of trying to find a way out – on the Saturday, 15 January, William signed a new promissory note to Jenkins & Bray for £840/14/-. On 28 January they brought an action against him in the Court of King's Bench for the sum due on this note. William was not in court for the hearing on 3 February; final judgement was obtained against him on 21 March. Four days later, William died in London.[81] It is tempting to guess that his death was suicide, but no evidence for this has been found.

Aftermath

William's will appointed Edward Daniel as his executor, and left him his law books and business papers, with the rest of his estate to his wife.[82] However as he died insolvent (as Edward Daniel testified in *Croome v Yescombe* in 1796, mentioned earlier), his effects were all sold. The sale advertisement shows that he had been living a comfortable life:[83]

BATH, April 6, 1774
TO be SOLD by Auction, by WM. CROSS, on Tuesday the 12th of April instant, and the following days,
    All the HOUSEHOLD FURNITURE, PLATE, LINEN, CHINA, BOOKS, &c. of Mr. YESCOMBE, Attorney, deceased, at his late Dwelling house in Monmouth-street; – consisting of standing beds with morine [stout woollen/cotton material used for curtains, *etc.*] and other furniture; goose feather beds, and bedding; mahogany furniture in dining, card, pillar and Pembroke tables, chests of drawers, a handsome bureau and book case with Chinese front, glaz'd; Wilton and Scotch carpets; a quantity of fine music of the late Mr. Chilcot's; a curious time piece in carv'd burnish'd gold; together with kitchen furniture, brewing utensils, &c.
Also, a post chaise, and a whisky [light two-wheeled one-horse carriage], in good condition.

His widow received nothing from his estate, but fortunately her marriage settlement meant that she still had some money of her own. Eighteen months later Sarah married again, to Thomas Elwes, a Bath apothecary.[84] Supporting William undermined Robert Yescombe's own finances – clearly the burden became too great, and from 1779 to 1781 he faced more than a dozen different actions for debt in the King's Bench; at least £6,500-worth of judgements were obtained against him. A settlement was negotiated with the creditors, under which Robert was forced to sell off his holdings of farmland around Wedmore – part of which had been in the family for at least 150 years, leaving nothing to the family but their house in Bristol. Bankruptcy was not an option, because the Bankruptcy Act of 1706 only covered debts incurred when carrying on a trade, so the only alternative would have been the debtors' prison. Robert's nephew Edward Bayntun Yescombe, the heir to the family estate, gave up any prospect of life as a country gentleman, but thanks to the influence of his maternal grandfather, Sir Edward Bayntun, he was able to secure an appointment as captain of a Post Office packet ship in 1787, and by the end of the eighteenth century he had restored the shattered family fortunes. Robert himself died in lodgings in Bath in 1815.

Notes

Abbreviations
BC   *Bath Chronicle*
BJ   *Bath Journal*
PRO   The National Archives (Public Record Office)

1   E.B.V. Christian, *A Short History of Solicitors* (Reeves & Turner, 1896), p.139ff.; Michael Birks, *Gentlemen of the Law* (Stevens, 1960), p.169. By the mid-eighteenth century attorneys had taken over conveyancing.
2   PRO/IR/1/20/100, 6 November 1755.
3   PRO/IR/1/52/116, 14 August 1755.
4   PRO/KB/172/1: Court of King's Bench, *Enrolment of Attorneys (Private)*, 27 November 1760; the entries for Robert and William can be found on the same page as their father 30 years earlier. There are no records of enrolments for the Courts of Exchequer and Chancery at this time.
5   Lambeth Palace Library: Vicar-General Marriage Allegations (licence 16 September 1760); City of Westminster Archives: Parish Register of St Clement Danes (marriage 18 September 1760).
6   *BJ*, 29 September 1760.
7   National Library of Wales: Eaton Evans & Williams (Haverfordwest) Deeds 403-407.
8   A glimpse can be found in an advertisement in *BJ*, 11 July 1768, for a horse he had lost while it was tied up overnight at The Circus.
9   *BC*, 21-28 November 1765 advertises the Kingsmead Street house as 'late in the Possession of Mr. Yescombe. Attorney'. In the edition of 21 November, there is another odd note – which looks as though it was inserted by accident – stating that this house was worth £500, with a rental of £35/10/- p.a.

10 Bath Record Office: 0005 (deeds).

11 *BJ*, 26 March-30 April 1770.

12 *BC*, 13 August-10 September 1761, BJ, 17 August-21 August 1761.

13 *BC*, 30 May 1765, *BJ*, 10 June-22 July 1765.

14 House of Lords Record Office: 12 Geo III (1772) c.134. This is the original enrolment of the Act as these 'estate acts' were generally not printed.

15 *Journals of the House of Commons*, Vol. XXXIII, p.789 (25 May 1772).

16 Surrey History Centre/G85/77; G85/12, 14 & 15.

17 Somerset Record Office/DD/DP/7/15.

18 Julian Pooley, 'Bray, William', *Oxford Dictionary of National Biography* (Oxford University Press, 2004).

19 *BC*, 14-21 December 1763; BJ, 12 December 1763.

20 R.S. Neale, *Bath 1680-1850: A Social History, or A Valley of Pleasure, yet a Sink of Iniquity* (Routledge & Kegan Paul, 1981), p.235.

21 Bath Record Office: O444 (deeds).

22 Neale, *op.cit.*, p.163.

23 British Library: Eg.MSS/3516 fos.36, 139-147.

24 Fawcett, *Bath Entertain'd: Amusements, Recreations and Gambling at the 18th-Century Spa* (Ruton, Bath, 1998), pp.4-9.

25 Olivier W. Ferguson, 'The Materials of History: Goldsmith's Life of Nash', *PMLA: Publications of the Modern Language Association of America*, Vol. LXXX (1965), p.372. The author is indebted to Mr Trevor Fawcett for this reference. Quotations are from Scott's letter books (British Library: Eg.MSS 3736-9).

26 *BC*, 19 March 1761, BJ, 23 March 1761; *London Gazette*, 17-21 March 1761.

27 *BC*, 21 May-11 June 1761; *BJ*, 25 May 1761.

28 Benjamin Boyce, *The Benevolent Man* (Harvard University Press, Cambridge, Mass., 1967), p.263.

29 Trevor Fawcett, *op.cit.*, pp.36-7.

30 [Oliver Goldsmith], *The Life of Richard Nash, of Bath, Esq.* (J. Newbery, London & W. Frederick, Bath, 1762), p.57; [Francis Fleming], *The Third Volume of the Life and Adventures of Timothy Ginnadrake, containing a Concise Account of the City of Bath, from the Year 1670, to the present Times* (Cruttwell, Bath, 1771), p.68. William Yescombe was a subscriber to the 1st volume of this work – undated, but probably published several years earlier, as the subscribers also include Thomas Chilcot, who died in 1766. Ferguson, *op.cit.*, pp.380-1.

31 *BC*, 13 August-17 September 1767.

32 PRO/C/12/1964/9 (pleas); C/12/1973/11 (interrogatories); C/33/433/241 (decree).

33 See William's advertisements relating to the estate in *BC*, 25 July-29 August 1765.

34 Neale, *op.cit.*, p.184.

35 Philip H. Highfill, Kalman A. Burnim and Edward Langhans, *A Biographical Dictionary of Actors, Actresses ... & other Stage Personnel in London, 1660-1800*, vol.9 (Southern Illinois University Press, Carbondale, Ill., 1984), pp.201-210 (but with only a short and confused reference to the Westgate Theatre affair).

36 *BC*, 1 & 8 March 1770; *BJ*, 5 March 1770.

37 [John Lee], *An Address to the Judges and the Public, on a decision lately made in one of our Courts of Judicature* (1772).

38 PRO/C/12/1891/39 (pleas); C/33/444/319 (order).

39 Somerset Record Office/DD/S/WI C/2307.

40 *BC*, 28 July-1 September 1763; *BJ*, 1 August-5 September 1763; *BC*, 5-19 December 1765; *BJ*, 16-23 December 1765.

41 Otto Emil Deutsch, *Handel – A Documentary Biography* (A. & C. Black, 1955).

42 Timothy Rishton, 'Chilcot, Thomas' in Stanley Sadie (ed.), *The New Grove Dictionary of Music and Musicians* (Oxford University Press, 2nd edn., 2000).

43 PRO/PROB/11/925.

44 *BJ*, 1 December 1766.

45 PRO/C/12/1929/32 (pleas); C/33/434/416 (order); C/38/629 (Master's certificate); quotations are from the pleas.

46 *BC*, 1-29 December 1766; *BJ*, 11 December 1766-1 January 1767.

47 Susan Sloman, *Gainsborough in Bath* (Yale University Press, New Haven & London, 2002).

48 *BC*, 6 August-17 September 1767.

49 C. Hoare & Co: Ledger 69/300, 11 July 1765, printed in Sloman, *op.cit.*, p.205 (chapter 2 of this book gives the background to Mrs Gainsborough's annuity).

50 Brice Seede worked in Bristol between 1753 and 1772, made harpsichords, and was well-known as an organ builder. (Christopher Kent, 'An Introduction to Brice and Richard Seede: Organ Builders of Bristol', *BIOS – Journal of the British Institute of Organ Studies*, vol.5 (1981), pp.83-97.)

51 *BC*, 1-8 January 1767.

52 For this sale see 'Aftermath' above, p.116.

53 *BJ*, 13 April, 14 & 28 December 1761; 19 April-18 June 1762.

54 *BC*, 30 August-6 September 1764.

55 *BJ*, 28 November 1768-21 August 1769.

56 Birks, *op.cit.*, pp.181-6. The first bank in Bath was the Bath Bank (or Old Bank), founded in 1768, followed by the Bath and Somersetshire Bank in 1775.

57 PRO/C/12/657/3 (pleas); C/12/483/18 (interrogatory); C/33/493/647 (order).

58 Julian Hoppit, 'Financial Crises in Eighteenth-century England', *Economic History Review*, 2nd Series, vol.XXXIX, 1 (1986), pp.39-58.

59 *Gentleman's Magazine*, vol.XLII (June 1772), p.293; cf. *BC*, 25 June 1772, and *BJ*, 29 June 1772, which print an almost identical paragraph.

60 Neale, *op.cit.*, p.235; Paul Langford, *A Polite and Commercial People: England 1727-1783*, (Oxford University Press, Oxford, 1989), pp.532, 570. Construction stopped in Edinburgh New Town for the same reason (James Buchan, *Capital of the Mind: How Edinburgh Changed the World* (Murray, 2003), p.200).

61 *The London Chronicle*, 15-18 August 1772.

62 *BC*, 11 October 1762.

63 Fawcett, *op.cit.*, p.49-51; the statement of Creaser's affairs in 1773 (see note 66) valued his interest at £120.

64 L.S. Pressnell, *Country Banking in the Industrial Revolution* (Oxford University Press, Oxford, 1956), pp.51-3.

65 *Felix Farley's Bristol Journal*, 17 & 24 October 1772. The latter issue includes a reply from 'Amor Justiciæ', who is clearly Creaser himself.

66 *BC*, 3 & 10 June 1773.

67 *The London Chronicle*, 11-13 August 1772.

68 *BJ*, 19 April-12 July 1773; *BC*, 1 July 1773.

69 *BJ*, 15 February 1773; this followed a further meeting of the creditors with the bankruptcy assignees on 8 February (*ibid.*, 4 February).
70 *BC*, 18 February 1773.
71 *BJ*, 22 February 1773.
72 *BJ*, 1 March & 27 November 1773, *BC*, 9 December 1773.
73 PRO/C/12/1945/71 (plea); C/33/440/437 (order); C/33/440/448 (order).
74 PRO/PROB/11/853/93.
75 PRO/KB/122/375/70, 376/1282; 382/132, 309 & 374.
76 PRO/C/12/906/41 (plea); C/33/440/455 (order); C/33/440/466 (order).
77 PRO/KB/122/428/697.
78 Bristol Record Office: Will of Ann Yescombe dated 7 December 1773, proved 14 June 1784 (*sic*).
79 Surrey History Centre/G85/14.
80 Surrey History Centre/G85/17.
81 *BC*, 31 March 1774; *Felix Farley's Bristol Journal*, 2 April 1774.
82 PRO/PROB/11/997/213.
83 *BC*, 7 April 1774.
84 *BC*, 21 September 1775.

Sarah Scott – A Female Historian in Mid-Eighteenth Century Bath

Holger Th. Gräf

The superb book by R.S. Neale has made Sarah Scott well-known as one of the witnesses of life and gossip in mid-eighteenth century Bath.[1] But she is by far more than one of the – in a continental perspective – enviably numerous authors of witty letters. She is also one of the novelists of distinction, though her writings seem not to have been widely discussed.[2] Nevertheless her literary work has experienced a considerable renaissance in recent years and at the conference on 'Women's writing in Britain 1660-1830' in Southampton in July 2003, an entire panel was dedicated to some of her novels. Strangely enough 'her historical works..., were always more consistently praised than her novels... and applauded as balanced and strong',[3] yet they are not looked at by modern historians. So the historical works of Sarah Scott form the basic theme of this paper. Her specific idea of history is studied by comparing her *History of Mecklenburgh* with the *History of Vandalia* by her contemporary Thomas Nugent (c.1700-1772). Finally the question is raised, why her *History of Mecklenburgh* was forgotten, marginalized? A promising answer to this question leads us to Bath. But first, her life and works will be sketched briefly.

The Life and Works of Sarah Scott, *née* Robinson

Sarah Robinson was born on 21 September 1720, probably at the country seat of her father in the village of Hutton Magna, 12 kms north of Richmond, Yorkshire, and baptised on 5 March 1721 in York.[4] Her father, Matthew Robinson (1694-1778), was descended from an old gentry family of that county. Around 1712 he had married Elizabeth Drake (c. 1693-1746), the daughter of a Cambridge landowner, who was a member of a Kent propertied family of office bearers and scholars. Twelve children – seven sons and two daughters reached adulthood – came from their marriage. The second husband of their maternal grandmother, Conyers Middleton (1683-1750), taught at the university of Cambridge. He was regarded as one of the 'classical republicans' of the early eighteenth century. In his house three younger brothers of Sarah were born between 1727 and 1731. During the long regular stays of the Robinson family in Cambridge, Middleton saw with notable success to the education of his grandchildren – including the two girls. Some of his grandsons studied in Cambridge. First-born Matthew (1713-1800)[5] was a Member of Parliament for Cambridge from 1747 to 1761. His brother William (1727-1803)[6] lived in Naples from 1760 to 1762 and later had a parish near Canterbury. He was a friend of the well-known poet Thomas Gray. Their sister Elizabeth, born in 1718, became in the 1750s a central figure of the so-called 'Blue Stocking feminism'.[7] The surviving personal letters show that they were – without exception – a family of talented, close brothers and sisters, who stayed in touch for the whole of their life.[8] Sarah's life was always tied to that of her older sister Elizabeth.

The family was undoubtedly wealthy, but the father's wish to move from Yorkshire to London could not be fulfilled. A life befitting their rank in the booming capital was too expensive and the family therefore moved to the country seat inherited by their mother in Mount Morris, Kent. Sarah had the worst future prospects of all the children: financial means were expended on the education and career of her brothers, and a marriage before her older sister was certainly out of question. The extraordinarily close relation between both sisters loosened in the short term, when in 1734 a friend of Elizabeth, Margaret Harley, married William Bentinck, Duke of Portland, and Elizabeth spent a lot of time in London to keep her company. Because of her lively and witty nature Elizabeth was soon successful in high society. Sarah, however, usually stayed in the country. A heavy smallpox infection in 1741 decreased her prospect of a socially advantageous marriage further. Elizabeth married Edward Montagu (1692-1775) on 5 August 1742. He was wealthy, due to coal mines, a grandson of the Earl of Sandwich and a Member of Parliament since 1734.[9] Marriage with a man twice as old as she but respecting her concerns had considerable advantages for Elizabeth: she obtained social reputation and the material independence to look after her literary and social interests.[10] From the 1750s her distinguished circle of 'Blue Stockings', to which the painter Angelika Kauffmann (1741-1807) belonged at times, was one of the most important salons at London. The couple lived in Yorkshire for most of the time, but also in Sandleford, Berkshire, where Sarah often paid longer visits. There, Edward Haytley (active 1740-1762), working often for the Montagus, painted her portrait in the 1740s.

Portrait of Sarah Scott by Edward Haytley, 1744.
(*From a Private Collection and reproduced here by kind permission of the owner*)

Mount Morris was the centre of Sarah's life until the death of her mother in 1746. After that her father, following his old wish, moved to London and lived there with a housekeeper. Sarah could not, was not allowed, or did not want to follow him. It was also out of the question to live in the shadow of her bright sister. Thus, she chose a restless life that was characterised by long visits to friends and relatives and stays in the elegant spas of Bath and Tunbridge Wells, the most important 'wedding markets' of the kingdom.[11] In Bath she got to know – at the latest in 1747 – Lady Barbara Montagu (died August 1765), a daughter of the Earl of Halifax, a few years younger than Sarah.[12] In August 1748 she moved into her house at Bath. Both lived on relatively modest allowances from their fathers. In 1750 Sarah Robinson published her first book, probably hoping to increase their household budget. In the same year George Lewis Scott (1708-1780) became 'sub-preceptor' of Prince George, the later George III, grandson of King George II.[13] Sarah had used her contacts in the background to support this appointment.[14] She had already met him, as a friend of her brother-in-law, at the end of the 1740s. His post was apparently the prerequisite for their marriage in London on 15 June 1751. With that, Sarah Scott approached the social and cultural centre of the country. The couple lived in Leicester Fields near the prince's residence at Leicester House, and moved some months later to Chelsea. But the marriage failed after nine months, causing a great stir. Scott left London with an allowance from her husband – £100 a year – and lived until her death with her friend Lady Barbara in Bath, spending the summers in Batheaston close by. This obviously scandalous step provoked a deep disagreement with her father. In Bath she initiated with Lady Barbara various charitable projects, concerning for example the employment of mentally and physically disabled servants. Thereby her financial difficulties increased, leading to her becoming a productive writer.[15] Many of her works found a quite positive reception by critics.[16] Contacts with court and London society, which arose out of the connections of her husband and her sister, fitted very well into her literary activity, and a long-term Sapphic friendship did not cause concern if it was seen without sexual connotation.[17]

The 'Blue Stockings' tried to create a kind of female republic of scholars. In the end, this was the only chance for women with academic and literary ambitions in an educational system that was shaped and dominated by men and that denied women access even to classical education. The works of Sarah Scott – she kept her husband's name after the separation – can be divided into two groups. On the one hand there are novels like *Millenium Hall* and *Sir George Ellison*. These works show a clear condemnation of moral and political failure as well as of the bad state of social affairs of her time. She criticises the discrimination against women in a sexist environment and condemns slavery in the colonies.[18] The solution to these problems she sees in a society based on a religious-utopia, transfiguring the hierarchic paternalistic feudal society.[19] The fundamental contradiction in this 'merry old England' ideology led in the end to her finding the events of the French Revolution repugnant, as did her sister and the 'Blue Stockings'. In her novel *Agreeable Ugliness*, written after her move to Lady Barbara Montagu's home, she tells the story of two sisters – one a bright beauty, the other a plain woman of education and virtue – whose juxtaposed adventures show the superiority of moral goodness over physical beauty. One has the idea that she put some autobiographical experiences from her relation to her sister Elizabeth into this.

In the second group of her publications – Sarah Scott's three historical treatises – her religious moralising attitude is also noticeable. In Scott's opinion the purpose of history is always to provide edifying and instructive models and examples for the present day. According to the then current idea of 'historia magistra vitae',[20] she published in 1760 (the year of the coronation of George III, the former 'student' of her former husband) a *History of Gustavus Ericson*. This is in our understanding no historical treatise, it is more like an early modern mirror for princes (*Fürstenspiegel*). There is no need to say that this work had to be published under the male pseudonym of Henry Augustus Raymond: an historical treatise by a female writer, moreover one who knew the king, could never have been published. The work – quite well reviewed by contemporaries – portrays the founder of the Swedish great-power as a religious, protestant, paternalistic, model king. The characterisation of his personality and policy becomes a governmental programme for an enlightened sovereign: promotion of trade and industry, deep respect for the sciences, welfare services for the poor and sick, founding of schools, hospitals and granaries. Scott's other historical works did not appear under her name either, but were published anonymously. Nevertheless the educated public knew of Sarah Scott's authorship.[21] The next historical publication was the *History of Mecklenburgh*, coming out in 1762 in two editions. Its origin is obvious and will shortly be dealt with below. Her last publication in 1772, *The Life of Theodore Agrippa D'Aubigné* (1552-1630), was also an historical work. Again the personality of the well-known Huguenot poet and the events connected with him, serve as *Exempla*

Historica for the discussion about personal freedom and religious dissent in those days: a controversy which had been discussed by England's educated public since the spectacular process of and the rigid censorship against John Wilkes (1727-1797).[22]

On the whole Scott's publications were more than the common works of an amateur, or the historical tales – dictated by events of the day – of a contemporary observing the current discussion. Basic geographical and historical knowledge combine in them with a good understanding of the relevant literature – the choice of that consulted in her *History of Mecklenburgh* already shows this.

The death of her brother-in-law Edward Montagu in 1775 made it possible for Elizabeth to make Sarah an allowance of £200 a year. The death of their father three years later brought Sarah another £50 annual income from the family's possessions in Yorkshire. Because of that she ceased to write, lived in London until 1784/5 and then moved to Catton near Norwich, where she died in 1795. In her last will she instructed that all private papers should be burned. Therefore her letters came down to us only in the estates of her family and friends. Although Sarah Scott never belonged to the inner circle of the 'Blue Stockings', she deserves our attention as an early 'professional' writer and as the author of the first English compendium of the history of Mecklenburg.

Sarah Scott and Thomas Nugent

The origin of the two earliest English works on the history of Mecklenburg is known and will be mentioned only briefly. On 8 September 1761, 22-years-old King George married 17-years-old Sophie Charlotte von Mecklenburg-Strelitz (1744-1818).[23] Until then this principality and its rulers were hardly known in England. If English society had some ideas of it they were rather obscure. On 9 July 1761 the famous writer Horace Walpole mocked in a letter about the English ambassador: 'Lord Harcourt is to be at her [Sophie Charlotte's] father's court – if he can find it – on the 1st of August ...!'[24]

The need for information was great: 'As soon ... as his Majesty declared his intention of taking the princess of Mecklenburgh for his consort, she became the general topic of discourse; and every Briton's thoughts were turned towards the family from which Great Britain was to receive its Queen', says Scott in the preface. However, in her letters she commented less enthusiastically on the new queen and the great public attention the young bride received. 'One would imagine that no king had ever married or any state ever had a queen before. The nation ... [is] ... absolutely frantic. I hear there is scaffolding enough erected against the coronation to hold two millions of people ...' she wrote to her sister-in-law in Naples on 14 September 1761.[25] Sarah's description of the appearance of the bride was not very benevolent: 'I understand she is very far from handsome. Her mouth fills great part of her face', which incidentally corresponds to the portrait of the queen by Thomas Gainsborough in Schwerin, Mecklenburg, 1781. But she admits that Sophie Charlotte had a good nature, was very lively and had a tremendous mental grasp. Expressing subtle irony she is surprised at the 'physical' capacity of the Princess of Mecklenburg: after ten days on board a ship and one day in a coach Sophie Charlotte arrived in London on 8 September and on the same day the wedding took place. After the wedding celebration 'she and the king were in bed, and *all* the night after her journey and so long a voyage. Nothing but a German constitution could have undergone it'.[26]

However these private remarks are to be judged, in the preface Scott declares her own curiosity to be the reason for her studies – financial interests seem to have been bad manners for writers even then: 'I confess I was myself no less curious on this subject than the rest of my countrymen'. And because no reliable and satisfying information was available she studied the authors 'from whom I could hope to receive any information for authentic particulars, relative to the house of Mecklenburgh'.[27] In 360 pages she compiles chronologically the history of Mecklenburg from the earliest days until the marriage of Princess Sophie Charlotte, without further subdivision into chapters. In the beginning there is a short overview of the constitution of the Holy Roman Empire, considering especially the relation between the emperor and the princes. As sources for the extensive account of the legendary prehistory Scott used the usual classical historians like Jordanes and Procopius, but also the *Annales Herulorum ac Vandalorum* by Nikolaus Marschalk, published in Rostock in 1521.[28] She describes the Vandals, claimed to be the direct ancestors of the people of Mecklenburg, as hospitable, charitable and just – quoting the chronicle uncritically. The part on modern history is mainly based on older works of Jean de Heiss, Samuel von Pufendorff and François de Bassompierre. Sarah used also quite recent publications, for example *The History of the Life of Gustavus Adolphus* by Walter Harte, published in 1759[29] or, for the time after the Treaty of Westphalia, Joseph Barre's *Histoire générale d'Allemagne*, ten volumes published in Paris 1748.[30]

The origin of Nugent's *History of Vandalia* was also the public interest in the royal wedding in 1761. But Nugent was neither forced to publish anonymously or under a pseudonym, nor to put forward curiosity as a reason for the work. On the contrary, as a member of the establishment[31] and as a history expert he recommended himself for such a task. In the preface it says: 'The following History derives its origin from the auspicious nuptials of the august pair, who so happily fill the throne of Britain. At the time when the eyes of the whole nation turned towards that princess, who ... was found worthy the affection of our most gracious sovereign, the author was solicited by some friends to represent the antiquity and splendor of her majesty's descent, in a consise history of the most serene house of Mecklenburg'. Nugent's treatise is also strictly chronological. Following the early legends, the work is more or less subdivided according to the reigns of the fabulous Vandal and Veneti rulers. In the first volume he starts with an extensive description of the geographic and topographic facts as well as a summary of the constitution of the Holy Roman Empire and its territorial states. After that the volume continues until the middle of the twelfth century. The second volume deals with the time from the Middle Ages until the Reformation, and the last volume ends with a description of Sophie Charlotte's journey to England and the wedding celebrations. Nugent studied much more literature than Scott. Not only did he publish his first volume four years later than Scott, he also travelled in 1766 – before he published the other volumes – for a few months through Mecklenburg. There he researched in libraries and archives and sought for discussions with native scholars. One of his most important sources for the first volume was Stephan Werner von Dewitz, an *envoyé extraordinaire* whom Nugent got to know in London between 1762 and 1765.[32] On his journey Nugent also got in touch with Lord Bassewitz, a minister of Duke Friedrich von Mecklenburg, and with experts of the history of Mecklenburg especially Angelinus Johann Daniel Aepinus,[33] Professor of rhetoric in Rostock and Butzow, and Samuel Buchholz,[34] preacher in Lychen. They made it possible for Nugent – unlike Scott – to study the relevant German and Latin historical literature intensively.[35]

Both authors, however, start with the complicated constitution of the Holy Roman Empire, the 'Germanic Body',[36] followed by a report on the great principalities. After dealing with the sovereignty of every prince in his own territory, they both give an account of the system of rule in Mecklenburg. With the emphasis on the sovereignty they obviously try to establish a certain equality between the bridal couple. Scott even describes this sovereignty as absolute: '... every Prince in Germany is absolute in his principality; and however insignificant his state may be, still he is above the laws'.[37] Nugent restricts it according to reality and the constitution of the empire: 'The princes are all souvereigns in their respective territories, having an absolute iurisdiction over their subjects, except where the diet or the supreme courts of iudicature think proper to interpose ... they exercise most acts of souvereignty that are not prejudicial to the empire'.[38] While Scott's statements on these general questions of the history of the Holy Roman Empire and its constitution are based on French treatises by Heiß von Kogenheim and Antoine de la Martinière, Nugent's knowledge came from Leibniz, Pufendorff and different German jurists.

Occasionally both used the same sources. In these parts one can see easily the contrasting fields of interest and the different personality of both authors. This can be exemplified by the description of the restitution of the rule of the dukes of Mecklenburg in Gustrow on 25 June 1631. Gustavus Adolphus attended the celebrations and both writers sometimes follow exactly the words in Harte's *Life of Gustavus Adolphus*. But they differ in an important detail. Nugent emphasises particularly that 'twenty hogsheads[39] of wine and forty of beer were given to the poor', and the King of Sweden even invited parents 'to bring their young children with them to taste the festal wine, that they might remember ... the restoration of their lawful sovereigns, as well as of their religion and liberty'.[40] A lot of alcohol, enjoyed in society as the promoter of loyal and religious feelings, was of course impossible for Sarah Scott. She portrays Gustavus Adolphus as a patriarchal educationalist who orders 'that all parents, should fully instruct their children in the nature of this Restoration, and teach them to remember ... the re-establishment of their lawful Sovereigns, of their religion, and of their liberty'[41] – no word about the pleasurable consumption of alcohol.

But it would be short-sighted and unjust to accuse Scott of being naive and seeing the king as a Nordic shining light, as did the biased popular Protestant literature of the nineteenth and twentieth centuries. Rather her point of view corresponds to the already mentioned idea of what kind of nature a prince and politician should have. Moreover, Scott has a specific understanding of politics and history. In principle, she has an enlightened notion that believes in a positive development of history and understands war as a secularised eschatological fight between good and bad. That did not concern eternal salvation, it was about the improvement of mankind in this world. So, a prince fought battles to promote common wealth. It is almost unnecessary to refer to the consequences for her treatise.

But, to return to Gustavus Adolphus: Wallenstein is portrayed as a blood-sucking usurper who exploits the country and oppresses the population, no matter if friend or foe.[42] In order to do that he gets support from sinister Southern European figures like the Italian Torquato di Conti who does not dare to fight an open battle against the 'lion from midnight'.[43] Instead they try to eliminate him with treason and deceitfulness – in vain of course. The death of the Swedish king in the battle of Lutzen is described by Scott in only two sentences, however she devotes more than one page to his personal qualities, mainly his humanity and his religiousness.[44] Nugent treats these events much more extensively. The attitude is basically the same. Torquato di Conti, who is not loved by his soldiers and is feared by the people, even gets the epithet of the devil – obviously the diametrical opposite of Gustavus Adolphus.[45] But – and attention has to be paid to that difference – in Nugent's work a more stereotypical male view of the war and his hero can be discerned. He devotes many pages to the detailed description of the campaigns and the different battles and sieges of the years 1630-32 – but never losing sight of the political dimensions of the events of the war. On the occasion of the battle of Lutzen Nugent sings an epic song:[46] on more than two pages he not only reports the death of the 'godlike hero, Gustavus Adolphus, the delight of his subjects, the terror of his enemies' and quotes his obligatory last words, he also recalls the 'brave and worthy commander' of the imperial troops, Lord Pappenheim, who also was mortally wounded at Lutzen.

The different ideas of war and history were not restricted to such sensitive topics as Gustavus Adolphus or the siege of Magdeburg.[47] Rather these attitudes characterised the complete treatise. For Nugent, who was much more familiar with continental court historiography, it was about striking out 'a history of ... powerful and warlike nations; a history representing the succession and memorable actions of their souvereigns'.[48] Scott however regrets that 'the history of Germany thus becomes entirely military; and consequently unentertaining'.[49]

Has Sarah Scott been forgotten or marginalised?

Nugent's description was historically and scientifically better researched: he had the matchless advantage of studying the historians of Mecklenburg. But both authors were known to their contemporaries, and although there are no figures about the number of copies published, Scott's *History* experienced two editions within one year, Nugent's only one. Thus, at the end a question has to be asked: has Sarah Scott been forgotten or marginalised? And if so, why did that happen? Today she is not one of the famous female authors of the eighteenth century. In Anglo-Saxon countries attention was paid to her in recent years only because of her novels. The *History of Mecklenburgh* satisfied only a short-term curiosity, a current interest in the new queen, not an interest in Mecklenburg. In Germany, even in Mecklenburg, Scott is forgotten. In 1944 she was still mentioned in a bibliography by Wilhelm Heess[50] and some short extracts were printed recently in a small anthology, edited by Jurgen Grambow.[51] But serious historical and literary studies of her life and her works are still to come.

The reasons for the priority Nugent enjoys in Mecklenburg are easy to understand: his journey in the country made him popular and the official character of his *History* got him suitable patronage. He established personal relations not only with scholars, but also with Sophie Charlotte's brother, Duke Adolf Friedrich IV.[52] The duke had already learned of Nugent and his work before, presumably from his ambassador Dewitz in London. He was in favour of the project and already in 1769, he engaged Andreas Gottlieb Masch the elder,[53] court chaplain in Neustrelitz, to do a translation of the *History*.[54] But it was never finished, or at least nothing was printed. Nevertheless, in 1781 a German edition of Nugent's letters on his journey was published and – the genre predestined for a literary success – established his fame in Germany. In England he was already well-known for the accounts of his travels.[55] In the year of his journey to Mecklenburg, Tobias Smollett's best-seller and trend-setter *Travels through France and Italy* appeared, in which Smollett fell back on Nugent's *Grand Tour*, published in 1749.[56] In 1768 – at the same time as Nugent's *Travels through Germany* – Lawrence Sterne's *Sentimental Journey through France and Italy* was published.

But what was the situation with Sarah Scott's *History of Mecklenburgh*? The inability of a female author of historical works to find appreciation has already been mentioned, but it is now necessary to draw attention to two sets of suspicious circumstances. It has to be made clear that Nugent knew Sarah Scott, if not personally, then at least her *History of Mecklenburgh*. After all they had the same publisher, Dilly and Millar. Moreover, Dr. Christopher Nugent, a doctor practising in Bath until 1764, was probably a brother or cousin of Thomas and mentioned in his will.[57] In view of Sarah Scott's charitable commitment in her long-standing place of residence, they had almost certainly met. So the question has to be raised, why Nugent, studying the literature intensely, did not take the only recent

English book about his topic into account? Misogynous arrogance may have led him to disregard a woman, but there are hints that most likely personal vanity and loyalty were crucial. Nugent's reference to a hardly important 'count Schomberg' in connection with conflict in Mecklenburg in 1630/31 may be significant.[58] Some pages earlier, some light is cast on the matter by the dedication of a portrait of Gustavus Adolphus 'To Ralph Schomberg', doctor of medicine and 'Fellow of the Society of Antiquaries', from 'His most Humble & Obedient Servant Thomas Nugent'.[59] Obviously Nugent wanted to honour his friend and connect him – genealogically wrongly – to the family of Schomberg, which had numerous different branches in France and England, that produced many army officers and civil servants. Ralph Schomberg (1714-1792) had established himself as a doctor in Bath in the 1750s and 60s, dedicating himself also to his literary ambitions – however, with limited success: 'Even the all-swallowing vase at Bath Easton was found to nauseate our Doctors compositions', Baker judged twenty years after Schomberg's death.[60] Apart from that, he was soon notorious as a plagiarist.[61] After he had embezzled money from a hospital fund, he had to leave Bath. Sarah Scott's literary reputation and her charitable commitment at her place of residence may have made her an enemy of Schomberg and because of that also of Nugent. But this is merely a speculation.

While Nugent's disregard can be explained by these personal reasons, the marginalizing of Sarah Scott by her contemporaries and following generations has other reasons. The main cause was the alleged proximity and sympathy of 'Blue Stocking' feminism to the French Revolution. In fact, all 'Blue Stockings' as well as Sarah distanced themselves early from the revolutionary events across the Channel, if they ever had any sympathies at all. In England from the middle of the 1790s, counter-revolutionary attitudes treated feminists as equivalent to Jacobins and the term 'Blue Stocking' connoted something negative until the twentieth century.[62]

Notes

1   Ronald Stanley Neale, *Bath 1680-1850: A Social History, or A Valley of Pleasure, yet a Sink of Iniquity* (Routledge & Kegan Paul, 1981), pp.17-27, 171, 319-321. On p.317 Neale acknowledges that Sarah Scott was 'one of the two sisters whose correspondence sets much of the scene for the description of the company ...' in Bath.

2   For her as a person, see Liz Bellamy, 'Scott, Sarah', in Janet Todd (ed.), *Dictionary of British Women Writers* (Routledge, 1989), pp.598-599, in which some details are not correct; Gary Kelly, *Sarah Scott, Bluestocking Feminism*, vol.5 (Pickering & Chatto, 1999), pp.ix-xxvii; and for relevant literature, Holger Th. Gräf, 'SCOTT, Sarah, geb.

Robinson, geb. 21.9.1720, get. 5.3.1721 York, gest. 3.11.1795 Catton bei Norwich', in *Biographisches Lexikon für Mecklenburg*, vol.3 (Rostock, 2001), pp.276-280. A first appreciation of her life and work from a feminist perspective was provided by Lynn M. Grow, 'Sarah Scott: A reconsideration', *Coranto. Journal of the friends of the libraries*, vol.9 (1973), pp.9-15. For a recent assessment see the entry by Gary Kelly in the new *Oxford Dictionary of National Biography* (Oxford University Press, 2004).

3 Elizabeth R. Napier, 'Sarah Scott (21 September 1723-30 November 1795)', *Dictionary of Literary Biography*, vol.39: *British Novelists, 1660-1800* (Gale Research Company, Detroit, Michigan, 1985), pp.413-418, especially 417-418.

4 21 September 1723 has been given for Sarah Scott's birthdate since the publication of the letters of Elizabeth Montagu, Emily J. Climenson (ed.), *Elizabeth Montagu, The Queen of the Bluestockings: Her Correspondence from 1720-1761*, 2 vols. (Murray, 1906), here vol.1, pp.116-117. See, e.g. Walter Marion Crittenden, *The Life and Writings of Mrs. Sarah Scott*, Phil. Diss. Philadelphia, 1932, p.13 and Napier, 'Sarah Scott', *op.cit.*, pp.413-418. Only Betti Rizzo established the real date from the baptismal register, see the 'Introduction', in Betti Rizzo (ed.), *The History of George Ellison by Sarah Scott* (University Press of Kentucky, Lexington, 1995), pp.xxxvii and xli.

5 Lewis Namier and John Brooke, *The House of Commons 1754-1790*, vol.3 (H.M.S.O., 1964), pp.367-368.

6 *Dictionary of National Biography* (*DNB*), vol. 17 (Oxford University Press, Oxford, 1917), pp.55-56.

7 Sylvia Harcstark Myers, *The Bluestocking Circle. Women, Friendship, and Life of the Mind in Eighteenth-Century England* (Oxford University Press, Oxford, 1990), pp.177-206, *passim*.

8 Kelly, *op.cit.*, p.x.

9 Namier and Brooke, *op.cit.*, p.153.

10 Kelly, *op.cit.*, p.xiii; Rizzo, *op.cit.*, pp.xi-xii; Harcstark Myers, *op.cit.*, pp.96-102.

11 Rizzo, *op.cit.*, p.xi. On the wedding market see Peter Borsay, *The English Urban Renaissance* (Oxford University Press, Oxford 1989), pp.243-248 with appropriate comments on Elizabeth Montagu.

12 Kelly, *op.cit.*, p.xiii.

13 *DNB*, vol.17, p.961.

14 Rizzo, *op.cit.*, p.xiv.

15 See the list of her works in Kelly, *op.cit.*, p.xxiv.

16 See the reviews in *Monthly Review* and in *Critical Review*, recorded in Rizzo, *op.cit.*, pp.xlii-xlv.

17 See Janet Todd, *The Sign of Angelica. Women, Writing and Fiction, 1660-1800* (Virago, 1989), p.115.

18 Apart from the relevant passages in Kelly and Rizzo see mainly Eve W. Stoddard, 'A Serious Proposal for Slavery Reform: Sarah Scott's Sir George Ellison', *Eighteenth Century Studies*, vol.28 (1995), pp.379-396.

19 Nicole Pohl, ' "Sweet Place, where Virtue then did rest": The Appropriation of the Country-House Ethos in Sarah Scott's Millenium Hall', *Utopian Studies*, vol.7 (1996), pp.49-59; Alessa Johns, 'Journeying towards Identity: Sarah Fielding, Sarah Scott and Feminist Utopianism in Eighteenth-Century England', in Raffaella Baccolini et al. (eds.), *Viaggi in utopia* (Ravenna, 1996), pp.319-325; Alfred Lutz,

'Commercial Capitalism, Classical Republicanism, and the Man of Sensibility in The History of Sir George Ellison', *Studies in English Literature 1500–1900*, vol.39 (1999), pp.557-574.

20 See Reinhart Koselleck, 'Historia Magistra Vitae. Über die Auflösung des Topos im Horizont neuzeitlich bewegter Geschichte', in Reinhart Koselleck (ed.), *Vergangene Zukunft. Zur Semantik geschichtlicher Zeiten*, 2nd. edn. (Suhrkamp, Frankfurt, 1984), pp.38-66.

21 After the anonymous publication of her last historical work in 1772 her authorship became known. See Paget Toynbee (ed.), *The Letters of Horace Walpole*, 16 vols. (Oxford University Press, Oxford, 1903-05), vol.VIII, p.170. Walpole had been acquainted with Sarah Scott for quite a long time, see the hand-written remark in his copy of the 2nd edn. of *Millenium Hall*, now in the British Museum. See John Doran, *A Lady of the Last Century (Mrs. Elizabeth Montagu)* (Richard Bentley, 1873), pp.104-105.

22 See the remarks of Horace Walpole in Toynbee, *op.cit.*, vol.VIII, p.170 as well as Peter D.G. Thomas, *John Wilkes: A Friend to Liberty* (Oxford University Press, 1996).

23 See Angelika Schmiegelow Powell, 'Sophie Charlotte, geb. 19.5.1744, Mirow (Mecklenburg-Strelitz), gest. 17.11.1818 (in Kew Palace bei London)', in *Biographisches Lexikon für Mecklenburg*, vol.2 (Rostock, 1999), pp.243-247.

24 Walpole to H. Mann, Strawberry Hill, 9 July 1761 in Toynbee, *op.cit.*, vol.V, p.73.

25 Doran, *op.cit.*, pp.94-95.

26 Doran, *op.cit.*, pp.97-98.

27 Scott, *The History of Mecklenburg, from the First Settlement of the Vandals in that Country to the Present Time* (1762), pp.ix-x.

28 Nikolaus Marschalk, *Annales Herulorum ac Vandalorum libri septem* (Rostock, 1521). Probably the new edition by Ernst J. Westphalen, *Monumenta inedita rerum germanicarum praecipue Cimbricarum et megapolensium* (Leipzig, 1739), was better known to Sarah Scott.

29 Walter Harte, *The History of the Life of Gustavus Adolphus, King of Sweden, surnamed, the Great*, 2 vols. (G. Hawkins, 1759).

30 Joseph Barre, *Histoire général d'Allemagne, 1648-1740*, 10 vols. (Delespine & Herissant, Paris, 1748).

31 Alan Valentine, *The British Establishment: 1760-1784. An Eighteenth-Century Biographical Dictionary*, vol.2 (University of Oklahoma Press, Norman, Oklahoma, 1970), names several current members of the Irish Nugent family.

32 See Thomas Nugent, *The History of Vandalia. Containing the Ancient and Present State of the Country of Mecklenburg; its Revolutions under the Vandals, the Venedi, and the Saxons. With the Succession and Memorable Actions of its Sovereigns*, 3 vols. (Hamilton, 1766-1773), vol.1, p.I. About Dewitz see Julius Freiherr von Maltzan (ed.), *Einige gute Mecklenburgische Männer* (Wismar, 1882), p.40-62. Dewitz presented his credentials in London on 13 December 1762 and had his last audience on 2 May 1765. See Friedrich Hausmann (ed.), *Repertorium der diplomatischen Vertreter aller Länder seit dem Westfälischen Frieden/Répertoire des représentants diplomatiques de tous les pays depuis la Paix de Westphalie*, vol.2: 1716-1763 (Zürich 1950), p.221.

33 See Niklot Klüßendorf, 'Aepinus, Angelinus Johann Daniel, geb. 10.5.1718 Rostock, gest. 28.2.1784 Rostock', in *Biographisches Lexikon für Mecklenburg*, vol.2 (Rostock, 1999), pp.14-17; Thomas Nugent, *Travels through Germany : Containing observations*

on customs, manners, religion, government, commerce, arts, and antiquities; With a particular Account of the courts of Mecklenburg ; in a Series of Letters to a Friend (1768; translation into German, Berlin 1781-82; new edition Schwerin 1998), pp.108-115 and 123-127.

34 Nugent, Travels, *op.cit.*, especially pp.199 and 279-281; *Allgemeine Deutsche Biographie*, vol.3 (reprint, Duncker & Humblot, Berlin, 1967), pp.480-481.

35 See Matthias J. Behr, *Rerum Mecleburgicarum libri octo* (Leipzig, 1741); Samuel Buchholtz, *Versuch in der Geschichte des Herzogthums Meklenburg* (Rostock, 1753); Hans Henrich Klüver, *Beschreibung des Herzogthums Mecklenburg* (Hamburg, 1728-1729); and in particular David Franck, *Alt- und Neues Mecklenburg* (Leipzig, 1753-1757); also Niklot Klüßendorf, 'Franck, David', *Biographisches Lexikon für Mecklen*burg, vol.2 (Rostock, 1999), pp.77-83. See other literary sources on Nugent, History, *op.cit.*, vol.1, Appendix iv, pp.451-452.

36 Nugent, *History*, *op.cit.*, vol.1, p.7; Scott, *History*, *op.cit.*, p.2.

37 Scott, *History*, *op.cit.*, p.5.

38 Nugent, *History*, *op.cit.*, vol.1, p.8.

39 A barrel containing 322 litres in the Hanseatic area.

40 Nugent, *History*, *op.cit.*, vol.3, pp.286-287.

41 Scott, *History*, *op.cit.*, p.263.

42 Scott, *History*, *op.cit.*, pp.246-249.

43 Scott, *History*, *op.cit.*, pp.250-252.

44 Scott, *History*, *op.cit.*, pp.271-272.

45 Nugent, *History*, *op.cit.*, vol.3, pp.272-273.

46 Nugent, *History*, *op.cit.*, vol.3, pp.300-301.

47 Scott, *History*, *op.cit.*, pp.260-261 and Nugent, *History*, *op.cit.*, vol.3, pp.281-282.

48 Nugent, *History*, *op.cit.*, vol.1, p.v.

49 Scott, *History*, *op.cit.*, pp.xi.

50 Wilhelm Heess, *Geschichtliche Bibliographie von Mecklenburg* (Rostock, 1944), 1st part, p.257.

51 Jürgen Grambow, *Die Rostocker Sieben und andere Merkwürdigkeiten*, 2nd ed. (Rostock, 2000), pp.27-29.

52 Nugent, *Reisen*, *op.cit.*, p.145. Nugent presented the duke with a copy of the first volume of the *History* and was therefore received by him in Neustrelitz and Mirow several times; see pp.166-168, 172-173, 287-289.

53 See *Allgemeine Deutsche Biographie*, *op.cit.*, vol.20, pp.550-551.

54 Nugent, *History*, *op.cit.*, vol.2, p.vii.

55 See Erwin Neumann, 'Ein aufgeklärter Ire in Mecklenbburg. Thomas Nugents "Travels through Germany" und ihre deutsche Übersetzung', in Wolfgang Griep (ed.), *Sehen und Beschreiben. Europäische Reisen im 18. und 19. Jahrhundert* (Heide, 1991), pp.185-196 here p.194.

56 Thomas Nugent, *The Grand Tour; or a journey through the Netherlands, Germany, Italy and France*, 4 vols. (1749, and two further eds.).

57 Valentine, *op.cit.*, pp.653-654, and *DNB*. Nugent, Christopher (1698-1775), doctor, born in Ireland, practised in Bath until 1764. There, in 1756, Edmund Burke got to know his daughter, whom he later married.

58 Nugent, *History*, *op.cit.*, vol. 2, p.275.

59 Nugent, *History*, *op.cit.*, vol. 2, p.263.

60 David Erskine Baker, *Biographia dramatica or a Companion to the Playhouse*, 3 vols. (Longman, 1812), recorded in British Biographical Archive, New York 1999. See A. Barbeau, *Life and Letters at Bath in the 18th Century* (William Heinemann, 1904), pp.224-229, for an account of the Bath Easton Vase, into which poems were placed to be drawn out and read at literary gatherings at Batheaston Villa.

61 Alexander Chalmers, *The General Biographical Dictionary*, 32 vols. (London, 1812-1817), recorded in British Biographical Archive, New York 1999.

62 Harcstark Myers, *op.cit.*, Epilogue and Kelly, *op.cit.*, p.xx.

Acknowledgments

I am very much indebted to Brenda June Buchanan for editing the text, giving important hints and not least for the possibility to have this essay published in *Bath History*. Moreover I wish to thank Marianne Alenius, Kopenhagen, for her invitation to present a paper on Sarah Scott at her panel on 'The Image of the Learned Women' at the 11th International Congress on the Enlightenment, Los Angeles, Ca., August 2003. Finally I wish to express my gratitude to my colleagues Niklot Klüßendorf for his steady interest which was always a decisive encouragement for my studies on Sarah Scott, and Anke Stößer for her help.

An Academy for Young Gentlemen:
John Naish and his School in Bath[1]

William Evans

Education in Bath at the start of the nineteenth century

Few traces remain of what Bath offered by way of education in the early nineteenth century, but there were certainly many children: it can be inferred from the census that at the turn of the century there must have been some 3,000 children aged 5 to 10 living in the four inner parishes of the city. Neither the affluent visitors (numbers declining) nor the genteel permanent residents (numbers rising) will have concerned themselves much about local schools. At the other end of the social spectrum, amongst those struggling for survival (numbers rising), education will not have been valued or affordable. But there must have been many families, respectable but not fashionable, whose activities serviced the visitors and the permanent residents and each other, who will have perceived education as an advantage in social or economic advancement.

At the start of the nineteenth century, demand for education will have been met in a number of ways.[2] Children from families who could afford it were most likely to be taught at home by a relation, tutor or governess. Bath newspapers carried advertisements for home tutors, some specializing in subjects like drawing, embroidery, dancing and music, as well as more traditional academic subjects like mathematics and, for the forward-looking, modern foreign languages. Few parents could afford, or might wish, to send their children to one of the small number of major public schools like Eton or Winchester.

For parents who wanted their children to have a classical education and could pay the fees there were grammar schools: at the turn of the century King Edward's prospered under Nathanael Morgan in buildings designed by Thomas Jelley and erected in 1754 in Broad Street. Here Thomas de Quincey had been a day pupil from 1796 to 1799, and was a dab hand at Latin verse. Between 70 and 80 pupils were taught by Morgan (a former fellow of King's College, Cambridge), assisted by an usher, two assistant masters (one of whom was Morgan's brother-in-law Thomas Wilkins, rector of Weston with Charlecombe), and a senior boy waiting to go to university. The two terms were divided by holidays, a month at Christmas and six weeks during June and July. Fees were about £26 a half-year, of which 2 guineas went to the Master, 5 shillings to the usher, 4 guineas for tuition, 4 shillings for a seat in church and 8 shillings for repairing shoes and stockings; 18 guineas was for bed and board. For half a guinea a pupil could be taught writing and accounts; and for a guinea a quarter, fencing, dancing and other social skills, but newspaper advertisements emphasized mainly the school's classical education. The boarders were mostly sons of neighbouring county families: some came from Cornwall.[3] According to the Charity Commissioners' report of 1820, by which time Wilkins had succeeded Morgan, the school had never received any boys 'on the foundation', that is sons of freemen nominated by the Corporation, though Wilkins said he was ready at all times to instruct the sons of freemen gratuitously if properly connected.

Children from poorer families might attend the Bluecoats charity school, founded in 1711 by Robert Nelson with help from the Society for the Promotion of Christian Knowledge, on a site donated by the Corporation. Bluecoats was for 'the education of poor children in the knowledge and practice of the Christian religion as professed and taught in the Church of England.' Pupils were nominated by subscribers. They came from honest, industrious and respectable Church of England working-class families in city parishes. 100 pupils, half of them girls, were taught basic literacy and numeracy, the bible and the catechism, and sang in the Abbey choir. Girls were also taught sewing, knitting and housewifery. Pupils could join at any age between 7 and 12; at 14 they were apprenticed or put out to service.[4]

Distinctions between King Edward's and Bluecoats were highlighted on mayor-making day, when a grammar school boy made a Latin speech to the Corporation, which local newspapers glowingly reported, sometimes with quotation and naming the speaker; and a Bluecoat boy (never a girl), whom the press did not normally name or quote, made a speech of thanks in English. The grammar school orator in 1807, called Kilvert, later became Morgan's assistant master, and went on to found his own private school at Claverton Lodge.[5]

At the turn of the century Bluecoats faced no sectarian competition. From 1785 Bath had about 30 Sunday schools, many with an Anglican flavour, some of which had a workshop or industrial school attached. Whilst the Corporation will have valued the influence of the grammar school and Bluecoats as part of its armoury of social control, different ideologies competing for control of the education of children from poor families had not yet emerged, and did not do so until about 1810.[6] From then on children from poor families might have received elementary education, if at all, at one of the early monitorial schools following the rigorous rote methods of Andrew Bell of the National Society (for the Education of the Poor in the Principles of the Established Church) or Joseph Lancaster, the 4th edition of whose *Improvements in education as it respects the industrous classes* was being advertised in Bath in 1806.[7]

In 1810 a group which the following year affiliated into the National Society opened a school in St John Street, moving to Kingsmead Square in 1814. It offered free elementary education in reading, writing and arithmetic, with compulsory church attendance and religious education according to the established church. It also ran a mixed Sunday school, an industrial school and a library.[8] Another school, appealing to Nonconformists, was sponsored by the Royal Lancasterian Society (renamed in 1814 as the British and Foreign Schools Society). Founded in Corn Street in May 1810 by voluntary subscription, and later moving to Walcot Street as the Bath and Bathforum school, it taught by the monitorial method up to 400 boys in reading, writing and arithmetic, with religious knowledge undenominational and optional.[9] A corresponding school for girls did not appear until 1814, in Grove Street, later moving to Morford Street. Subscribers nominated the pupils. Some children will have attended dame schools, many of which delivered no more than incompetent childminding.

The gap in the middle of the education market was filled by small private academies teaching children from families who paid fees. In 1805 Bath had at least 24 boarding schools, of which 11 were for boys; of those, one was preparatory only, one was a grammar school in the strict sense, and two were run by clergymen.[10] Some had talented teachers: in 1809 the mathematician William Horner left Kingswood School (not yet in Bath) to set up his own academy in Grosvenor Place.[11] Those for girls were in effect finishing schools for the fashionable world, but some may have trained for housekeeping. Some, for boys, offered a predominantly commercial or military curriculum; others classical and commercial, like Mr Durban's in Guinea Street. They advertised in the *Chronicle* and the *Journal*, with varying degrees of specificity, offering a choice of location, subjects, times, age ranges, day or boarding options, and fees. In 1806 Miss Rundall advertised her 'seminary' at Cumberwell House (some 6 miles out of Bath) but did not say exactly what she taught. Mrs Turmeau at 21 Westgate Buildings taught French, English, writing and arithmetic to young ladies, with evening classes in French only. On Combe Down Mrs Bonner ran an 'initiating academy' for 'young gentlemen from the age of 4 to 8 years', boarding.[12] The Revd Dr Keith's at Summer Hill, Upper Bath Road, also advertised, as did two dancing academies. At Bloomfield Place, Miss Aldritt ran a boarding seminary for ladies, and for boys aged 4 to 7; she charged 20 guineas a year plus extra for washing, and also extra for teaching reading, orthography, English grammar and geography, needlecraft ('for ladies'), writing and arithmetic, French, music and dancing. Contrast Miss Thomas at 2 Lower James Street, who taught writing and arithmetic at half a guinea a year, and for another half-guinea, plain and ornamental needlework. At West Hall, a mile from Bath, Mr Masters offered military, naval and commercial studies and classical literature, as did Mr Barber at Grosvenor Place, but without the literature.[13] At 6 Lansdown Road, Mr Hunt offered French, Latin, Italian and geography with globes, with an evening school 'for young ladies and gentlemen 5 to 8'. The overall picture is of small businesses in private houses, offering to different sectors of the market different packages, some fixed, others optional, some limited by the skills of the proprietor, others employing part-time teachers as required when parents were prepared to pay an extra charge for a particular subject.

Even with this array of educational opportunity, for Quakers the selection of a school was difficult. They valued education, both in itself and as a means of advancement. Many will not have wished their children to attend Church of England schools, especially ones like Bluecoats where the catechism was taught; and from many Anglican schools they would have been barred in any event. Military academies were ruled out on grounds of conscience. Private commercial schools might have lacked the moral and religious ethos and content a Quaker demanded of a school and its curriculum. As a result, some Quakers sent their children to boarding schools founded by Quaker meetings explicitly for children from Quaker families: one was at Ackworth in Yorkshire, and another at Sidcot in Somerset. Other Quakers formed their own schools, and ran them as businesses. One such was John Naish, who opened a school in Bath in 1806.

John Naish's ledger

The main surviving trace of John Naish and his school is a thick, narrow, stumpy ledger, bound in white vellum, unadorned, unlabelled, untitled. It found its way into the account books of Bristol College, a school which opened in 1831, whose documents were deposited in Bristol Central Reference Library.[14] The book contains no explicit indication of what or whose it was, but it offers five clues: entries for payments to a

Lancasterian school: so the proprietor was not an Anglican or Roman Catholic, but probably a Nonconformist; all dates are in the format 1 Mo 1, so the proprietor was almost certainly a Quaker: consistent with that is an account headed 'Tithes' but completely blank; entries for payments to 'Bath monthly meeting' and 'Quarterly meeting', so the proprietor was a member of the Society of Friends in or near Bath; an entry for a payment to Sidcot School (opened 1 September 1808): so the school to which the Ledger relates was not Sidcot; and fifthly, an entry for rent for 1 Hatfield Place in 1813.

There is a Hatfield Place in Bath: it is a house in Hatfield Road, which runs from Wellsway to Bloomfield Road at its junction with Englishcombe Lane, high up and at that time out of town: the temptations of the sulphurous pit would have been at some distance, albeit downhill all the way. Browne's *New Bath Directory* for 1809 lists Mr John Naish at Hatfield Place, without attributing any occupation. But the *New Bath Directory* for 1812 has an entry for 'Naish J, academy for young gentlemen, 1 Hatfield Place, Wells-road.'

So the Ledger is that of John Naish of Bath, Friend, and proprietor of a school for boys at 1 Hatfield Place, Bath.

View of 1 Hatfield Place, Bath, now arranged as two houses known as Hatfield Place and Hatfield House. (*Photograph by the author*)

John Naish

John Naish the schoolmaster was the son of Francis, a silversmith (1752-1785), and Susannah Naish (1756-1822) of Bath. Susannah Naish, daughter of William and Susannah Evill, was brought up a Baptist, married Francis Naish in 1778, but was left a widow in 1785 with four young children.[15] She joined the Friends and wielded much influence.[16] Her circumstances enabled her to arrange for her sons John and William Naish to attend Ackworth School in Yorkshire from 1793 to 1796; William is recorded as having come from [Flax] Bourton in Somerset and he stayed at Ackworth until 1799.[17] From 1796 to 1803 John Naish was an apprentice schoolmaster at Ackworth.[18] He then went to Sheffield and there taught as a schoolmaster: he is so described when on 16 January 1806 he married Catharine Trickett at Sheffield Friends' meeting. Catharine was the daughter of Robert, a cutler, and Catherine Trickett of Hill-foot in Yorkshire.[19] The North Somerset Monthly Meeting on 28 April 1806 received a certificate of removal for John and Catharine Naish from Balby Meeting, Yorkshire. Young Sturge the land surveyor was detailed to get the measure of them, with friends approved by the women's meeting.[20]

John and Catharine Naish were to have four children while they were at Hatfield Place: Francis (31 March 1808); Robert (11 April 1809); Phebe (18 August 1811); and Thomas (14 May 1813).[21] That John Naish was made of stern stuff is suggested by his own report about sufferings to the North Somerset Monthly Meeting at Sidcot on 30 October 1809. He had been fined £20 by Bath magistrates for refusing to do militia duty. He had not paid the fine, but distress had not been levied.[22] The same meeting investigated with disapproval the conduct of Joseph Sewell, who had been fined £10, but had acquiesced in his employer paying the fine for him.[23]

John Naish the schoolmaster is often referred to in Monthly and Quarterly Meeting minutes as John Naish of Bath, to distinguish him from two others of that name:

(1) John Naish of Congresbury. He is mentioned in the North Somerset Quarterly Meeting minutes, but does not feature in this story. The son of Joseph and Betty Naish (*née* Willmott) of Flax Bourton, born 1786, he married Lydia Eddington in 1810 and became a shopkeeper at Congresbury; he died in 1875, aged 88.[24]

(2) John Naish of Bathwick. Bath directories list a John Naish who was a horsedealer at 19 Bathwick Street, though by 1812 he had moved to 35 Bathwick Street (or Bathwick Street had been renumbered). He is not John Naish the school proprietor, but the Ledger of John

Naish's school does refer to him: towards the end of the Ledger is an account headed '1813 Estate of John Naish', to which another hand has added 'Bathwick'. The account opens with an entry dated 26 April 1813 for £24 cash found in the deceased's pocket (a horse sold or to be bought?); there are items for horses, the cost of the funeral, and payments 'to Sarah' (his daughter or widow?). The burial was at Flax Bourton on 27 April 1813.[25] The register records that he was a horse dealer from Bath, but 'not a member of our Society,' which is consistent with an entry in the estate account in the Naish school Ledger for the payment of tithes. The *Bath Chronicle* 29 April 1813 and the *Bath & Cheltenham Gazette* of the previous day report the death on 23 April 1813 of John Naish, 'formerly an eminent tanner in Lambridge, a man much respected by an extensive circle of friends.' The corresponding entry in the *Bath Journal*[26] calls him John Nash, gives his address as Sydney Place, and describes him as formerly proprietor of the tan-yard at Lambridge.

Why should this estate account have been written in the school Ledger? The accounts in the Ledger are not confined to the school: some deal with other trades, for example the sale of porter, and some deal with Meeting expenses. One possibility is that John Naish the schoolmaster wound up the estate of John Naish the tanner and horsedealer; perhaps they were related.

What sort of school?

John Naish does not appear to have advertised his school in the Bath newspapers: that suggests that it was intended for children from a wider area; but he does not appear to have advertised in regional papers either, such as the *Exeter Flying Post*, which suggests his school may have been intended for Quaker families only. Before moving back to Bath from Yorkshire, he issued a prospectus:[27]

John Naish respectfully informs his Friends, that he intends to open a Boarding school at No 1 Hatfield Place, three quarters of a mile from Bath.
For Thirty* boys at 35 guineas per annum.
The situation is pleasant and healthy, and the premises are large and commodious.
The school is intended to be opened the 1st of the 2nd Month, 1806.
Applications are requested to be made either to SUSANNAH NAISH, Kingsmead Terrace, Bath; or to JOHN NAISH, No 17, Allen-Street, Sheffield.
* This number will not be exceeded – The Languages and Drawing to be paid for extra, each 3 guineas per annum – Entrance money 2 guineas.

In contrast to the control over the establishment of new businesses exercised by the Leeds Meetings,[28] the minutes of the North Somerset Monthly Meeting do not contain any resolution authorising John Naish to set up the school. That may reflect different practice, or Susannah Naish senior's clout.

Curriculum and staff

Naish's prospectus set out both his proposed curriculum and his principles of education, with much that modern educators would applaud:

> The children will be instructed in Reading, Writing, English Grammar, Arithmetick, Book-Keeping, the Mathematicks, Geography, History, and such of the Languages as their parents may desire, in Drawing, if required, and in some other branches of Learning.
>
> For the effectual accomplishment of the important designs of Education, it seems necessary that the teacher be well acquainted with the minds of his pupils; JN will therefore endeavour to establish a free and familiar intercourse between him and his scholars. When by this means he has obtained an easy access to their minds, and acquired over them that influence which he trusts will result from their confidence in his endeavours to promote their welfare, he hopes it will be easy to direct and guide their exertions, and to establish such principles and habits in their minds as will qualify them for useful and honourable stations in future life.
>
> With respect to his mode of teaching, it may be proper to observe, that he will always endeavour to make his pupils acquainted with the elementary principles of those Sciences which they profess to study, and to adapt his instruction to their peculiar habits of thinking.
>
> Spelling and Reading claim great attention; they will in some measure be considered as the groundwork of Literary Education.
>
> Writing will be taught in its various branches, and regard had both to elegance and usefulness.
>
> In the study of Grammar, their attention will first be directed to the radical principles of language, the teacher having invariably found a familiar explanation of these the best introduction to a well-grounded knowledge of the particular rules. They will frequently be exercised in Composition on easy and familiar subjects; and attention will be paid to their style of conversation.

In Arithmetick, besides the proper management of figures, they will be instructed in the general properties of numbers, and will mostly be exercised with such questions as are the likeliest to occur in real business, and it will be deemed highly useful to make them conversant with the most approved methods of Book-keeping.

The Mathematicks it is hoped may be made to expand and strengthen the intellectual powers.

The study of Geography will be preceded by that of the simple parts of Astronomy, because the children must be acquainted with the nature of latitude, longitude, the meridians, equator, &c, before they can make a right use of maps and globes.

Their Historical and Biographical Reading, the teacher hopes, will furnish him with opportunities of instilling just and generous sentiments into their minds.

The Languages will be taught by approved masters.

Such parts of Natural Philosophy as are adapted to their capacities will be explained to them in familiar lectures, illustrated by a suitable philosophical apparatus.

For their further Improvement, a proper assortment of books will be provided, to the reading of which they will be encouraged to allot a part of their leisure time.

J NAISH is aware that the most punctual performance of what he has now mentioned does not comprise the whole of his business. His oversight of the children will not cease with their regular hours of study, because he well knows that at other times there will be frequent opportunities of giving them general and miscellaneous information, of teaching them to act well, and think correctly. It will be his duty to attend to every circumstance that is likely to affect the forming of their minds, and to encourage their applications for advice and information.

Though the children will be taught to consider a strict attention to their studies as a serious and indispensable duty, yet the teacher hopes he shall be able to render the performance of it pleasing, and to impress them with a just sense of the usefulness of learning.

It will be regarded as an object of considerable importance to make suitable provision for their amusement, and in all other respects to study their comfort and accommodation. This it is considered will tend to produce in them a disposition favourable to the purpose of education.

It is not stated what the 'suitable provision for their amusement' was; it is not clear whether games were played, but in the Ledger Richard Davis' account is debited with a sum for '2 skins for covering balls.' What that resulted in is suggested by several entries for 'cash, boys, for damage;' an account headed 'Glazier' might explain of what sort.

How John Naish delivered his curriculum can be gleaned from the Ledger entries. He employed as schoolmaster Richard Davis. Although the Ledger begins at the start of 1809, it includes an account for Davis, copied from a loose paper account tucked into the Ledger, which acknowledges that he was employed from 5 September 1806, some seven months after the opening date given in John Naish's prospectus. Davis' salary was £63 a year, and from the books credited to him he seems to have taught French as well as English. Davis was absent ill from December 1808 to March 1809, and got no pay. In the accounts for 1811 Daniel Deboudry is employed as teacher at £63 a year. As he is credited with a copy of Weekes' *Rhetorical Grammar* and Cicero's orations, perhaps he taught Latin. In 1812 there appear to be other teachers, John Rae, and R. Wallis, the latter being paid 'for 3 boys extra,' so presumably he taught an optional subject such as French or Latin. In 1813 there is a teacher called Thomas Jones.

Of particular note (as it may explain what happened to the Ledger) is the account of John Sanders. That for 1810 includes £17 2s 6d for his bill for drawing, implying that he was not at that time John Naish's employee. His account also includes £10 for a telescope and £3 13s 6d for a microscope: obtained, perhaps, from Darton & Co, whose account includes an item for newspapers as well as instruments and unspecified goods, which may have included some of the 'philosophical apparatus' referred to in the prospectus. In 1811 Sanders is employed as drawing master, on a salary of £40 15s. It is tempting to speculate whether John Sanders might be:

(1) John Sanders or Saunders (1750-1825), who studied and exhibited at the Royal Academy 1769-1773.[29] He was living in Bath in 1792; taught painting and drawing at 9 Lansdown Place in 1793,[30] where he was a tenant of the Sharples and did damage by nailing pictures to the stucco walls;[31] moved to Beach's studio at 2 Westgate Buildings in 1799; and enjoyed some success there as a portrait painter. He painted Judith Countess of Radnor in 1821, and Fanny D'Arblay mentions him as having painted Princess Charlotte.[32] He appears to have moved in 1802 into his son's premises at 4 Green Park and then 3 Westgate Buildings. Late in 1824 he moved to Clifton, Bristol, to a relation's house at 1a Clifton Place, and died there early in 1825.[33] Or,

(2) His son John Arnold Sanders, born probably before 1789[34] in London, who had a drawing academy at 4 Green Park, Bath in 1802;[35] offered landscape and perspective at 19 Kingsmead Street in Bath and 1 Clifton Place, Bristol in 1815;[36] and married Fanny Hippisley at Shepton Mallet on 21 October 1815.[37] He taught drawing at the Bristol Hotwell in 1816 and possibly later,[38] but is said to have got involved with a pupil. He emigrated to Canada in 1832-33.[39]

John Naish had other employees. In 1809 he employed three female servants (explained in the 1810 summary account as a cook, housemaid and nursemaid), two at 9 guineas and one at 6 guineas a year; a man (Moses?) employed for 40 weeks (term time only?), at 8s a week 'allowing 20% as given him.' There was also a Charlotte Hart employed at 18 guineas a year (governess/matron?), who also got one and three quarter yards of cassimere at 10s.[40]

Lowest paid of all was George Robinson, credited 5s a quarter, later increased to 6s, but to whom £8 was debited for clothing. He was John Naish's apprentice, presumably an apprentice schoolmaster. His account includes a debit for 'a horse cloth lost, 4s 6d.' Whether that was the occasion of a quarrel between them the accounts do not say, but there was a serious rift: John Naish reported to the North Somerset Monthly Meeting on 28 January 1811 that there was a dispute. The background to the disagreement is not clear. In October 1799 Brighouse Monthly Meeting in Yorkshire had disowned George Robinson's father (of the same name) for not paying his debts. He must have asked to be reinstated, because on 19 May 1809 the Brighouse meeting asked the Rochester Monthly Meeting in Kent to visit him and enquire, which the Rochester Friends did, but not with much hope. In September 1809 the Bath Meeting asked the Rochester Meeting for a certificate for George Robinson junior, which was agreed on 11 October 1809. The Rochester Meeting on 6 March 1811 received from the North Somerset Monthly Meeting a note of dissatisfaction, not about George Robinson junior, but about his father's conduct 'in relation to something unpleasant between his son & a member of that Monthly Meeting to whom his son is apprenticed.' The committee appointed at Rochester reported on 7 March 1811 that it did not think George senior should be advised to take his son away, but that John Naish should have got the overseers of his own local meeting to help sort it out. Consideration was adjourned in the hope that an accommodation could be reached.[41] Evidently it was: the dispute, which the North Somerset minutes referred to as a misunderstanding, ended on 26 August 1811 with the issue of a clear certificate of removal for George Robinson to Rochester, so presumably the apprenticeship was discharged and George went home to this father.

In 1809 John Naish billed fees for just over 30 pupils at 35 guineas each per year. Such a fee implies claims to quality, but it was not as expensive as King Edward's. Some parents paid extra for Latin and French. Robert Fox's outstanding debt from 1808 implies that young Joshua was taught Spanish, but that appears to have been a one-off: the prospectus said languages would be taught as a parent might require. There are items for English readers, an English dictionary, '48 copies of exercises on histories of England', 6 Payne's *Geographies*,[42] and a year's subscription to Upham's library: John Upham was a bookseller in Lower Walks, Bath.[43] In 1810 Naish appears to have sold some books to Sidcot school. There is also a payment of 11s to R. Smith of Ackworth, which might be another school-connected payment. French required the purchase of *Gil Blas* and *Les Jardins*. Other works purchased included Douce's *Illustrations*[44] and Malcolm's *Anecdotes*.[45] The accounts include items for quills, drawing paper, and a sheet of parchment (6s 6d: for a legal agreement? for teaching handwriting? for binding the Ledger itself?)

Pupils

Not all pupils were local: the Ledger confirms the prospectus's description of the venture as a boarding school. With the help of the *Dictionary of Quaker Biography* in Friends House Library it is possible to identify some of the 37 fee-payers and hence some of the pupils, but only tentatively, because few addresses are given; mutual aid, charity and the practice of set-off of one debt against another, mean that the person billed was not necessarily the parent of the pupil; and some items are so large as to imply more than one pupil.

Information has been assembled on the following fee-payers: George Eaton was probably the ironmonger in Bristol, whose son Joseph (1792-1858) later established the *Bristol Temperance Herald*; Luke Evill is almost certainly John Naish's cousin, an attorney who practised at Green Street in Bath;[46] Edward Fox (1749-1817) was probably the merchant of Wadebridge whose son Francis was born in 1797; the family were related to the Weres of Wellington in Somerset; Dor[othy] Fox (1766-1842) *née* Hingston, the widow of Robert Were Fox, merchant of Wadebridge was one of two Dorothy Foxes in the 1809 list of Friends ordered to be drawn up by the West Devon Monthly Meeting;[47] John Grace (1771-1851), merchant of

Gloucester, Lodway (near Pill in North Somerset) and Bristol, had four children including James (born 1797) and Josiah (1799); Walter Prideaux (1779-1832), the banker from Plymouth, who appears in the 1809 West Devon list under Kingsbridge/Modbury, had a son Charles (1809-1893) who rose from apprentice to inspector to general manager to chairman in the family firm; William Shorthouse (1768-1838), a Birmingham chemist, had a son Joseph, born 1797; John Southall (1763-1828), a Leominster mercer, had sons Samuel (1793), Thomas (1794) and William (1797); John Thomas (1752-1827) is likely to have been the grocer at Bristol Bridge who later interested himself in the Somerset Coal Canal and the Kennet and Avon Canal; in 1812 he retired to Prior Park, so was a comparatively near neighbour of John Naish; his sons included Edward (1794) and Joseph (1797); John Tuckett (1758-1845) may have been the merchant from Bristol who moved to Plymouth and had children including Edward (1798); Thomas Were (1771-1833), a Bristol merchant, had a son Thomas (1800); Dev[ereux] Bowly was a banker from Cirencester.[48]

Other fee-payers are not so easily identifiable. Was Edmund Barritt from Purleigh in Essex? Who was Frank Cookworthy? Rachel Fox? Was David Cox of Essex or Gloucester? Was Geo Fisher the one from Lancaster? Was Stephen George from Rochester, or the Bristol sugar trader of that name? Was David Coe the father of Joseph Coe the Bath haberdasher? Was Josh Gibbins from Aston near Birmingham or Stourbridge? Was John Hinton the grocer from Plymouth Dock (Devonport) who married at a Friends' meeting in 1784?[49] Was James Leman the Bristol attorney of that name? And who were William Boultbee, George Arthur, B. Chorley, William Tay, Josh Young?

As might be expected from the location of the school, the list has a strong westcountry flavour, but the prominence of Cornwall and Plymouth names suggests there may have been no comparable school at that time for the sons of affluent Friends in the far southwest.

One pupil had a separate account of his own. In just five lines of accountancy Wm Boultbee was charged for Alfred Boultbee's tuition to Christmas 1808; then for board only; 2 guineas for a physician; £3 9s for an apothecary (William White); and £16 6s for the undertaker's bill.

John Naish and Sidcot

One local event which may have had some implications for John Naish's school was the opening of Sidcot School, about 24 miles from Hatfield Place. F.A. Knight has told[50] how Sidcot came to be founded.

In 1779 the Friends' Yearly Meeting purchased the premises of the former foundling hospital at Ackworth in Yorkshire, and opened a boarding school there. In 1784 John Benwell, who had a school at Yatton, and whose brother Joseph Benwell had a school at Longfield, moved to Sidcot and opened a school there for 45 boys. At the Yearly Meeting in 1807 unnamed Friends from the West of England discussed opening an Ackworth-type school near Bristol, agreed on the need, and decided to raise it at the Bristol and Somerset Quarterly Meeting. Held at Glastonbury in June 1807,[51] the Quarterly Meeting approved of founding in one of the western counties 'an Institution somewhat similar to that at Ackworth, for the education of a smaller number of the children of Friends in low circumstances.' The Quarterly Meeting appointed a committee to move the matter forward which included John Benwell, Joseph Naish and 'John Naish (of Bath).' The three men appointed superintendents of the school included John Benwell and Joseph (but not John) Naish. Joseph Naish (1750-1822) was the son of John and Elizabeth Naish of Flax Bourton. He was placed with a Bath tradesman, returned to Flax Bourton as a tanner (so was his father John Naish of Lambridge?), married Betty Willmott of Claverham in 1771, and moved in 1789 to Congresbury, where he met John Benwell.[52]

The provisional or general committee, appointed by the Quarterly Meeting, met at Bridgwater on 15 September 1807 and decided to raise £7000 to establish a school within reach of Bristol. When the committee met in Bristol on 15 December 1807, with £4000 subscribed, it agreed to buy John Benwell's house and 14 acres at Sidcot, Benwell and his wife Martha to act as unpaid superintendents but with free board and lodging until permanent staff were recruited. This was agreed by the Yearly Meeting in 1808.

The possibility of competition with other schools, including private schools owned or run by Friends as individuals as distinct from Friends' Meetings, was noted: Sidcot was intended for

> the offspring of poor Friends, or of those who cannot well afford to send them to other boarding schools. They are not to encourage the sending of those whose parents or guardians can conveniently send them to other boarding schools.

That stipulation may have been made to protect the interests of proprietors like Naish, and might even have been made at his instigation: his school at Hatfield Place was already running. When Ackworth opened it had caused the closure of several schools that had been established by Meetings.[53]

At the first meeting of the General Committee of Sidcot School on 15 July 1808, the fees were fixed at £14 a year plus 4s 4d pocket money. John Naish was charging two and a half times that. The curriculum was to be Reading, Writing, English Grammar, Arithmetic and Geography. The girls were to learn sewing and knitting as well. All were to undertake domestic work; the girls were to mend the boys' linen, and the senior boys were to work on the land and in the gardens. In 1808 the Committee included Joseph Naish, but neither John Naish nor John Benwell. However, in 1811, the North Somerset Monthly Meeting gave John Naish permission to attend the Sidcot School Committee (28 January 1811); he had attended the Ackworth general meeting on 29 July 1807.[54]

Sidcot opened on 1 September 1808 with six boys and three girls. Numbers rose to 32 in 1809, 67 in 1812, 75 in 1815, and 85 in 1820. During its early years there were staffing difficulties. The first schoolmaster, on £40 a year, left after two months. A husband and wife team appointed in 1810 on £120 a year left after 18 months. Joseph Naish, filling in as unpaid superintendent in 1817, gave notice of his intention to resign within a year because of friction between his predecessor's widow and another woman member of staff who left in 1818; Joseph himself resigned in 1820, by which date John Naish's school at Hatfield Place, and the Ledger entries, had ceased.

What other business connections did John Naish have?

There was an S. Naish at 7 Kingsmead Terrace in 1809: she must be the Susannah Naish who is named in John Naish's school prospectus as one to whom applications might be made. The Ledger mentions two Susannah Naishes: senior (John Naish's mother) and junior (his sister-in-law). Susannah Naish senior is recorded as having lent some £75 for 3 years at 5%, the rate of interest on all borrowings in the Ledger but one. Susannah Naish junior's account has several entries, including meat, cash advanced to C. Naish (John Naish's wife Catharine), 'pictures of orchard', a bed, a lye but[t], a swing and 6 sheets of drawing paper.

William and Susannah Naish were advertising themselves as selling general groceries, teas and British wines at 21 New Bond Street in 1809,[55] and they were still there in 1812.[56] It is clear from the Ledger that John Naish traded with them: they supplied meat and groceries. William Naish features prominently in the accounts, on occasion as the funder of Meeting expenses, as John Naish's debtor and creditor, and as one who paid some of the pupils' fees. Perhaps not too much should be made of that, as one of the striking features of the Ledger is the way in which balances were struck after setting debts off against each other, often with many parties involved. Not all cases were as simple as that of Robert Fox of Falmouth, whose 9s debt for a Spanish grammar for Joshua and 30 yards of cord was 'discharged by gift of a hat to Francis.'

The *Bath Journal* for 3 February 1812 carried an announcement that Swetman & Co's Brown Stout Porter business would be removing from Broad Street to 21 New Bond Street (William & Susannah Naish's shop), where it would be carried on under the name of Naish & Co. The Ledger shows that some time before 1812 Josiah Swetman helped not William but John Naish to open a trade in London porter in Bath. There are entries for carriage of samples to Bristol and Sheffield, which implies that the business was seeking to use the Naish family's local connections there. Amidst entries for bottles and corks is one for a payment of £10 to Josiah Swetman 'for his services before the opening of the trade.' Josiah Swetman then gets a salary of £60. After sales totaling just over £40, John Naish appears to have sold the stock to William and Susannah Naish, for a price left with them, but on which they would pay interest. On 24 February 1812 the Bath & North Somerset Monthly Meeting authorised Josiah Swetman's removal to Bristol.[57] Commencing September 1812, the Ledger records, William and Susannah agreed to allow John Naish 3% 'on all the London porter sold in Bath.'

There is also an account with James White, under which John Naish paid a cash dividend of 6% on a sum of about £100, plus some £14 'profit and loss', possibly as part of the terms of a business loan. John Naish borrowed other money at simple interest, all at 5%. The lenders were: Susannah Naish senior: £74 15s 6d; Thomas Sanders: £300; Samuel Smith: £100, increased in 1812 to £400; Robert Trickett (Catharine's father, presumably): £200. These evidently were the providers of working capital for John Naish's school. At least two, possibly three, were relations of John Naish.

Some accounting aspects of The Ledger

Five pages of the Ledger have been cut out. The index implies the missing accounts were for R. Wallis (one of the schoolmasters), A. Pye, T. Witton, John Thomas (who had a school fees account), a Meeting (presumably North Somerset), Glazier and Butcher; and the debit side of the bank account. The document contains both business and household items, and also entries for expenses of Friends' Meetings, which appear in various individuals' accounts. It is not possible to reconcile these with the accounts of the Meetings, which have suffered fire damage and are largely illegible.[58]

The Ledger is kept in conventional double entry. As some of the items are difficult to reconcile with the annual summary accounts, and some of the contra items are not in the accounts where you might expect them to be, it is possible that John Naish may not have grasped the principles fully, or accounting conventions may have changed. Set-off is frequent, as is satisfaction in kind. Many accounts are paid by bill of exchange. There are transactions with a bank, not named. Prescott's is mentioned in a note to one of the estate accounts, but that may be because John Naish the horsedealer banked with them.

The 1809 figures include an account headed 'Taxes'. This includes not only the expected items for window tax, poor rate, highway rate and property tax (including property tax on interest on loans), but also items for house, servant, carriage, horse and dog, the last 3s 6d. This might suggest that John Naish treated as a tax all outgoings, whether or not they were strictly taxes: thus the 1811 summary account includes under the heading Taxes, his subscriptions to Sidcot School and a Lancasterian school (begun in Bath in 1810 and referred to earlier), and two subscriptions to the Bath Meeting. But he has a separate account for house contents insurance (£800 in 1809, reduced to £500 later), the debit entry being to cash, not taxes.

One outgoing which had a separate account was John Naish's horse. Again, a mini-saga in a few lines. It cost him £37 16s; there were bills for hay, corn, the saddler, medicine, shoeing, and the blacksmith. Running costs totalled £16 15s. 5½d. Twice, John Baker was paid 1s 6d for mending a whip (though this is not in the Horse account, so it may have been used in the school). The horse was sold for £20. Mileage is not recorded.

John Naish rented 1 Hatfield Place. The rent was £67 a year in 1809 and 1810, paid to John Hensley, possibly of Bathwick Street;[59] but in the year of his death, £100 was paid to Richard Bailey or Bayly (who is not named in Bath directories). John Naish rented a field to Thomas Wright, later to Captain Thornhill;[60] and a cellar to Hester Bishop, who in 1805 and 1812 had an ironmongery and brazier's business at 25 Broad Street.[61]

The school was profitable. In 1809, on a turnover of £1,213, John Naish made £251, a profit of 20% on turnover and 26% on outlay. The summary figures for 1810 are not totalled, which suggests he had not put all the expenses in, but on the figures listed he made £547 net on a turnover of £1,250, a profit of 43% on turnover and 77% on outlay.

Unlike a modern educational establishment or even its grammar school contemporary, the business was not, in money terms, labour-intensive: of the expenditure for 1809, 65% went on food (more than half on meat and bread) and drink; 18% on domestic expenses (including food as well as soap, candles, brushes and starch); 7% on rent; giving a total of 90% plus 10% on staffing costs. Compare King Edward's, where food and domestic expenses accounted for nearly 75% of the bill, teaching for 25%.

Some of the accounts do not tally. In particular, the totals of the individual accounts for beer and wine are lower than the amounts for those items stated in the annual summaries. Some of the entries are puzzling, for example in 1813, '3 shares of engraving J T Adams's profile.' John Till Adams had an account for books, so could have been a bookseller or publisher, but the subject was perhaps John Till Adams (1748-1786), a doctor in Bristol who married Ann Fry in 1777 and had 'a large connection among the Quakers of Bristol'.[62] He was 'a talented man whose early death was greatly lamented.'[63] Perhaps John Naish thought him a good role model. John Sturton the mason got paid £9 11s 6d 'for putting up the steamer': some sort of boiler?

The annual summary for 1810 is incomplete. There are no annual summaries for later years, though there are entries in individual accounts. Perhaps there were other account books, now lost. Perhaps John Naish tired of accounting: he will not have been the first. Perhaps the school folded. It looks very much as if John Naish the schoolmaster took his leave about the same time as John Naish the horsedealing tanner. The *Bath Chronicle* for 6 May 1813 carried an advertisement:

TO SCHOOLMASTERS

To be let, very pleasantly situated within a mile of Bath, a HOUSE, and extensive Premises, conveniently fitted up for a genteel establishment, and the School Business, which business has been carried on there for several years. The School Furniture, in good condition, to be sold – applications (post paid) to be made to WN, 21 New Bond Street, Bath.

Evidently William Naish was selling his brother's former premises and business stock; the school was being sold as a going concern. Perhaps John Naish had died. There was no report or notice in local newspapers, and no mention in the relevant quarterly or monthly meeting minutes. There is no entry for any Naish in Gye's *Bath Directory* of January 1819.

John Naish after the Ledger

After John Naish died, Catharine Naish appears to have returned to Sheffield. The youngest three of their four children were pupils at Ackworth School between 1819 and 1827, and are all described as of Sheffield: Robert from 1819 to 1823; Phebe from 1823 to 1825; and Thomas from 1824 to 1827.[64] Their mother Catharine was principal mistress (that is, governess) at Ackworth from 1827 to 1830.[65] Thomas, like his father, stayed on at Ackworth as an apprentice schoolmaster from 1827 to 1832, in which year he died at the school.[66] The others died in the 1830s and 1840s, two of them at Sheffield: the *Annual Monitor* also records the death of a Catharine Naish at Sheffield in 1840, describing her as the widow of John Naish of Bath.

Hatfield Place still stands. Built in 1804 on the site or foundations and cellars of a much older (possibly fifteenth-century) farmhouse, it was one of four large houses (the others were Bloomfield House, Westfield House and Devonshire Cottage) in an area then known as The Gore. Some time after 1864 the building was divided into two, and there are internal signs of extensive structural alteration. Half retained the name Hatfield Place, the other half was called Hatfield House.[67] The cellars, of early date, which John Naish sublet to Hester Bishop the ironmonger, include traces of ovens and flues.

Notes

1   This article is based on an account that first appeared in the *Journal of the Friends Historical Society*, Volume 58, No.3 (1999).
2   For examples from the eighteenth century see T. Fawcett, *Voices of Eighteenth-Century Bath* (Ruton, Bath, 1995) under *Education*.
3   J. Wroughton, *King Edward's School at Bath 1552-1982* (King Edward's School, Bath, 1982), pp.52, 61ff.
4   R.B. Hope, 'Educational development in the city of Bath 1830-1902, with special reference to its interrelations with social and economic changes' (unpublished thesis, University of Bristol, 1970), p.45.
5   K.E. Symons, *The grammar school of King Edward VI. Bath* (Bath, 1930), p.271. From parish records this was probably John Kilvert.
6   J. Haddon, *Bath* (Batsford, 1973), pp.161-162.
7   *Bath Journal*, 15 September 1806.
8   *Original Bath Guide*, 1830, pp.93-95; Hope, 'Educational development', p.47.
9   Hope, *Educational development*, p.46.
10 *Holden's Triennial Bath Directory*, 1805-1807 (Holden, *TBD*).
11 G.M. Best, *Continuity and change: a history of Kingswood School 1748-1998* (Bath, n.d.), p.51.

12 *Bath Journal*, 13 January 1806.

13 *Bath Journal*, 20 January 1806, 7 and 14 July 1806.

14 City of Bristol Reference Library (CBRL), B11644-11651.

15 For the Evill family, see T. Fawcett, *Bath Commercialis'd: shops, trades and market at the 18th century spa* (Ruton, Bath, 2002), pp.133-134.

16 Bristol & Somerset Quarterly Meeting 3/1823, Somerset County Record Office (SCRO), DD/SFR 2/2, 108.

17 Typescript of Ackworth School registers, Friends House Library (FHL).

18 Ackworth School register of trustees and officers, FHL, p.38.

19 Yorkshire Quarterly Meeting marriages digest, FHL.

20 Wilts County Record Office (WCRO), 1699/25.

21 Digest register of births for Bristol & Somerset Quarterly Meeting, 17th century to 1837, Bristol Record Office (BRO), FSCF/R1/1(a)4.

22 There is no entry in the Bristol and Somerset Sufferings Book 1794-1827, SCRO, DD/SFR 9/1.

23 WCRO, 1699/25.

24 *Dictionary of Quaker Biography* (*DQB*), FHL.

25 North Somerset burial records, National Archives, RG6/39.

26 26 April 1813.

27 FHL Tract Vol. N/179A.

28 A. Prior & M. Kirby, *The Society of Friends and the Family Firm, 1700-1830*, Lancaster University Management School Discussion paper EC 11/93 (Lancaster University, 1993).

29 A. Graves, *Royal Academy of Arts: a Complete Dictionary of Contributors and their Work from its Foundation in 1769 to 1904* (Henry Groves & Co. & George Bell and Sons, 1905).

30 *Bath Chronicle*, 14 November 1793, p.1.

31 T. Fawcett, manuscript notes on Sanders in Bath Victoria Art Gallery (Fawcett, VAG.).

32 E. Bénézit, *Dictionnaire Critique et Documentaire des Peintres, Sculpteurs, Dessinateurs et Graveurs* (Librairie Gründ, Paris, 1976); (Bénézit's *Dictionnaire*).

33 *Dictionary of National Biography* (*DNB*), XVII.747.

34 Not 1801 as per Bénézit's *Dictionnaire*, as he married 1815.

35 Fawcett, VAG.

36 *Bath Chronicle*, 2 February 1815, p.3.

37 Shepton Mallet parish registers, 1815, 85.

38 Anonymous notes in Bristol Museum and Art Gallery.

39 Bénézit's *Dictionnaire*, but no source is quoted.

40 Cassimere, a fine wool twill: *OED*; of medium weight, soft, patented by Francis Yerbury of Bradford, 1766; mentioned in an advertisement in the *Bath Chronicle*, 16 January 1806, for a young man desirous of learning the manufactory of cloth, cassimere and fancy articles. Information from Rachel Boak, Museum of Costume, Bath.

41 Rochester Monthly Meeting Minutes, Centre for Kentish Studies, N/FrM 1/1.

42 John Payne, *Geographical Extracts, forming a general view of Earth and Nature, with maps* (G.G. & J. Robinson, 1796).

43 Holden, *TBD*.

44 Probably Francis Douce, *Illustrations of Shakespeare and of ancient manners; with dissertations on the Clowns and Fools of Shakespeare; and on the collection of popular tales, entitled Gesta Romanorum and on the English national drama* (Longman, Hurst, Rees and Orme, 1807).

45　James Petter Malcolm: one of *Anecdotes of the Manners and Customs of London during the eighteenth century, with a review on the State of Society in 1807* (1808); or *Anecdotes of the Manners and Customs of London, from the Roman invasion to the year 1700* (Longman, 1811); or *Miscellaneous anecdotes, illustrative of the manners and history of England, during the reigns of Chas II, Jas II, Wm III and Q. Anne,* (1811).

46　Holden, *TBD*. For the Evills, see T Fawcett, *Bath Commercialis'd*, pp.133-134.

47　A.D. Selleck, 'Plymouth Friends', in *Transactions of the Devonshire Association*, vol.99, p.213-261. See p.248.

48　*Bath Chronicle*, 25 March 1813 reports the death of his second son: 'He was sitting at dinner, when he fell down and instantly expired.'

49　*Exeter Flying Post*, 17 June 1784, 3d.

50　F.A. Knight, *A History of Sidcot School*, (Dent, 1908). (Knight, *Sidcot*).

51　Knight, *Sidcot* says July, but the minute book in SCRO, DD/SFR 2/1 is clear.

52　*DQB*, FHL.

53　Knight, *Sidcot*.

54　Bristol & Somerset Q.M. minutes 17/6/1807, SCRO, DD/SFR 2/1.

55　*Bath Chronicle*, 3/8/1809.

56　Browne's *New Bath Directory*, 1812.

57　WCRO, 1699/25.

58　WCRO, 1699/54.

59　Holden, *TBD*. Hensley Road is close to Hatfield Place.

60　Thornhill felt it necessary to advertise in the local newspaper following litigation in the King's Bench: *Bath Chronicle*, 16, 23 and 30 January 1806.

61　Holden, *TBD*.

62　G. Munro Smith, *History of Bristol Royal Infirmary* (Arrowsmith, Bristol, 1917), p.474.

63　*DQB*, FHL.

64　Typescript of register of Ackworth pupils, FHL.

65　Register of Ackworth trustees and officers, FHL.

66　Ackworth register of trustees and officers, FHL.

67　Information from current owner of the present Hatfield Place, Dr Bruno Bubna-Casteliz.

Acknowledgements

I would like to thank Malcolm Thomas (Librarian, Friends House Library), Russell Mortimer of Leeds, and West Kent Monthly Meeting of the Society of Friends, for information and permission to use documents; Roger Angerson and the late Kathleen Cottrell of Bristol for reading drafts of this note, and offering guidance; Dr Bruno Bubna-Casteliz and Mr and Mrs Chris Brigden, current owners of Hatfield Place and Hatfield House, for access to and information about the later history of the house, and for permission to inspect deeds and take photographs; Sheena Stoddard of Bristol City Museum and Art Gallery, Sarah Kelly of the Victoria Art Gallery, Bath, Dr Ann Sumner of the Holburne Museum, Bath, and Trevor Fawcett of the History of Bath Research Group, for information about John Sanders and John Arnold Sanders; and Rachel Boak at the Museum of Costume in Bath for information on fabrics.

I am grateful for the use of public facilities and the help of staff at the Bath and Bristol central reference libraries; the Westcountry Studies Library, Exeter; the Centre for Kentish Studies; the Bristol, Somerset and Wiltshire record offices; and the Bolland Library of the University of the West of England, Bristol.

Brunel in Bath

R. Angus Buchanan

I.K. Brunel was a thoroughly Metropolitan man. Despite having been born in Portsmouth, where his father, Marc Brunel, had been commissioned to install an ingenious series of block-making machines in the Royal Dockyard, the family moved to London when he was only a child, and his home remained there for the rest of his life. He travelled widely, both on his professional business and on journeys of exploration when the opportunities occurred, but once he had set up house in Duke Street, Westminster, above the offices of his busy engineering practice, this became his permanent home. Many business commitments, from bridges and railways to docks and ship-building, drew him to Bristol and the West Country, but he did not make his home there. During the last decade of his life he bought an estate at Watcombe, near Torquay, and spent a great deal of effort on planning its garden and the house which he intended to occupy on his retirement. When he died in 1859, however, at the age of 53, work on the house had only just begun and the scheme was abandoned by his family, even though the house subsequently built upon the site bears his name. It is, in any case, hard to imagine Brunel settling comfortably to the life of an English country gentleman.[1]

The implication of this metropolitan emphasis is that any associations between Brunel and Bath were incidental to his major preoccupations, and dependent mainly on professional considerations. It was only as the result of an accident that he came to the West Country in the first place, as he required a long convalescence after nearly drowning in the inundation of the Thames Tunnel in January 1828. He had been working on the tunnel, as Assistant Engineer to his father, for three years when this occurred. The accident enabled him to submit an application to the competition for a bridge across the Avon Gorge in Clifton, and when he emerged successfully from what turned out to be a rather convoluted process, he applied his youthful energy to its construction. The fact that the funds ran out and the bridge was not finished in his lifetime did not prevent Brunel from making some crucially important contacts in Bristol, and these led on to a series of formative professional commitments. First, he was engaged to recommend improvements to the Bristol docks, which were urgently in need of measures to overcome silting. Then came the commission to become engineer of the Great Western Railway. This led on

Fig.1 I.K. Brunel as a young man, from the portrait by his brother-in-law John Horsley, painted c.1844.

to Brunel's involvement with ship construction, as the s.s. *Great Western* was conceived explicitly as an extension to New York of the enterprise after which it was named. The dock works undertaken by Brunel in Bristol were not large, but they included his successful solution to the silting problem of the Floating Harbour and the renewal of the southern entrance lock at Cumberland Basin, both of considerable significance to the prosperity of the mercantile community in Bristol. The Great Western Railway quickly became one of the huge railway systems which grew in Britain in the middle of the nineteenth century, and Brunel presided over every detail of its design and operation. Brunel's initiation into shipbuilding, moreover, led on to the superbly innovative s.s. *Great Britain*, the first large iron ship, and the first to be powered by a screw propeller, and ultimately to the gigantic s.s. *Great Eastern*, which obsessed him in his closing years in the 1850s. In a very real sense, therefore, it was the Bristol region which launched I.K. Brunel on his extraordinarily meteoric and creative career, and the city of Bath played a significant part in this relationship.

There can be little doubt that Brunel's family had a special affection for Bath. His father is on record as having spoken approvingly of the city, and seems to have considered it as a retirement home because in 1832 he described a visit to Bath in his diary: 'Went round to inspect houses – found many that would suit and very moderate in rent – a splendid town Bath is'.[2] I.K. Brunel himself seems to have found it a congenial place for a stop-over on busy journeys connected with his engineering business. On Census Night in 1841 (7th June) he was staying at the *Lion Hotel* in High Street, presumably in connection with preparations for the opening throughout of the Great Western Railway from Paddington to Bristol Temple Meads which occurred at the end of that month.[3] The hotel was in Market Street, on the site later occupied by the northern extension of the Guildhall, and it had previously been known as the *White Lion*. Brunel is given as 'Civil Engineer', aged 35, and he is listed alongside two Solicitors, two Merchants, a Surgeon, and a 'Short Hand Writer'.

Brunel did a lot of travelling by stage coach before he became engaged on railway work, and even then it was several years before enough track had been laid to make railway travel a satisfactory alternative. He liked horses, and wrote a short treatise on the horse as a draught animal for the Society for the Diffusion of Useful Knowledge.[4] When it was feasible he enjoyed riding, although from the surprising number of accidents which he reports he does not seem to have been an accomplished horseman.

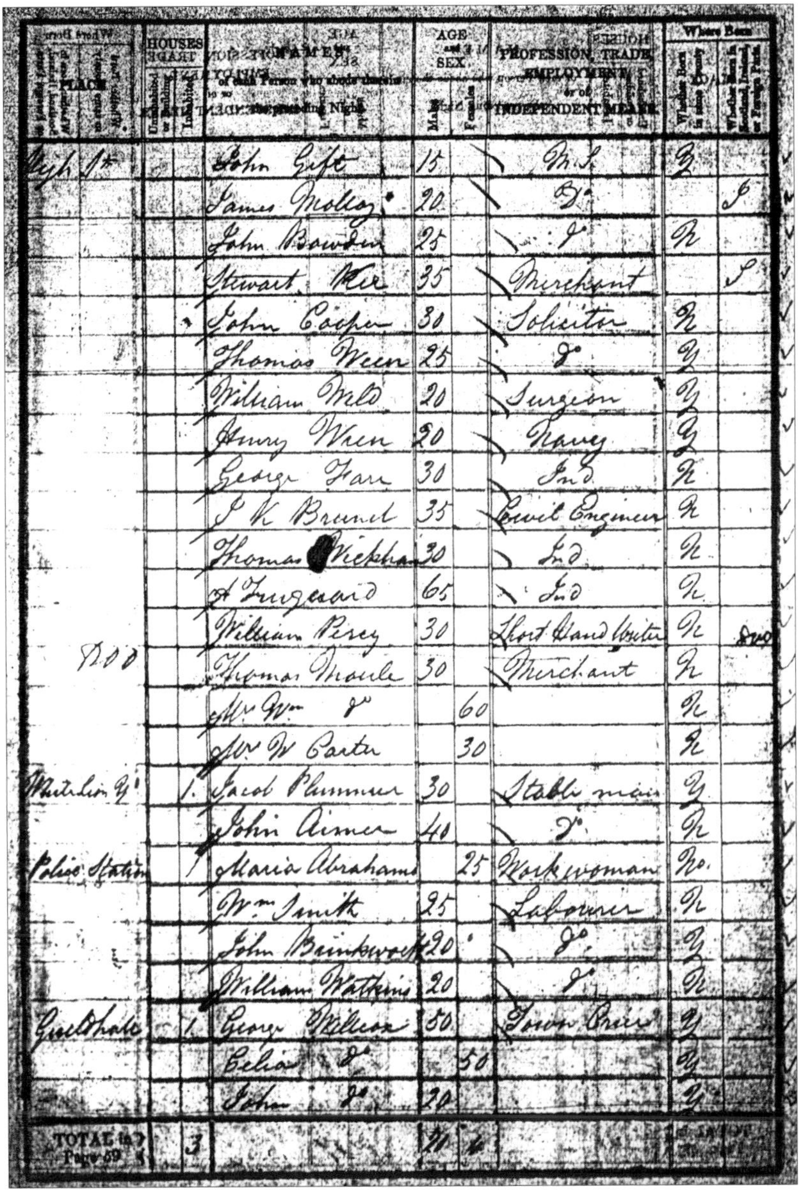

PLACE	HOUSES	NAMES	AGE & SEX	PROFESSION, TRADE, EMPLOYMENT or of INDEPENDENT MEANS	Where Born
		John Gift	15	M.S.	B
		James Molloy	20	D⁰	S
		John Bowden	25	D⁰	R
		Stewart Kee	35	Merchant	S
		John Cooper	30	Solicitor	R
		Thomas Ween	25	D⁰	R
		William Wild	20	Surgeon	R
		Henry Wren	20	Navy	R
		George Farr	30	Ind	R
		I K Brunel	35	Civil Engineer	R
		Thomas Nickham	30	Ind	R
		A Fougeraid	65	Ind	R
		William Percy	30	Short Hand Writer	R
		Thomas Maule	30	Merchant	R
		Mr Wm D⁰	60		R
		Mr W Carter	30		R
Whitchin D⁰	1	Jacob Plummer	30	Stable man	R
		John Aimer	40	D⁰	R
Police Station	1	Maria Abrahams	25	Work woman	No
		Wm Smith	25	Labourer	R
		John Brinkwork	20	D⁰	R
		William Watkins	20	D⁰	R
Guildhall	1	George Williams	50	Town Crier	R
		Eliza D⁰	50		R
		John D⁰	20		R
TOTAL Page 39	3				

Fig.2 Page from the Census Returns for 1841 showing the entry for I.K. Brunel who was staying at the Lion Hotel, demolished in the 1890s to make way for the northern extension of the Guildhall. (*Microfilm in the Podium Library, B&NES Library Services*)

For the most part, therefore, he depended on coaches to get him around the country. He particularly enjoyed travelling on top of the coach, and regarded this as the only seemly way for a young man to travel, inside accommodation being intended for ladies and the elderly. His diaries contain many references to long journeys, frequently in most inclement weather, and there is a delightful account of a journey which he made from Paris to London in the hard winter of 1828-1829, when with two companions he contrived to maintain warmth and high spirits by filling all the space around them with straw picked up at the inns where the coach stopped. At the height of his railway work, he designed a coach for himself which contained all his office services and a bed, so that he could live in it for days if necessary.[5]

It is likely that Brunel frequently stayed in hotels in Bath, although the first visits to the West Country of which we have any record took place when he was staying in Bristol, to promote the Clifton Bridge scheme. He won the competition for this in March 1831, with the design for the elegant suspension bridge that was completed on the site as a memorial to him in 1864. Interesting accounts survive of two of his early visits to Bath. The first of these was on 17th September 1830, when he drove over from Bristol to canvass support for the Clifton Bridge and called on William Beckford (1759-1844), the fabulously rich eccentric antiquarian who had built the fantastic Gothic mansion at Fonthill in Wiltshire but then moved to Bath, where he lived in Lansdown Crescent. Brunel probably had an introduction from one of the powerful circle of Bristol Merchant Venturers who had befriended him and may have been amongst those who accompanied him. We are fortunate in having the young engineer's own account of the meeting in his Private Diary:

> After Breakfast went to Acraman's and all started for Bath. Called on English's. Went to Beckford. Well received – an agreable [sic] gentlemanly well informed man – talking a great deal, evidently very warm and always in motion – his house a pattern of elegance – splendour rendered agreable and unostentatious by purity of taste – and well studied luxury in the highest degree – painting gems and articles of virtu crowded in costly cabinets and on beautyful tables – He entered warmly into the bridge affair admiring much the giants hole plan and praising strongly the architecture I had adopted – approving of Egyptian but condemning in strong terms all the others. On the whole I was highly delighted and only regretted that Benyon was not with us.[6]

It is not apparent whether or not Beckford's moral support was subsequently given any substance, and I have no record of any other communication between the two men. But Brunel was back in Bath in June 1831 – to attend the Bath Races on Lansdown where he 'met a number of Bristol people – did a little bridge business'.[7] The previous day, he recorded: 'rode over to Bath – called on Mr Ellacombe in my way – Arrived late in Bath'.[8] Henry Thomas Ellacombe (1790-1885), Vicar of Bitton, between Bath and Keynsham, had served as an Assistant Engineer to Marc Brunel, before going into Holy Orders and acquiring a considerable reputation as a local historian and antiquarian.[9] A month later, Brunel came over from Bristol again, to visit the Murhill quarry near Winsley, in the Limpley Stoke valley, as a possible source of stone for his bridge: 'some excellent stone – very hard and durable but too white'.[10] He chose instead for the two towers some grey pennant sandstone.

The other substantial visit in these early years in the relationship between Brunel and Bath was the occasion in 1833 when he was consulted in connection with the arbitration of a dispute between the trustees of the Black Dog Turnpike Trust and the trustees of the Kennet & Avon Canal. The point at issue appears to have been the anxiety of the Canal proprietors and their officers about the risk of landslipping which could be triggered off by the construction of the new Black Dog Trust road, up the Limpley Stoke Valley from Bath to Warminster. The danger was not imaginary, as the canal builders had themselves struggled with the instability of the ground in this valley, and the imposition of road works on the hillside above them could not be construed as a benefit to their property. So it was agreed to seek the advice of two prominent engineers, the veteran tramway and mechanical engineer William Brunton, and the young Brunel who had just been appointed Chief Engineer to what was soon to become the Great Western Railway. On a Monday morning in March 1833, the week after his appointment to the GWR had been confirmed, Brunel took a day off from the task of surveying the route for his masterpiece by making a site visit. He had an appointment with McAdam, acting for the Black Dog trustees, so this was probably William McAdam Sr, who was Surveyor to the Trust. In this post he was somewhat at loggerheads with his father, the venerable John Loudon McAdam, who was Surveyor to the Bath Turnpike trustees, who had their own reasons for being suspicious of the Black Dog project. And William McAdam's son, William Jr, would also have been in difficulties, as he had responsibilities to the Bath Trust whilst contriving to help his father on the Black Dog.[11] Brunel's appointment with the two Williams was probably at their office in Westgate Buildings, although it could have been at the elder William's home in Norfolk Buildings:[12]

> Started at 6 ½ on horseback to Bath – had a fall at starting – arrived at Mr McAdams at ¼ 9. After waiting a little for Brunton, breakfasted. Brunton came, proceeded with him & Mc & Son on foot to Claverton. The proposed road runs for a short distance parallel to the Canal. The side of the Hill is a rotten disruption [?] oolite laying on clay. Many slips have occurred owing no doubt to the washing of the clay by the rain and considerably assisted by the bad management of the canal. Blackwell, the Canal engineer, a bigotted obstinate practical man, says the road will make the hill slip – but would not tell us why. Cotterell, a quaker [?] surveyor attending on the part of Vivian the Landowner who opposes, could not or would not either say how or why. Merriman the Canal solicitor appeared to think his advisers rather uninfluenced [?] by reason. After a useless discussion during which Merriman twice said that Mr B[lackwell] would not of course be convinced and did not come to be convinced (Mr M the last time tried to say this as a joke tho' perfectly true) we parted. Mr Tring our solicitor took my card and promised to let me know in good time when they went into Committee. Brunton & I then returned to McAdams, wrote our opinions separately & sealed. Rice [?] & I returned to Bristol.[13]

From this diary entry it is clear that Brunel had resolved the dispute in favour of the proposed road, which was duly built but which has had trouble with landslipping on this stretch ever since.

Once Brunel had begun to tackle the railway project which he was determined to make 'the finest work in England', it became by far the most important contribution which he made to the landscape and social life of Bath. But before going on to consider this contribution, there is a curious link between Brunel's family and the Bath district which is worth mentioning. Brunel's mother, from whom he acquired his middle name, had been Sophia Kingdom (1775?-1855), the daughter of William Kingdom, a naval contractor in Plymouth. Sophie was the youngest of sixteen children, and although little is known about her family, one of her sisters, Elizabeth Kingdom (1761-1856), had married Thomas Mudge (1760-1843), a lawyer with an interest in clock-making derived from the fact that he was the son of Thomas Mudge (1717-1794), a celebrated

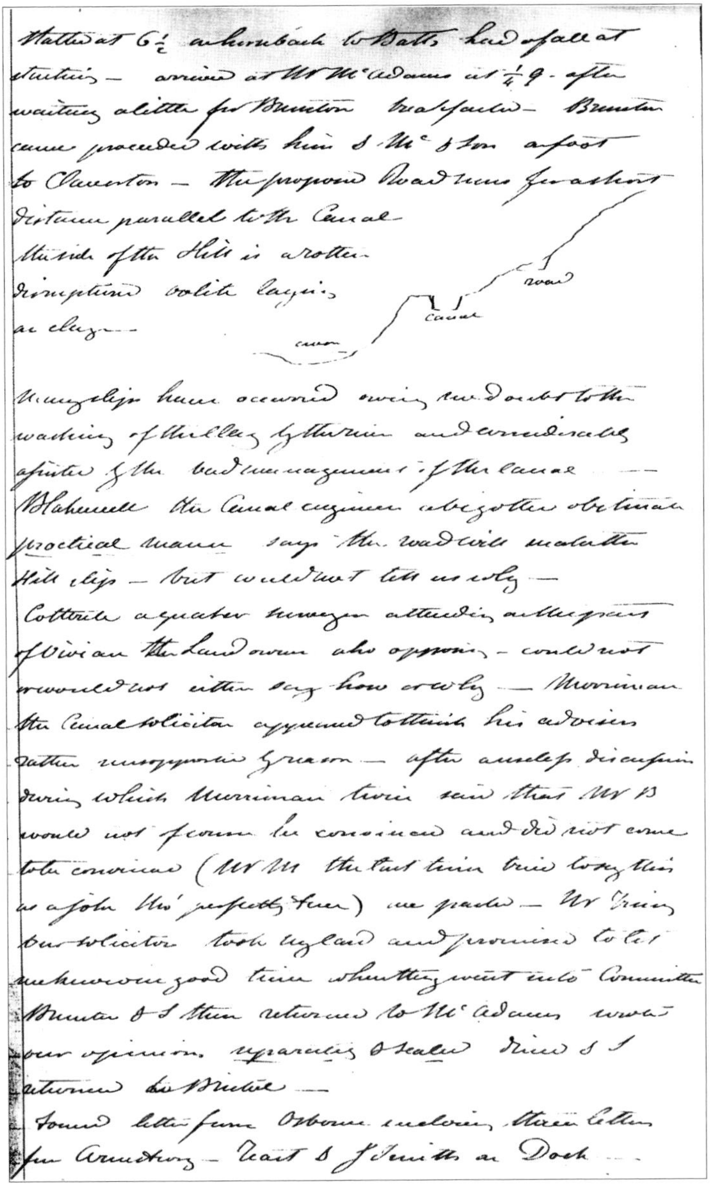

Fig.3 Page from I.K. Brunel's Private Diary for March 1833 regarding his visit to adjudicate between the Black Dog Turnpike Trust and the Kennet & Avon Canal Company. (*Brunel Collection, Bristol University Library*)

166

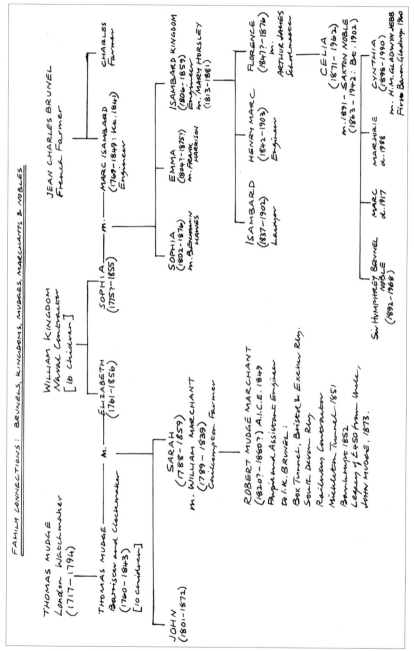

Fig.4 Family Tree, showing the relationships between the Brunels and the Marchants of Chilcompton.

maker of clocks and watches. It seems that Thomas Mudge the younger and Elizabeth, who had a large family of their own, moved at some time to live in the countryside in Somerset, and it was there that their second daughter Sarah (1786-1859) met and married a well-to-do farmer from Chilcompton called William Marchant (1789-1839). It is likely that this is the same William Marchant as the one named as the occupier of Norton Green Farm in 1822.[14] He had died in 1839, so that Sarah was a widow at the time of the visit by the Brunels.[15] William and Sarah had at least one son, Robert Mudge Marchant, who trained under I.K. Brunel, served as an assistant engineer to him, and subsequently quarrelled with him. Before that, however, Sarah and her family had probably been the hosts of Marc and Sophia Brunel on at least one country holiday, and possibly more.

The visit about which we know was in 1843. Sir Marc Isambard Brunel, who had been knighted the previous year as the Thames Tunnel works approached completion after eighteen years of epic labour and anxiety, had been advised by his doctors to take a rest. He was already 74 years old and had suffered a stroke from which he had made a reasonable recovery, but both he and his wife needed some respite from the pressures of a busy professional life. It seems probable that Sophia, Lady Brunel, got in touch with her widowed niece Sarah Marchant, who invited the senior Brunels to spend several weeks with her family in Chilcompton. The village is six miles south of Bath, towards the Mendip hills, in undulating farmland which was then enjoying additional prosperity from the exploitation of the coal measures beneath its fertile soil. It consists mainly of small farms, but it has a pleasant church and churchyard in the bottom of the valley, and provides abundant rural calm. So it was here that Marc and Sophie came to spend much of what was for them an eventful and exciting summer near Bath. It could not have been very restful, but it certainly made a change.

Marc Brunel was a diligent diarist, although most of the entries in his journal were concerned with business and professional matters. Even when he was supposed to be relaxing on holiday, he recorded little about his place of residence or his hosts except for some brief and perfunctory references. He records the journey down to Bath on 3rd June 1843: 'Journey to Bath by the Railway ... agreeable company in the coach, the Bishop of Rippon [sic] Yorkshire and Lord Barrington.'[16] Three days later they moved on to Chilcompton: 'reached this place in good time. Fine but Hilly Roads'.[17] But once established, his diary continued to be preoccupied with business matters. Marc waited anxiously for the post every day, expecting to be kept informed regularly about activities at the Tunnel, and he became very restless when there was no news. He kept a particular check on the number of visitors to the Tunnel, which had been opened to the public in March. Amazingly, by July a million people had paid to walk through it – which is all they could do, because the approaches allowing vehicular traffic through it had still to be built, and were indeed not built until the Tunnel became part of the London Underground system in the 1860s.[18]

On 18th July, Marc (and Sophie?) travelled into Bath 'by the Chilcompton conveyance' on the invitation of a Mrs Brake who had hired the whole carriage for herself and friends, and then on into Bristol (by Railway?) to *Watt's Hotel*, 'The Hotel where Isambard has put up his family and friends'.[19] The next day, 19th July, they attended the launch of the s.s. *Great Britain*, which was floated out of the dry dock in the port of Bristol in which it had been constructed, with due pomp conducted in the presence of HRH Prince Albert. Marc was understandably impressed and proud of his son's achievement, which led him to reflect on his own experiments with screw propulsion many years before. The party returned to Chilcompton via Bath on 21 July, although a passage has been excised from the journal at this point. On Sunday 23rd July, Marc recorded: 'At Chilcompton – in very good health and much improved by the Trip to Bristol and Clifton'.[20]

Five days later, however, Marc Brunel was thrown into a panic when news reached him that the Queen had made an informal visit with her husband to the Thames Tunnel. Apparently Prince Albert had returned to Windsor greatly enthused with the engineering skills of the Brunels, and had promptly persuaded the Queen to accompany him on a visit to the Tunnel, and they made the expedition on 28th July. As conceiver, inspirer and engineer of the Tunnel, Marc was mortified at being absent on the occasion of her visit, and immediately felt constrained to seek a Royal Audience in order to explain what he regarded as his dereliction of duty. So on the morning of 31st July he was given a lift into Bath in Mr Marchant's gig and caught a train to London. Three days later he managed to encounter the Royal Train at Slough, and 'secured a brief audience'.[21]

I.K. Brunel did everything he could to look after his father on this occasion and to facilitate the Royal meeting. When that had been achieved, however, Marc did not immediately return to his wife in Somerset, but found business to detain him in Town until the end of the month. Then, on 30th August, he returned to Chilcompton:

'Set off at 6 from Paddington – a very agreeable run – reached Bath at 10 o.c., long before Mr Marchant could be there according to the notice sent – <u>But he had come early</u> and we set off at 2 p.m.'[22]

Reunited with Sophie, they appear to have spent the autumn quietly in the countryside, with occasional outings to Cheddar (on 12th September); to Hornisham, for Longleat (on 25th September); and to Bath (on 1st November), when he was pleased to meet his son's chief assistant engineer, Mr Hammond, who could bring him up to date with IKB's movements.[23]

Then, on the 10th November, old Thomas Mudge (Sarah Marchant's father) died, and Marc Brunel records attending the funeral: 'of our old friend and relative Mr Mudge who departed this life at the age of 82, 10m, 4 days. Buried in Chilcompton Churchyard'.[24] The following week he records 'an agreeable ride' to the neighbouring village of Clutton, about six miles away:

CLUTTON – went to this place with Mr Marchant, Mrs Marchant and Mr Robt. Mudge and self for the object of obtaining a Tomb Stone to be laid over our friend and relative ...[25]

But Marc was restless to return to the London scene, and just before Christmas 1843 he left Sophie to spend several more weeks with the Somerset family and returned to town. On Christmas Day he wrote to his wife: 'giving her some more correct particulars of every thing before us chiefly what is expected from me at this moment'.[26] He had effectively spent half the year in Chilcompton.

I.K. Brunel figures in the background of his parents' activities in the summer and autumn of 1843. There is no indication that he ever visited the Chilcompton relatives himself, although it is difficult to imagine that he would not have done so at some time. One curious link, however, is that Robert Mudge Marchant, the son of William and Sarah, did join his staff and worked as an assistant engineer for him.[27] But Marchant quarrelled with Brunel and appears to have left in something of a huff. He took up railway contracting and entered into some dubious partnerships which then came to grief, most notably in the case of the Mickleton Tunnel. This was undertaken for the GWR extension from Oxford to Worcester, and when in 1851 the contractors failed to complete the tunnel on time, Brunel raised a large band of railway navvies to evict them from the site in an operation that became known as the Battle of Mickleton Tunnel.

It was an act of risky legality, but it seems likely that Brunel knew his man and correctly surmised that Marchant would back down if pushed hard enough.[28] Brunel certainly received abusive letters from his cousin-once-removed, to which he responded in February 1852 by threatening to return further letters unread.[29] But as far as the tunnel was concerned, Brunel achieved his objective.

Which brings us back to railways and to the main contribution of Brunel to the Bath landscape – the Great Western Railway. As we have seen, from the moment he was appointed Chief Engineer to the putative company in March 1833, Brunel was involved with the line which he projected, with Bath as an important stop on the route between London and Bristol. The line was built from both ends, with stretches opening as soon as they became usable. The Eastern Division, out of Paddington, was under the supervision of a London Committee of directors, while a Bristol Committee was responsible for the Western Division. The two sections met at the Box Tunnel, which was the final link to be completed in 1841. Here we are only concerned with the Western end, and particularly with three parts: the approach to Bath from Bristol; the line from Bath to the Box Tunnel; and, in between, the Bath Spa Station, situated on the north side of the River Avon, with a bridge at either end.

Brunel quickly resolved any doubt about the best route between Bristol and Bath by opting firmly for that following the River Avon for most of the way rather than the northward swing though Downend and Mangotsfield favoured by his assistant Townshend and some of the directors. A preliminary survey was rapidly made, taking the line east from the site in Temple Meads where the terminus to the new railway would be built, across the Feeder Canal and the River Avon, and then keeping south of the river all the way to Bathford except for the short excursion north of the river to what became the site of Bath Spa Station. Brunel took care to keep the line throughout this section well above possible flood levels, with embankments through the river meadows and long viaducts in Bath itself. As with all the early main railway lines, the construction work was done by many small contractors, and Brunel struggled with several of indifferent quality on this stretch. With two of them, Ranger and David McIntosh, he subsequently became involved in tortuous claims for compensation.[30] Despite these difficulties, the engineering work was eventually accomplished to Brunel's complete satisfaction.

Eastwards from Temple Meads Station in Bristol, no attempt was made to follow the river through the Crews Hole valley. Instead, the line passed through Brislington in a series of short tunnels, before emerging on the river bank and following it to Keynsham. At Saltford it cut through the low ridge of Liassic limestone on which the village stands by a short tunnel, and then swept across the river meadows to approach Bath through Twerton. In doing so, it went under the Bath-Bristol Turnpike Road at Newbridge, with a skew bridge carried on iron posts giving it the name 'Cross Post Bridge' (see the drawing shown in Fig.11 on p.175). Here, quite unexpectedly, the assistant engineers conducting the excavation found that they were driving the line through a Roman Villa site. Brunel's Resident Engineer for the Bristol Division was G.E. Frere who, together with the Assistant Engineer T.E.M. Marsh, showed considerable archaeological perception, and managed to persuade Brunel to allow a short delay so that the site could be surveyed. Marsh, who went on to become an accomplished amateur archaeologist, was then only nineteen. He was allowed two months to excavate and record the site, and supervised the raising of two mosaics, one of which was installed as a feature on Keynsham Station for several years before being removed to Bristol Museum. It has the popular 'Orpheus' motif, with surrounding animals.[31]

Another short tunnel and cutting brought the line into Twerton. This previously detached village had become in effect an industrial suburb of Bath in the eighteenth century. There had been several industries based on water power from the two large weirs, including a brass mill and a logwood mill, but the dominant enterprise in the early nineteenth century was woollen textile manufacture.[32] There was a large mill on the south bank of the river, with many small streets of artisan housing running at right-angles to the river. There can be no doubt that Brunel's railway was a major disruption to the community of Twerton, as it cut through this network of streets with a long brick and masonry viaduct of 28 arches. Some compensation was provided by building homes into several of the arches, and these appear to have remained in use for many years. The viaduct alongside the re-aligned Lower Bristol Road was faced in masonry, and a platform was built on the viaduct for Twerton Station, no longer in use.[33] After a low cutting at Oldfield, there was another viaduct of 73 arches which carried the line to the timber-arched skew bridge by which Brunel crossed the river to approach Bath Spa Station.

Immediately to the east of the station, St James's Bridge carried the line back to the south side of the river with a single masonry arch over the water and two subsidiary arches. Thereafter, the line made a graceful sweep to the north-east, involving a surprisingly tight-radius curve which was only acceptable on a high-speed route because trains would

172

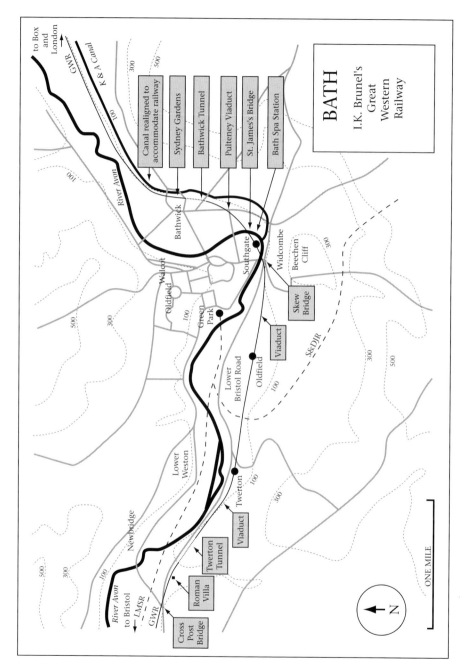

Fig.5 Map showing the route of I.K. Brunel's Great Western Railway through Bath.

Fig.6 Twerton Station on the GWR, now closed, from a postcard of c.1910.

Fig.7 Castellated viaduct on the GWR opposite Southgate, Bath. (*Photograph by the author, 1990*)

be slowing down in the vicinity of the station. This stretch carried the railway over Pulteney Road by a neat three-arch bridge faced in Bath stone. This was somewhat disfigured by subsequent restorations using blue engineering brick instead of stone, but it survived until replaced in the 1970s by the present box-girder single-span viaduct which is less elegant but provides for an easier flow of modern traffic on the main road route through the city from east to west.

174

Fig.8 Lithograph of the timber skew bridge approaching Bath Spa Station from the west, from J.C. Bourne, *History and Description of the Great Western Railway*, 1846.

Fig.9 Lithograph depicting the construction of the Great Western Railway as it approached Bath Spa Station from London, also from J.C. Bourne, *History and Description of the Great Western Railway*, 1846.

A short cutting and tunnel brought the railway into Sydney Gardens, where Brunel contrived a vista of great theatrical quality, with promenaders having an opportunity of seeing trains on his railway, gliding – as it were – across a stage. It is sobering to reflect that, only a generation before, the Kennet & Avon Canal had taken a parallel cut through the Gardens, and that neither engineering exercise appears to have aroused effective resistance. But whereas the canal company had been content to hide their intrusion in a carefully executed cut spanned by small iron bridges, Brunel had sought maximum presentation of the railway as a piece of public relations. Every effort seems to have been taken to supplement rather than detract from the recreational amenities provided in the Gardens, even though a maze was destroyed in order to accommodate the railway. A drawing in Brunel's *Sketchbooks* of a single-storey pavilion with a veranda, placed directly alongside the railway lines, shows a grandstand that would have provided fine views of passing trains, perhaps with refreshments available, that was sadly never built.[34]

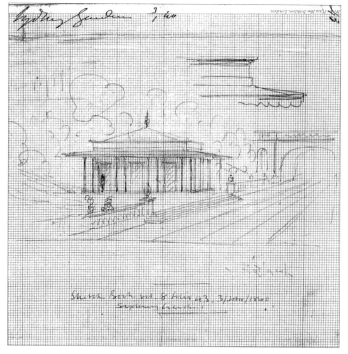

Fig.10 A drawing from I.K. Brunel's *Sketchbooks* showing the pavilion designed for Sydney Gardens but never built. (*Brunel Collection, Bristol University Library*)

Emerging from Sydney Gardens, it was necessary to arrange a short alteration in the course of the K & A Canal where both railway and canal turned eastwards again, with the canal being at the higher level at this point. This modification was accomplished by moving the canal several yards to the east and by building a substantial retaining wall alongside the railway. Then across the meadows, but still comfortably above the flood levels, and over the Avon for the last time with an elegant masonry bridge, and on with another bridge across the Bradford-on-Avon road, and so up the valley of the By Brook to Box. There was a wrangle over property rights at Bathampton which caused a small deviation from the original alignment, and provision was made for a junction with the line which eventually went up the Limpley Stoke valley to Frome and Westbury. Brunel had avoided this route for his main line, but with its links through the Vale of Pewsey to Newbury and Reading it eventually became part of the GWR network.[35]

Fig.11 A drawing from I.K. Brunel's *Sketchbooks* showing the Cross Post Bridge. (*Brunel Collection, Bristol University Library*)

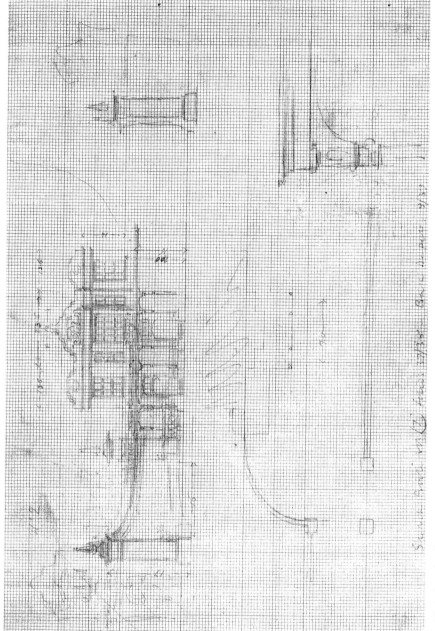

Fig.12 A drawing from I.K. Brunel's *Sketchbooks* showing the façade of Bath Spa Station. (*Brunel Collection, Bristol University Library*)

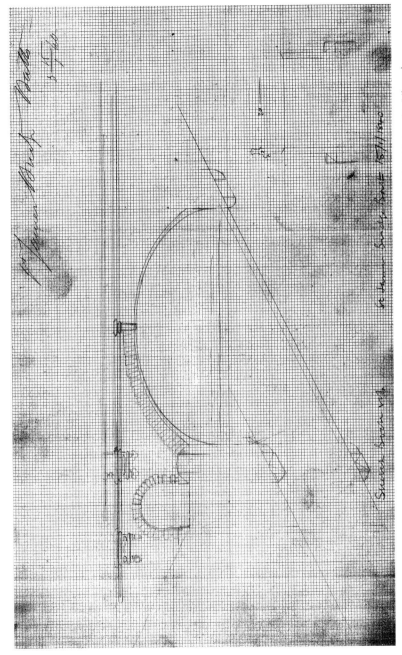

Fig.13 A drawing from I.K. Brunel's *Sketchbooks* showing St. James' Bridge. (*Brunel Collection, Bristol University Library*)

179

The Box Tunnel, 1¾ miles long, was the last section of the original GWR main line to be completed. It was a major excavation, involving many teams of navvies over several years, working simultaneously from both ends and from faces at the bottom of the six ventilation and supply shafts sunk along the line of the tunnel. One important by-product of the work was that it opened up another supply of excellent quality Bath stone from the beds of oolitic limestone through which the tunnel was cut. As with most civil engineering works of any magnitude in the nineteenth century, there was a price to pay in human suffering and loss of life. There may have been as many as a hundred fatalities during the course of the construction of the Box Tunnel, but it is a curious reflection of the indifference to such matters at the time that there is no exact record of the number. The work was finished, and the line opened throughout, on 30th June 1841.[36]

Perhaps in deference to Bath, Brunel chose a muted classicism to present the western portico of the Box Tunnel, twice the height of the internal bore, but providing a fine landscape flourish to the line on its departure from the Bath region. But maybe not, because the vagaries of Brunel's styles represent exuberance rather than any consistent pattern, and in Bath Spa Station itself, where he might have been expected to show some deference to Palladian influences, there is no such influence to be seen. The style adopted for the façade, which in all its essential features was as it is today, is the same Tudor Cottage/Romantic that he had used on the Temple Meads offices (see the drawing shown in Fig.12 on p.176). The station was built with a shed-roof, again like that at Temple Meads, using timber beams balanced on iron columns, meeting corresponding beams from the other side in the middle and anchored at the outer end in the external walls.

The point of this arrangement was to avoid undue loading on the external walls, which were carried over the arches of the viaduct on which the station was built. It was less satisfactory than the Bristol station, with the columns too near the edge of the platforms, and the whole roof was removed in the 1890s and replaced by the canopies over the two main platforms. Other modifications have been made, such as the removal of the two additional sets of rails that allowed for by-passing and parking rolling stock, and of course the whole track was re-laid with the conversion from the broad gauge to standard gauge, which was completed in 1892. Brunel's brilliant innovation had enabled the GWR to achieve the regular high-speed passenger services that he had envisaged, but his success had stimulated the standard gauge engineers to improve their own performance, with the result that the broad gauge had become increasingly uncompetitive and expensive to maintain. But one welcome legacy of the broad gauge was the comparative spaciousness of its tunnels, viaducts and stations, at a time when standard gauge speeds were being increased by the introduction of High Speed Trains in the last quarter of the twentieth century.

Amongst other features of Bath Spa Station which have changed since Brunel's time, the removal of the large water tank which was a standard feature of nineteenth century stations is worth a mention. Also, the signal-box incorporated in the canopy above the 'down' platform has gone fairly recently, and the goods yard has been obliterated. This was awkwardly built at right-angles to the main line at the western end of the 'up' platform. Access was by means of a turn-table taking one wagon at a time. It was convenient for servicing the power generating station when this was built on the adjacent site in the 1890s, but when that closed down after the Second World War, the goods yard was closed and became a car park.

Changes have also been made in the bridges between which the station stands. Small but unsightly repairs have been made to the main masonry arch of St James's Bridge, although it is otherwise unaltered (see the drawing shown in Fig.13 on p.177). The timber skew bridge (shown in the lithograph in Fig. 8 on p.172), however, was replaced by a wrought-iron girder bridge in 1878. This had been a remarkable specimen of Brunel's virtuosity, demonstrating his mastery of timberwork in large structures. He used the same skills later on timber viaducts to carry his Cornish railway over the deep valleys in that county. The bridge in Bath, crossing the river at an acute angle just upstream from the ancient Bath Bridge, had been built in two arches of laminated timber, across cast-iron columns in the middle of the river, and it had done good service. But the directors of the GWR had been alarmed by the collapse of the 'Halfpenny' Footbridge behind the station in 1877. This had been a timber bow-structure, which fell into the river with a considerable loss of life when it became overloaded with people streaming across to attend the Bath & West Show being held that summer on Beechen Cliff, the hill immediately south of the river.[37] It led to some nervousness about large timber structures, and the main line bridge was consequently replaced. The new footbridge, also an iron girder construction, was built by T.E.M. Marsh, Brunel's Assistant Engineer who had conducted the excavation on the Roman villa at Newbridge, and who had acquired a practice in the city as a Consulting Engineer.

Bath Spa Station survives as a distinct Brunel feature in the townscape. We have already observed Brunel's penchant for theatrical flourishes in the display of the railway in Sydney Gardens, and an element of the same quality can be found in the station, with its approach from the city via Manvers Street, although he was not able to carry out the idea of a 'grand approach' in detail. It occurs also in the façade which the railway viaduct presents across the river to Southgate, with its turrets and castellations in good quality Bath stone. These features show Brunel's understanding of the Bath market. He does not adopt its Palladianism, but neither does he try to impose himself and his railway on the city: he salutes it respectfully but a little jauntily as he passes by, inviting its citizens to travel out into a wider world. The citizens of Twerton who had been bulldozed out of their homes by the advent of the railway would not have appreciated it in the same way. But they had less voice and, more significantly, less money than the visitors who would come flocking into the city through the new mode of high-speed passenger transport. From their point of view, as from that of posterity, Brunel's Great Western Railway was comfortably assimilated into the Bath landscape as a desirable and agreeable feature.

I.K. Brunel thus made an impressive mark on the City of Bath, with his great railway to the West sweeping gracefully through its parks and

across its river, and with its elegant station and viaducts. His descendants retained the family attachment to the city: his son Henry made several visits, and his granddaughter Celia, who became Lady Noble, made her home in the Royal Crescent.[38] Brunel has been commemorated in the city with a plaque in Sydney Gardens, recalling the opening of the line from Bristol to Bath in 1840. In addition to all its other charms and claims to fame, Bath is justified in taking some pride in its association with this dynamic man who did so much to stimulate the industrialisation of the nation and to demonstrate the value of the new modes of rapid transport which he put at the disposal of society.

Fig.14 The Brunel Society plaque to I.K. Brunel in Sydney Gardens, unveiled on 30th June 1977. (*Photograph by the author*)

Fig.15 Celia Brunel, Lady Noble, granddaughter of I.K. Brunel, from an oil on canvas painting by Walter Sickert in 1905. (*Victoria Art Gallery, Bath & North East Somerset Council*)

Fig.13 The unveiling of the Brunel Society plaque to I.K. Brunel in Sydney Gardens, 30th June 1977: the Mayor and Mayoress of Bath, Councillor and Mrs R.C. Rosewarn; the President of the Brunel Society, R. Angus Buchanan; and, in the pale coat, Cynthia, Lady Gladwyn, great-granddaughter of I.K. Brunel.
(*Reproduced from the Brunel Society Newsletter, No.24, October 1977*)

Notes and References

This essay was first presented as a lecture to the History of Bath Research Group on 7th January 1998. I am grateful to members of the Group who, then and subsequently, have made constructive comments that have enabled me to improve the text. I am particularly grateful to the Editor of *Bath History* for her support and helpful suggestions, and to Hilary Strickland for her help in preparing the map on p.172.

1   For a general account, see R. Angus Buchanan, *Brunel: The Life and Times of Isambard Kingdom Brunel* (Hambledon and London, 2002). The system of referencing used in the book has been adopted here, viz: PLB = Private Letter Books, PerD = Personal Diary, PriD = Private Diaries. Most of the archival material on the Brunel family is in the Special Collections at the University of Bristol Library and, as ever, I am indebted to the Archivists, Michael Richardson and Hannah Lowery, for their skilful assistance.

2   Paul Clements, *Marc Isambard Brunel* (Longman, 1970), p.201: no reference is given for this citation, and I have so far failed to identify it in the Diaries of Marc Brunel, which are in the archives of the Institution of Civil Engineers. But I have no reason to doubt its authenticity.

3   I am grateful to William and Pauline Hanna for drawing my attention to this entry. It is from the 1841 Census transcript, Enumeration District No.5, p.3 of 20: Registration District: Abbey, Parish St Peter & St Paul, ED 5, p.59. A copy is available on microfilm in the City of Bath Library.

4   William Youatt (ed.), *The Horse* (Baldwin and Cradock, 1831).

5   Charles MacFarlane, *Reminiscences of a Literary Life* (Charles Scribner's, 1917), pp.280-293, recalls the journey from Paris. For an account of Brunel's own coach, his black britzska or 'Flying Hearse', see L.T.C. Rolt, *Isambard Kingdom Brunel* (Longmans Green, 1957: Penguin edition, Harmondsworth, 1989), p.105.

6   IKB's Private Diaries, in the Bristol Collection: PriD, 17 Sept 1830: Brunel's idiosyncratic spelling has been retained, but the punctuation has been tidied up slightly. Acraman, English and Benyon were all Bristol businessmen with an interest in the Clifton Bridge. The reference to the 'giant's hole' is to a feature in the limestone cliff at Clifton known by this name which appears in one of the drawings for the projected bridge made by Brunel.

7   PriD, 17 June 1831.

8   PriD, 16 June 1831.

9   For Ellacombe, see R. Beamish, *Memoir of the Life of Sir Marc Isambard Brunel* (Longman, Green, Longman and Robert, 1862), pp.115-124.

10 PriD, 11 July 1831.

11 W.J. Reader, *Macadam* (Heinemann, 1980), pp.152-154.

12 The *Bath Directory* for 1841 gives the address of William McAdam, General Surveyor of Roads, as 13 Norfolk Buildings (p.107). But there was also a 'General Office of Roads', at Westgate House, 17 Westgate Buildings (p.220), with 'Wm. McAdam, gent.' being given as the General Surveyor, so it seems probable that the rendezvous was here.

13 PriD, 11 March 1833.

14 David J. Strawbridge, *Meandering through Chilcompton*, (Strawbridge, Chilcompton, 1985), p.92. For background information about the Mudge and Marchant families, I am grateful to the late Frank D. Smith of Bolton, Lancs, who sent me some long com-

munications on the subject. Thomas Mudge Jr is listed in Ian White, *Watch and Clock Makers in the City of Bath*, (Antiquarian Horological Society, Wadhurst, 1996), p.94.

15 The date of death, 1839, is given on the Marchant family tree provided by Frank Smith.

16 MIB Diaries, 3 June 1843.

17 MIB Diaries, 6 June 1843.

18 MIB Diaries, 11 July 1843, mentions the millionth visitor.

19 MIB Diaries, 17-18 July 1843.

20 MIB Diaries, 23 July 1843.

21 MIB Diaries, 3 August 1843. The Marchant mentioned here was probably Robert Mudge Marchant, his father having died in 1839.

22 MIB Diaries, 30 August 1843.

23 MIB Diaries, 1 Nov 1843.

24 MIB Diaries, 16 Nov 1843.

25 MIB Diaries, 22 Nov 1843.

26 MIB Diaries, 25 Dec 1843.

27 IKB: PLB 5, 26 and 29 March 1847.

28 For a summary of the 'Battle of Mickleton Tunnel', see R. Angus Buchanan, *op.cit.*, p.158. For a fuller account see: David Brooke, 'The "Great Commotion" at Mickleton Tunnel, July 1851', *Journal of the Rail and Canal Historical Society*, 30 (1990), pp.63-67.

29 IKB, PLB 8, 16 Feb 1852.

30 E.T. MacDermot, *History of the Great Western Railway* (Great Western Railway, 1927; rev. ed. C.R. Clinker, Ian Allan, 1964), vol.1, p.55. See also David Brooke, 'The Equity Suit of McIntosh v. The Great Western Railway ...', *Journal of Transport History*, third series, 17 (1996).

31 For an excellent summary of IKB's work on the Bristol-Bath stretch of the GWR, see MacDermot, *op.cit.*, esp.pp.54-58 of vol.1 of the revised edition. See also Colin G. Maggs, *The GWR Bristol to Bath Line* (Sutton Publishing, Stroud, 2001). For the excavation of the Twerton Roman Villa, see *History of Bath Research Group Newsletter* 34 (September 1997), reporting the meeting on 15 May 1997 when James Russell gave an account of the work: see also his article in *Bath & Avon Archaeology*, vol.9 (1992), pp.2-23.

32 See Nicholas von Behr, 'The Cloth Industry of Twerton from the 1780s to the 1820s', in *Bath History*, vol.VI (Millstream Books, Bath, 1996), pp.88-107.

33 See Maggs, *op.cit.*, p.68 for an illustration of this station; also p.66 for a picture of the masonry face of the viaduct and a cross-section of the internal arrangement of one of the dwellings.

34 The maze had been a popular feature of the Gardens until it was destroyed to make room for the GWR. The drawing of the pavilion is in the Brunel Collection, *Sketchbook*, vol.8, folio 43, and is dated 3rd January 1840.

35 There is a plan of the Bathampton deviation in the Bristol Collection.

36 MacDermot, *op.cit.*, p.66

37 See R.Angus Buchanan, 'The Bridges of Bath', in *Bath History*, vol.III (Alan Sutton, Gloucester, 1990), pp.1-21.

38 Lady Noble (1871-1962) moved to No. 22 Royal Crescent towards the end of her life, and became a well-known figure there and in the Pump Room. Her portrait by W.R. Sickert, painted in 1905, is in the Victoria Art Gallery, Bath. It pre-dates Lady Noble's residence in Bath, but it has found an appropriate home in the city.

Index to *Bath History* Volumes 1-X by Author

Index to *Bath History* Volumes 1-X by Title